JADEN CROSS

Hands-On Modern App development
with C# 8

Contents

Introduction: Navigating Modern App Development with C# 8

Overview of Modern App Development: Trends and Needs
In recent years, app development has undergone a profound transformation, driven by rapidly evolving technologies, consumer demands, and business needs. For developers, staying current with these trends isn't just about keeping up; it's about building resilient, scalable, and competitive applications. In this section, we'll explore the key trends and requirements in modern app development and how the C# 8 language empowers developers to address these demands effectively.

1. The Push for Cross-Platform Solutions

A defining characteristic of today's app landscape is the necessity for cross-platform functionality. Users expect seamless experiences across devices—desktop, mobile, and web—whether for enterprise solutions or personal use. To meet this demand, developers must build apps that run efficiently on multiple platforms with minimal modification.

Cross-platform frameworks, such as .NET Core and Xamarin, have gained popularity because they reduce the development effort and ensure consistent user experiences across devices. By enabling developers to write once and deploy everywhere, C# 8 and .NET Core support a flexible approach to cross-platform development. These tools not only save time but also reduce costs and streamline maintenance. With C# 8's rich set of features, developers can create responsive, user-friendly applications that perform well regardless of the platform.

2. Cloud-Integrated and Distributed Applications

The rise of cloud computing has revolutionized how we think about storage, data processing, and scalability. Cloud integration is now essential for most applications, particularly enterprise-level solutions. Modern applications often need to support vast amounts of data, integrate with third-party APIs, and provide real-time interactions across geographically dispersed users. As a result, developers are increasingly adopting cloud-native development practices, leveraging platforms like Microsoft Azure, AWS, and Google Cloud.

C# 8 is well-suited for building cloud-native applications. It offers language features that simplify asynchronous programming, making it easier to work with distributed systems and network operations. For example, async streams in C# 8 allow for more efficient handling of real-time data, enabling developers to create responsive applications that adapt to fluctuating network conditions. This is essential for applications that rely on cloud APIs and need to maintain high performance even with large-scale data operations.

3. Microservices Architecture for Scalability and Flexibility

To build scalable and maintainable applications, developers are increasingly moving toward microservices architecture. In a microservices model, applications are broken down into independent services that communicate over APIs. This approach enables teams to deploy, scale, and manage each service independently, resulting in more agile development processes and easier scalability.

Microservices architecture aligns well with C# 8 and .NET Core, which provide built-in support for creating APIs and managing inter-service communication. Features like default interface methods in C# 8 make it easier to build flexible service contracts, while .NET Core's lightweight runtime allows services to be deployed efficiently in containerized environments such as Docker. As businesses prioritize quick deployment and frequent updates, the modularity offered by microservices makes C# 8 a valuable tool for modern development.

4. Security as a Core Requirement

With cyber threats becoming more sophisticated, security has become a fundamental concern for app developers. Users and organizations expect applications to protect sensitive data, enforce authentication, and comply with data protection regulations. This focus on security is especially important for applications that handle personal information, financial data, or critical business processes.

C# 8 offers features that promote more secure coding practices. For instance, nullable reference types can help developers prevent null reference exceptions, a common source of runtime errors that can potentially lead to vulnerabilities. By enforcing nullable checks, C# 8 encourages developers to write more reliable, error-resistant code. Moreover, C# integrates well with .NET Core's extensive security libraries, which include support for secure encryption, token-based authentication, and authorization protocols. For developers, this means that C# 8 can be the foundation for building applications that meet the highest security standards.

5. The Rise of Artificial Intelligence and Machine Learning

As artificial intelligence (AI) and machine learning (ML) become integral to modern applications, developers are increasingly incorporating AI-driven features, such as recommendation systems, predictive analytics, and natural language processing. These capabilities enhance the functionality of applications, allowing them to deliver more personalized and intelligent user experiences.

While C# may not be the primary language for machine learning, Microsoft has introduced tools like ML.NET, which enables developers to build and integrate machine learning models directly within C# applications. By combining C# 8 with ML.NET, developers can build data-driven applications that adapt to user behavior, improve efficiency, and provide intelligent insights. The seamless integration of ML into C# applications empowers developers to stay competitive in a landscape where AI capabilities are becoming expected features.

6. User-Centric Design and High Performance

Modern app development is not only about adding features but also about ensuring that applications are fast, efficient, and user-friendly. Performance optimization and a focus on user experience are essential, especially in a market where users have numerous alternatives. Applications that lag or respond poorly to user input are quickly abandoned in favor of faster, more reliable options.

C# 8 supports performance optimization through its language features. Indices and ranges, for instance, simplify the handling of data and allow for cleaner, faster code when working with large datasets. Additionally, C#'s robust memory management and garbage collection allow developers to maintain high performance even in memory-intensive applications. By enabling developers to optimize code more easily, C# 8 helps ensure that applications remain responsive, reliable, and efficient—key factors in providing a top-notch user experience.

7. Collaborative Development and Version Control

With teams now working remotely and collaborating across locations, the development process has become more collaborative. This shift has led to a greater reliance on tools for version control, CI/CD pipelines, and code review processes. For developers, it's essential to write code that is modular, understandable, and easy to maintain.

C# 8 supports these collaborative requirements by promoting code clarity and maintainability. Features like static local functions allow for better encapsulation within methods, making code more modular and less prone to bugs. Additionally, C# integrates smoothly with Git for version control, and with tools like Visual Studio and Azure DevOps, developers can implement CI/CD pipelines to automate testing, deployment, and updates. For developers working on complex, team-driven projects, C# 8's features make collaborative development more efficient and less error-prone.

8. Automation and DevOps Integration

Automation is now a central component of modern development, helping to reduce time to market and improve code quality. As companies increasingly adopt DevOps practices, developers are tasked with integrating their code into CI/CD pipelines, automating testing, and monitoring application performance.

C# 8, in conjunction with .NET Core, is well-suited for DevOps workflows. Automated unit tests can be implemented with frameworks like xUnit, while .NET Core's compatibility with Docker containers allows for straightforward deployment. C# 8's compatibility with these tools and practices ensures that applications can be deployed faster, maintained with fewer errors, and easily updated in response to user feedback.

9. Data-Driven Development and Analytics Integration

Today's applications need to gather, process, and analyze large amounts of data to generate insights. Whether through embedded analytics, user behavior tracking, or data visualization, the demand for data-driven development is higher than ever.

C# 8 simplifies data manipulation with enhanced LINQ capabilities, enabling developers to filter, query, and aggregate data efficiently. Moreover, its compatibility with various database solutions, from SQL Server to NoSQL databases, makes it a flexible choice for data-driven development. With tools like Entity Framework Core, developers can manage complex data models and perform data analysis directly within their applications. This capability aligns well with modern applications that rely on data to drive user engagement and inform business decisions.

The trends in modern app development highlight an industry that is both rapidly evolving and increasingly complex. For developers, this environment demands a language that is versatile, powerful, and capable of meeting diverse requirements. C# 8 addresses these needs by offering a comprehensive set of tools and features that align well with the trends and requirements of modern app development. Whether it's cross-platform compatibility, cloud integration, security, or machine learning capabilities, C# 8 empowers developers to build applications that are ready for the demands of today's market. This book will explore these features in depth, guiding you through the essential skills and knowledge you need to create competitive, future-ready applications with C# 8.

Why C# 8: Exploring the Power of New Features
Advancements in Code Safety and Reliability

One of the standout features of C# 8 is its support for nullable reference types, a tool that fundamentally changes how developers handle references and null values. Traditionally, reference types in C# could be assigned null, a value that often led to NullReferenceException errors if not properly checked before accessing. This problem has been a notorious source of bugs and crashes in applications, particularly in complex codebases where null values might propagate unexpectedly.

Nullable Reference Types

C# 8 addresses this issue by allowing developers to explicitly define whether a reference type can accept nulls. With nullable reference types enabled, the compiler issues warnings whenever potentially null references are accessed without proper checks. This simple change encourages safer code practices by helping developers proactively avoid null-related errors, which can be particularly problematic in large applications where they might be hard to trace. Not only does this lead to more robust applications, but it also fosters a coding style that prioritizes clarity and predictability.

Default Interface Methods

In addition to nullability improvements, C# 8 introduces default interface methods, a feature that significantly enhances flexibility when working with interfaces. Before C# 8, developers were required to implement any changes in all derived classes if an interface was modified—an approach that often resulted in breaking changes and code duplication. With default interface methods, developers can now define implementations directly in interfaces, enabling them to introduce new functionality without impacting existing code. This feature is particularly useful in maintaining backward compatibility, making it ideal for evolving codebases where incremental feature additions are common.

Enhanced Asynchronous Programming with Async Streams

Asynchronous programming is essential for applications that need to handle tasks concurrently or process large volumes of data in real-time. C# has long supported asynchronous programming with the async and await keywords, but C# 8 takes this further with async streams, which allow developers to handle streams of data asynchronously.

The Benefits of Async Streams

Async streams, introduced through the IAsyncEnumerable<T> interface, enable developers to consume data in a more natural and responsive way. Rather than waiting for an entire data set to be available before processing, async streams allow applications to process each item as it becomes available. This is especially useful in applications that handle real-time data feeds, such as live chat systems, data monitoring dashboards, or IoT device data processing. By using async streams, developers can build applications that are both more efficient and more responsive, adapting to the demands of asynchronous workflows with ease.

This feature not only simplifies code but also optimizes performance by reducing memory overhead. For applications where resources are limited or where responsiveness is critical, async streams provide an elegant solution. By fully integrating async streams into its asynchronous programming model, C# 8 makes it easier for developers to implement high-performance applications without compromising readability or maintainability.

Pattern Matching Improvements for Cleaner Code

Pattern matching, a feature introduced in C# 7, receives a significant upgrade in C# 8 with new types of patterns that make code more expressive and concise. Pattern matching in C# allows developers to match objects against specific shapes or types, simplifying logic and reducing the need for verbose if-else statements. C# 8 introduces additional patterns, including recursive patterns and property patterns, which provide greater flexibility when working with complex data structures.

Recursive Patterns

Recursive patterns are especially useful for applications that rely on hierarchical data structures or nested objects. With recursive patterns, developers can decompose data structures in a single, cohesive statement, which simplifies code and improves readability. For instance, if an application involves traversing tree-like data structures—such as XML documents or abstract syntax trees—recursive patterns can significantly reduce the code required to access and manipulate specific elements.

Property Patterns

Property patterns, on the other hand, allow developers to directly match specific properties within an object, without needing to create multiple nested checks. This improvement makes pattern matching ideal for situations where different behaviors need to be applied based on an object's properties, such as in rules-based applications or data validation tasks. With these new capabilities, pattern matching becomes a more powerful tool for structuring logic, enabling developers to create more concise, readable, and maintainable code.

Indices and Ranges: Streamlined Data Manipulation

Working with data is a core part of most applications, and C# 8 introduces indices and ranges to make data manipulation more intuitive. This feature simplifies the way developers work with collections, particularly arrays and lists, by allowing them to specify indices from the end of a collection, as well as ranges to create slices of data.

Using Indices and Ranges

Previously, accessing elements from the end of a collection required cumbersome calculations that involved manually determining the length of the array or list. In C# 8, the ^ operator allows developers to access elements starting from the end of a collection, making this process much more straightforward. For instance, myArray[^1] accesses the last element in the array, while myArray[^2] accesses the second-to-last element. This syntax enhances code readability, particularly in cases where data structures represent ordered information, such as time-series data or logs.

Ranges, represented with the .. operator, allow developers to create subarrays or slices effortlessly. For example, myArray[1..3] would create a new array containing elements from index 1 to index 2. These features streamline common data manipulation tasks and reduce boilerplate code, making applications both easier to write and to maintain. For data-intensive applications, especially those that involve frequent slicing or indexing, this feature in C# 8 is a valuable enhancement.

Static Local Functions for Better Encapsulation

In large codebases, encapsulation and modularity are essential for maintainability. C# 8 introduces static local functions, which can be declared within a method and marked as static to ensure they don't capture any external variables. By preventing variable capture, static local functions help developers write more predictable and optimized code, particularly in performance-sensitive applications.

Advantages of Static Local Functions

Static local functions are beneficial in scenarios where a function is only relevant to a specific block of code, such as in a data processing routine or algorithm implementation. Marking these functions as static forces the compiler to treat them as standalone blocks, which can lead to performance improvements by avoiding closures. This feature is particularly useful in scenarios that involve high-frequency data processing, where every bit of performance optimization counts.

Streamlined Interface Management with Default Interface Methods

As applications evolve, interfaces often require updates to accommodate new functionalities. Traditionally, this has been challenging in C#, as modifying an interface required updating every implementation of that interface. C# 8's default interface methods provide a solution by allowing developers to define default implementations for methods within interfaces. This feature promotes backward compatibility, enabling developers to extend interfaces without breaking existing code.

Practical Applications of Default Interface Methods

Default interface methods simplify maintenance in projects with large or complex hierarchies, especially those involving multiple teams or modules. For instance, if an application interfaces with various external services, developers can use default interface methods to add new behavior without updating every implementation. This feature helps manage versioning and facilitates a more modular design, making C# 8 ideal for projects where scalability and maintainability are key priorities.

The features introduced in C# 8 represent significant advancements in both language design and practical functionality. By improving code safety, enhancing asynchronous programming, and simplifying data handling, C# 8 aligns with the demands of modern app development. Its tools for nullability, pattern matching, async streams, and default interface methods allow developers to write cleaner, more efficient, and more maintainable code.

Who This Book is For: Developers, Hobbyists, and Industry Professionals

Developers: From Beginners to Intermediate Coders

For developers, this book offers a practical roadmap to mastering C# 8's newest features. While foundational knowledge of programming in C# is recommended, this book is designed to be accessible for those with basic to intermediate coding experience. The content progresses logically, ensuring that readers can build on their understanding as they go.

Newer Developers

If you're relatively new to programming, this book will guide you through essential language concepts and real-world applications. While some familiarity with C# basics will help, this book aims to reinforce that foundation by explaining advanced topics in an understandable way. Each chapter begins with clear, approachable explanations before delving into more intricate details, making this book an excellent resource for those still building their skills.

With hands-on examples and exercises, you'll gain a comprehensive understanding of C# 8's capabilities, from nullable reference types to async streams. The book emphasizes not only how to use these features but also why they matter in real-world scenarios. By the end, you'll have gained practical experience with the tools and techniques that professional developers use daily.

Intermediate Developers

If you've worked with C# in the past and have a grasp of the language, this book is designed to deepen your expertise. You'll encounter new concepts that expand your understanding and discover ways to optimize and improve your code. We'll focus on strategies to help you write cleaner, more efficient code, utilizing features like pattern matching and default interface methods to their fullest potential.

Through project-based learning, you'll see how these concepts apply to real applications. This approach not only strengthens your knowledge but also prepares you for advanced challenges, whether you're interested in building scalable cloud-based applications or optimizing performance in complex data-driven projects.

Hobbyists and Independent Developers

App development isn't limited to the workplace. For many, coding is a passion and a form of creative expression. This book caters to hobbyists who are eager to experiment, build personal projects, or explore the possibilities of C# 8 in modern app development. If you're working on side projects, building an indie game, or creating tools for your own use, this book will provide you with the technical insights to bring your ideas to life.

Why C# 8 Appeals to Hobbyists

The features in C# 8 simplify complex tasks and streamline workflows, which is ideal for independent developers working on solo projects. For example, async streams make it easier to manage data from external sources or asynchronous operations, while pattern matching allows for more intuitive control structures. These tools save time and reduce complexity, allowing hobbyists to focus more on the creative aspects of their projects.

We also include practical projects that can be adapted to a variety of personal interests, from creating desktop applications to experimenting with cross-platform development. Each project is designed to be approachable and engaging, providing hobbyists with the satisfaction of completing a functional app while learning valuable new skills. Additionally, these exercises emphasize code readability and modular design, making it easy for hobbyists to revisit, expand, and share their projects with others.

Industry Professionals: Seasoned Developers, Engineers, and Architects

For industry professionals—whether you're a software engineer, a technical lead, or an architect—this book serves as an in-depth guide to leveraging C# 8 for enterprise-grade applications. As an experienced developer, you'll find that this book dives into the intricacies of C# 8, offering insights and techniques for optimizing code, improving maintainability, and building scalable solutions.

Key Benefits for Professionals

Professionals working on large-scale projects will appreciate the book's focus on best practices, performance optimization, and maintainability. For instance, we explore how nullable reference types can reduce null-related bugs, which is especially valuable in complex codebases. Similarly, features like default interface methods and static local functions streamline code organization, enabling cleaner, more modular code that's easier to maintain and refactor.

This book also addresses topics critical to enterprise applications, such as microservices architecture, cloud integration, and data-driven development. Each of these sections includes practical advice on how to implement these solutions in C# 8, from setting up distributed systems to handling asynchronous data streams effectively. By the end, professionals will have a deeper understanding of how to use C# 8 to build resilient, high-performance applications that meet industry standards.

Bridging the Gap Between Legacy Systems and Modern Applications

Many industry professionals are tasked with maintaining legacy systems while also adapting to new technologies. C# 8's backward-compatible features, such as default interface methods, provide a unique advantage in these scenarios. This book discusses strategies for incrementally modernizing codebases, allowing professionals to incorporate the latest C# 8 capabilities without disrupting existing systems. This approach makes it easier to bridge the gap between legacy applications and modern demands, positioning companies to stay competitive while maintaining the integrity of established software.

Educators and Trainers

For educators and trainers in software development, this book offers a structured approach to teaching modern C# concepts. The progression from foundational principles to advanced topics makes it an ideal resource for coursework or training programs. Each chapter includes hands-on projects and exercises, providing students or trainees with opportunities to apply theoretical concepts in practical ways.

Instructors can use this book to supplement classroom learning or guide students through self-study. With detailed explanations, real-world applications, and examples that reinforce key concepts, educators can provide a well-rounded curriculum that prepares students for the demands of modern app development. Additionally, this book's focus on best practices ensures that students learn not only how to use C# 8 but also how to adopt coding habits that promote quality and maintainability.

IT Managers and Technical Decision-Makers

While IT managers and technical leads may not need to write code daily, understanding the capabilities of C# 8 can inform better decision-making for technology strategy and team development. This book provides insights into how C# 8's features align with current development trends, such as microservices and cloud integration, helping leaders make informed choices about tech stacks and infrastructure.

By understanding the tools and techniques available in C# 8, technical managers can set realistic expectations for development timelines, encourage best practices, and support their teams in adopting efficient coding patterns. This perspective ensures that decision-makers are not only aligned with the technical side of app development but are also empowered to advocate for sustainable, scalable solutions that benefit their organizations.

This book is designed to meet the needs of a diverse audience. Whether you're a developer, a hobbyist, or an industry professional, the concepts, projects, and best practices included here are tailored to help you succeed in today's demanding development environment. With a focus on practical application and real-world scenarios, this book aims to equip readers with the skills to build, maintain, and optimize modern applications using C# 8.

Structure of the Book: What to Expect and How to Use I
  An Overview of the Book's Structure

The book is organized into three main parts, each designed to gradually build your understanding of C# 8 and its application to real-world development challenges. While each chapter builds upon the last, the book is structured to allow you to dive into individual sections based on your learning needs and experience level.

1. **Foundation and Core Concepts**: The initial chapters establish a strong foundation, covering essential C# 8 language features, object-oriented principles, and the basics of building modular and reusable code. This

part is essential for readers who may be new to C# 8 or are looking to refresh their knowledge. It introduces nullable reference types, default interface methods, and other key features that will serve as building blocks for later, more complex topics.

2. **Application of C# 8 in Real-World Scenarios**: The middle chapters guide you through applying C# 8 to specific development scenarios, such as cross-platform app development, cloud integration, and asynchronous programming. Here, we explore how C# 8's new language features can streamline data handling, improve asynchronous workflows, and support scalable, distributed applications. This part includes hands-on projects that allow you to implement what you've learned, reinforcing both your understanding of the language and its application in a practical context.

3. **Advanced Techniques and Best Practices**: The final chapters delve into advanced topics, such as performance optimization, design patterns, and DevOps integration. This part is geared toward readers looking to refine their skills and build applications that meet the highest standards of performance, maintainability, and scalability. We discuss best practices for version control, testing, and continuous integration, equipping you with the tools to handle complex project requirements and collaborate effectively in team settings.

How Each Chapter is Structured

To ensure a cohesive learning experience, each chapter follows a consistent structure designed to reinforce learning through both theory and practice.

1. **Introduction and Objectives**: Each chapter opens with a brief introduction to the concepts and features that will be covered. Objectives are clearly outlined, giving you a sense of what you'll achieve by the end of the chapter and how it fits into the larger framework of app development.

2. **In-Depth Explanations of Key Concepts**: Core concepts are explained in detail, with a focus on clarity and practical application. We break

down complex topics into manageable sections, ensuring that each concept is thoroughly covered before moving on to more advanced material.

3. **Real-World Examples**: To demonstrate how these concepts apply in real-world scenarios, each chapter includes examples that reflect common development challenges. These examples are designed to help you see the relevance of each feature and understand how it can be used to solve practical problems.

4. **Hands-On Projects and Exercises**: Most chapters include a hands-on project or exercise where you'll apply what you've learned. These projects build progressively, allowing you to work on a complete application or series of modules as you progress through the book. By the end of each chapter, you'll have developed concrete skills that you can apply to your own projects.

5. **Key Takeaways and Best Practices**: Each chapter concludes with a summary of key points and best practices. This section is intended as a quick reference guide for revisiting core ideas and reinforcing important concepts, making it easy to review material later as you continue building your skills.

Suggested Reading Path

This book is designed for both sequential reading and modular exploration, so you can approach it based on your learning goals:

- **For Beginners and Intermediate Developers**: It's recommended to follow the book in sequence, starting with foundational concepts and progressing through each chapter. This path ensures a strong understanding of core principles before tackling more advanced topics. As you build a complete app through the exercises, you'll gain experience with C# 8's language features in a structured, guided format.
- **For Experienced Developers and Professionals**: If you're already familiar with the basics of C#, feel free to focus on specific sections that align with your goals. For instance, if you're interested in microservices

or cloud integration, you might start with the chapters on distributed applications. The book is structured to provide context and examples for each topic independently, allowing you to choose chapters that offer the most immediate value to your work.

- **For Educators and Trainers**: Educators can use this book to structure coursework or training sessions by selecting chapters that match the syllabus. The hands-on projects and exercises are designed to be suitable for classroom or workshop settings, providing students with a balanced mix of theory and practical experience.

Making the Most of Hands-On Projects

Throughout the book, you'll work on several hands-on projects that grow in complexity. These projects are more than exercises; they are practical applications that reinforce the chapter's material and allow you to apply what you've learned to real scenarios.

For best results:

- **Follow Along with Each Step**: While it may be tempting to skip ahead, following each step carefully ensures that you don't miss important details. Each project is designed to help you build specific skills, and jumping ahead may mean missing essential context.
- **Experiment with Code Modifications**: Feel free to modify the code in each project to explore different solutions or add your own ideas. Experimenting with the code reinforces your understanding and allows you to see how changes impact the application.
- **Document Your Work**: Take notes as you progress through each project. Documenting your approach, the challenges you encountered, and how you resolved them can help reinforce learning and serve as a valuable reference for future projects.

Leveraging Additional Resources

While this book is comprehensive, app development is a vast field with continual advancements. To further enrich your learning experience, each chapter includes recommendations for additional reading and online resources where relevant. These resources allow you to delve deeper into specific topics, stay updated with the latest developments in C# and .NET, and connect with communities where you can learn from others.

Building a Portfolio Through Progressive Projects

One of the unique aspects of this book is the progressive nature of the hands-on projects. By the time you reach the final chapters, you'll have completed a series of projects that demonstrate your skills in modern app development. These projects can serve as portfolio pieces, showcasing your expertise in C# 8's advanced features, cloud integration, cross-platform development, and more.

For readers who are building their resumes or portfolios, this book offers an opportunity to compile a set of fully functional applications that illustrate your mastery of modern C# practices. Each project is designed with real-world relevance in mind, making it an ideal addition to your portfolio or GitHub profile to impress prospective employers or clients.

This book is designed to be a lasting resource that you can return to as you advance in your career. Beyond serving as a learning tool, it's also structured as a reference guide. Each chapter's Key Takeaways section makes it easy to quickly revisit core concepts, while the hands-on projects provide a practical foundation that you can build upon with future projects.

Setting Up Your Development Environment: Essential Tools and Software

1. Choosing the Right IDE: Visual Studio and Visual Studio Code

For C# development, Visual Studio and Visual Studio Code (VS Code) are the most popular Integrated Development Environments (IDEs) due to their robust feature sets and Microsoft's continuous support.

Visual Studio (Recommended for Comprehensive Development)

Visual Studio is an all-in-one IDE designed specifically for .NET and C# development, making it ideal for complex projects and enterprise applications.

Visual Studio includes tools for debugging, profiling, and testing, as well as support for source control and deployment pipelines, which makes it particularly useful for larger projects and professional development.

- **Download and Installation**: Visit the Visual Studio download page and select the Community, Professional, or Enterprise edition, depending on your needs and budget. The Community edition is free and offers all essential features, making it an excellent choice for personal and educational use.
- **Workload Selection**: During installation, select the **.NET desktop development** and **ASP.NET and web development** workloads. These workloads install all the necessary libraries, frameworks, and dependencies for C# 8, web applications, and desktop applications.
- **Extensions**: Visual Studio supports a wide range of extensions to enhance your development experience. Consider installing:
- **ReSharper** for advanced code refactoring and analysis
- **GitHub Extension for Visual Studio** for streamlined GitHub integration
- **Azure Functions and WebJobs Tools** for cloud-based projects

Visual Studio Code (Recommended for Flexibility and Lightweight Needs)

Visual Studio Code is a lightweight, extensible code editor that is highly customizable and supports a wide range of programming languages and frameworks. While it lacks some of the advanced features of Visual Studio, it's ideal for developers who prefer a minimal setup or need to work across various languages in addition to C#.

- **Download and Installation**: Visit the Visual Studio Code website to download the latest version. It's available for Windows, macOS, and Linux.
- **Essential Extensions for C#**:
- **C# by Microsoft**: Provides syntax highlighting, IntelliSense, and

debugging features for C#.

- **Live Share**: Allows real-time collaboration with other developers, a useful tool for pair programming or team-based projects.
- **Azure Functions**: Useful for developing cloud-integrated applications.
- **Docker**: Essential if you plan to containerize your applications for microservices or cloud deployments.
- **Settings and Customizations**: VS Code offers extensive customization options. Configure settings like auto-save, format on save, and keyboard shortcuts based on your workflow preferences.

2. Installing the .NET SDK

The .NET SDK (Software Development Kit) includes all necessary libraries, compilers, and tools to build, run, and publish .NET applications. With .NET Core's cross-platform capabilities, you can develop C# applications on Windows, macOS, or Linux. The latest .NET SDK is essential for developing with C# 8 features.

- **Download and Installation**: Download the latest .NET SDK from Microsoft's .NET website. Choose the SDK version compatible with your operating system. The installer includes the .NET runtime, which is required for running .NET applications, and the CLI (command-line interface), which provides essential commands for creating, building, and running projects.
- **Verifying the Installation**: After installation, verify that the SDK is correctly installed by running the following command in your terminal or command prompt:

```bash
dotnet --version
```

- This command should return the installed version of the SDK, confirming a successful setup.

3. Configuring Git for Version Control

Git is a version control system that helps track changes in your code, collaborate with other developers, and manage code revisions. It's a fundamental tool in modern development, especially for projects that require collaboration or long-term maintenance.

- **Download and Installation**: Install Git from git-scm.com. After installation, configure Git with your username and email address:

```bash
git config --global user.name "Your Name"
git config --global user.email "your.email@example.com"
```

- **Using Git with Visual Studio and VS Code**: Both Visual Studio and Visual Studio Code offer integrated Git support. In Visual Studio, open the Team Explorer tab to access Git functionalities. In VS Code, the Source Control tab allows you to manage repositories, stage changes, and push to remote repositories.
- **Integrating with GitHub**: For online repository management, consider creating a GitHub account. GitHub repositories provide versioned cloud storage for your code and facilitate easy collaboration with other developers. You can create repositories, track issues, and manage pull requests directly from Visual Studio or VS Code.

4. Setting Up Docker for Containerized Development

Docker enables you to package applications into containers, ensuring that they run consistently across different environments. Containers are especially useful for microservices and cloud-based applications, where each service may have its own dependencies.

- **Download and Installation**: Install Docker from Docker's website. Docker Desktop is available for Windows and macOS; Linux users can follow the instructions on the site for their specific distribution.
- **Docker Integration in Visual Studio and VS Code**: Visual Studio includes Docker support, allowing you to create, run, and debug containers directly from the IDE. VS Code also offers a Docker extension, providing similar functionality within a lightweight environment.
- **Configuring Docker with .NET Applications**: After installing Docker, you can containerize .NET applications by adding a Dockerfile to your project. Visual Studio can automatically generate this file and integrate Docker commands, making it easy to build and run containers.

5. Database Management Tools

Many modern applications are data-driven, so having the right database tools is essential. For C# development, SQL Server and SQLite are popular choices, but you can also work with PostgreSQL, MySQL, or NoSQL databases like MongoDB.

- **SQL Server**: SQL Server is Microsoft's flagship database solution and integrates seamlessly with C# and .NET applications. You can download SQL Server Express for free or use SQL Server in the cloud via Azure SQL Database.
- **SQLite**: SQLite is a lightweight, file-based database ideal for small applications or as a testing database.
- **Database Management Tools**: Install SQL Server Management Studio (SSMS) or Azure Data Studio to manage SQL Server databases, run queries, and perform administrative tasks. These tools provide a graphical interface for database operations, making them valuable for testing and development.

6. Testing Frameworks and Debugging Tools

Testing is essential in modern development to ensure code quality, functionality, and performance. Visual Studio includes built-in support for popular testing frameworks, while VS Code allows easy integration with these tools.

- **xUnit and NUnit**: These are widely used testing frameworks for C# that support unit and integration tests. Visual Studio supports both xUnit and NUnit with minimal setup.
- **MSTest**: Microsoft's own testing framework, MSTest, is also supported in Visual Studio. It's a straightforward option for users who want a testing framework with full IDE integration.
- **Debugger Tools**: Visual Studio's debugger is one of its strongest features, providing breakpoints, variable watches, and step-through capabilities. VS Code also includes a debugger with support for C# breakpoints, allowing you to inspect code flow and identify issues during runtime.

7. Setting Up Azure for Cloud Integration

Microsoft Azure is a powerful cloud platform that supports .NET applications natively. If you plan to build cloud-based applications, setting up an Azure account provides access to services like Azure App Services, Azure SQL, and Azure Functions.

- **Creating an Azure Account**: Sign up for a free Azure account at azure.microsoft.com. The free account provides credits to explore Azure services, which is especially helpful for learning and experimentation.
- **Azure Tools for Visual Studio and VS Code**: Visual Studio includes Azure integration, allowing you to deploy directly to Azure services from the IDE. For VS Code, the Azure Account and Azure App Service extensions provide similar functionality, making it easy to manage Azure resources and deploy applications without leaving your editor.

8. Additional Tools and Plugins for Enhanced Productivity

A productive development environment often includes additional tools that streamline workflows and improve code quality.

- **Postman**: An API client that simplifies API testing, Postman is useful for developers working with web services and REST APIs. It allows you to test endpoints, manage requests, and debug HTTP requests.
- **Fiddler**: Fiddler is a web debugging proxy tool that logs HTTP(S) traffic. It's valuable for diagnosing network issues, especially in web and cloud applications.
- **Live Server (for VS Code)**: This extension provides a local server for web development, allowing you to preview changes in real-time as you edit files. This tool is useful for front-end developers or when testing web-based interfaces in cross-platform applications.

Final Configuration Tips

Once your environment is set up, consider customizing settings based on your preferences. Here are a few final tips:

- **Configuring Code Formatting**: Both Visual Studio and VS Code offer formatting options. Configuring your IDE to automatically format code on save can improve readability and standardize your code, which is especially beneficial for collaborative projects. In Visual Studio, you can set formatting rules under **Options > Text Editor > C# > Code Style**, while VS Code offers a **Format on Save** option under **Settings**.
- **Environment Variables**: If your application requires sensitive information like API keys or database connection strings, avoid hard-coding these values directly in your code. Instead, set up environment variables on your development machine. This approach is more secure and allows for easier configuration across different environments (e.g., development, staging, and production).
- **Version Control Settings**: Configuring Git for branch naming conventions, commit signing, and push restrictions can help maintain consistency and integrity in your version history. Tools like GitLens for VS Code provide enhanced Git insights, showing the history of changes to individual lines of code and integrating with services like GitHub or GitLab.

Testing Your Environment Setup

After installing and configuring your development environment, it's a good idea to perform a few basic tests to ensure everything is working as expected. These tests also provide an opportunity to familiarize yourself with the workflow you'll use throughout the book.

Creating a Sample .NET Project

Creating the Project: Open your IDE and create a new console application. In Visual Studio, select **Create a new project > Console App (.NET Core)**, and in VS Code, you can use the terminal:

```bash
dotnet new console -o SampleApp
```

Writing a Test Program: Open Program.cs in the SampleApp folder and replace the default code with a simple test program. For example:

```csharp
using System;

class Program
{
    static void Main(string[] args)
    {
        Console.WriteLine("Environment setup successful!");
    }
}
```

Building and Running: Run the application to ensure that your setup is correct. In Visual Studio, click **Start**; in VS Code, use:

```bash
dotnet run
```

You should see the output "Environment setup successful!" in the console, confirming that your C# environment is operational.

Testing Git Integration

Initialize a Repository: In your sample project folder, initialize a new Git repository:

```bash
git init
```

Make an Initial Commit: Stage and commit your project files:

```bash
git add .
git commit -m "Initial commit"
```

Push to a Remote Repository: If you have a GitHub account, create a new repository online and link it to your local project:

```bash
git remote add origin https://github.com/yourusername/SampleApp.git
git push -u origin master
```

This confirms that Git is properly set up and that you're ready to work with version control throughout the book.

Docker Test: Running a Sample Container

To verify Docker installation, run a sample Docker container:

Pull a Sample Image: Pull an official .NET image from Docker Hub:

```bash
bash

docker pull mcr.microsoft.com/dotnet/core/runtime:latest
```

Run the Container: Start the container:

```bash
bash

docker run -it mcr.microsoft.com/dotnet/core/runtime:latest
```

If the container runs successfully, Docker is set up and ready to be used for containerizing and deploying .NET applications.

Wrapping Up: Ready to Code

With your development environment fully set up, you're ready to dive into the hands-on projects and advanced features of C# 8 covered in this book. As you progress, this setup will allow you to seamlessly build, test, and deploy applications, providing a streamlined workflow to support your learning and productivity.

Remember to keep your environment up to date—both Visual Studio and .NET SDK receive frequent updates, which often include important bug fixes and performance improvements. A well-maintained setup not only enhances your development experience but also ensures compatibility with the latest tools and libraries.

Getting Started with C# 8 Fundamentals

Introduction to C# 8: Language Basics and Syntax Refresh
C# has consistently evolved since its inception, maintaining a strong presence in modern software development. With C# 8, Microsoft has introduced features that not only simplify programming but also promote safer, more efficient, and maintainable code. Before diving into these new capabilities, it's essential to revisit the fundamentals of C# syntax and structure to ensure a solid foundation for understanding advanced features.

This section will cover the following topics:

- Basic Syntax and Structure
- Core Language Constructs
- Data Types and Variables
- Control Flow Statements
- Methods and Parameters
- Error Handling and Exceptions

Each of these elements forms the backbone of any C# application, and a comprehensive understanding is necessary to utilize the language to its fullest potential.

Basic Syntax and Structure

The basic structure of a C# application reflects its roots in object-oriented programming (OOP), where everything is organized within classes. Each C# program starts with a Main method, which serves as the entry point. Let's begin by examining a simple example of a C# program:

```csharp
using System;

namespace HelloWorldApp
{
    class Program
    {
        static void Main(string[] args)
        {
            Console.WriteLine("Hello, World!");
        }
    }
}
```

Explanation of Key Elements

1. **Namespace**: Namespaces are used to organize code and prevent naming conflicts. The System namespace, for example, contains fundamental classes and methods, such as Console.
2. **Class Declaration**: class Program defines a class, which is a blueprint for objects. Classes encapsulate methods, fields, and other data members.
3. **Main Method**: The Main method (static void Main(string[] args)) is the starting point for a C# application. The static keyword signifies that Main can be called without instantiating the Program class, and void indicates that it does not return a value.
4. **Console Output**: Console.WriteLine("Hello, World!"); outputs text to the console. The Console class provides various methods for input and output, widely used for debugging and simple applications.

Core Language Constructs

C# offers a comprehensive set of language constructs that support object-oriented, structured, and even some functional programming approaches. Understanding these constructs will help establish a flexible coding style as we proceed.

Variables and Data Types

C# is a statically typed language, meaning each variable's type must be explicitly declared. Here's an example:

```csharp
int age = 30;
double height = 5.9;
string name = "Alice";
bool isDeveloper = true;
```

Each of these lines declares a variable with a specific data type:

1. **int**: Represents integer values.
2. **double**: Stores decimal values with a high level of precision.
3. **string**: Stores text.
4. **bool**: Holds true or false values.

Type Inference with var

C# supports type inference, allowing you to use the var keyword to let the compiler deduce the variable type based on the assigned value:

```csharp
var salary = 50000;     // int
var pi = 3.14159;       // double
var greeting = "Hello"; // string
```

Type inference can make code more concise, but it's recommended to use explicit types for readability, especially in complex or team-based projects.

Control Flow Statements

Control flow statements determine the flow of execution in a program, including conditional statements and loops.

Conditional Statements

if-else: The if statement allows you to execute code conditionally. If the condition is true, the code block inside if runs; otherwise, the else block (if present) executes.

```csharp
int number = 10;

if (number > 5)
{
    Console.WriteLine("Number is greater than 5");
}
else
{
    Console.WriteLine("Number is 5 or less");
}
```

switch: The switch statement evaluates a variable and executes code based on the matching case. With C# 8, switch expressions allow more concise and readable code.

```csharp
string day = "Monday";

switch (day)
{
    case "Monday":
        Console.WriteLine("Start of the work week.");
        break;
    case "Friday":
        Console.WriteLine("End of the work week.");
        break;
    default:
        Console.WriteLine("Middle of the week.");
        break;
```

```
}
```

Loops

for: The for loop is used for executing code a specific number of times, typically when the number of iterations is known.

csharp

```csharp
for (int i = 0; i < 5; i++)
{
    Console.WriteLine("Iteration: " + i);
}
```

while: The while loop continues executing as long as a condition remains true. It's useful when the number of iterations is unknown.

csharp

```csharp
int count = 0;
while (count < 5)
{
    Console.WriteLine("Count is: " + count);
    count++;
}
```

foreach: The foreach loop iterates over elements in a collection, such as an array or list.

csharp

```csharp
string[] colors = { "Red", "Green", "Blue" };

foreach (string color in colors)
{
    Console.WriteLine(color);
```

```
}
```

Methods and Parameters

Methods in C# allow you to encapsulate code, improving readability and reusability. Methods can have parameters, return values, and optional arguments.

Basic Method Structure

```csharp
public int Add(int a, int b)
{
    return a + b;
}
```

In this example:

- public is the access modifier, indicating the method is accessible from outside the class.
- int is the return type, specifying that the method returns an integer.
- Add is the method name.
- (int a, int b) are the parameters, allowing values to be passed to the method when it's called.

Method Overloading

C# supports method overloading, which allows multiple methods with the same name but different parameters.

```csharp
public int Add(int a, int b) => a + b;
public double Add(double a, double b) => a + b;
```

Here, the Add method can handle both integer and double values due to overloading.

Data Encapsulation and Access Modifiers

Encapsulation is a core concept in object-oriented programming, providing mechanisms to restrict access to data within a class. Access modifiers in C# define the visibility of classes, fields, and methods:

- **public**: Accessible from any other code.
- **private**: Accessible only within the containing class.
- **protected**: Accessible within the containing class and derived classes.
- **internal**: Accessible only within the same assembly (project).

Example of Data Encapsulation

```csharp
public class BankAccount
{
    private decimal balance;

    public void Deposit(decimal amount)
    {
        if (amount > 0)
        {
            balance += amount;
        }
    }

    public decimal GetBalance()
    {
        return balance;
    }
}
```

In this example, balance is private, meaning it cannot be directly accessed outside BankAccount. Instead, the Deposit and GetBalance methods control how balance is modified and accessed.

Error Handling and Exception Management

Error handling is essential in writing robust applications. C# uses exceptions to manage errors and unexpected behavior, ensuring that applications can handle faults gracefully.

Try-Catch-Finally

The try-catch-finally construct allows you to handle exceptions in a controlled manner:

```csharp
try
{
    int result = 10 / 0;
}
catch (DivideByZeroException ex)
{
    Console.WriteLine("Division by zero is not allowed: " +
    ex.Message);
}
finally
{
    Console.WriteLine("Execution completed.");
}
```

In this code:

- **try**: Contains the code that may cause an exception.
- **catch**: Handles specific exceptions, such as DivideByZeroException.
- **finally**: Executes regardless of whether an exception occurred, often used for cleanup operations.

Understanding C# syntax and foundational structures provides a reliable base for tackling more advanced features. C# 8 builds on these concepts, introducing new capabilities that enhance code readability, safety, and performance. By revisiting these basics, you're setting yourself up to apply new techniques with greater confidence, ensuring that you can use C# 8's features effectively in real-world applications.

Nullable Reference Types: Writing Safer Code

One of the most significant and widely anticipated features introduced in C# 8 is nullable reference types, a concept that fundamentally changes how developers handle null values in their code. Traditionally, null references have been a common source of bugs and runtime errors, often resulting in NullReferenceExceptions when code attempts to access members of a null object. In larger or complex codebases, null values can easily propagate through methods and classes, making it difficult to trace the source of these errors.

Nullable reference types provide a new approach by enabling developers to explicitly declare when a reference type can or cannot be null. This feature helps prevent null-related errors at compile time rather than runtime, improving code safety, readability, and reliability. In this section, we'll explore how nullable reference types work, the benefits they offer, and how to implement them effectively.

Understanding Nullable Reference Types

Before C# 8, all reference types in C# were nullable by default. This meant that any object of a reference type (e.g., string, class, object) could be assigned a null value, even when that was not intended by the developer. With nullable reference types, C# 8 introduces a distinction between non-nullable and nullable reference types, allowing the compiler to check for potential null assignments and alert the developer when a null value might cause an issue.

Non-Nullable Reference Types

In C# 8, reference types are treated as non-nullable by default. This change means that if you declare a variable as a reference type without explicitly marking it as nullable, the compiler assumes that the variable should never hold a null value. For example:

```
csharp
```

```
string message = "Hello, World!"; // Non-nullable
```

In this code, message is a non-nullable reference type, meaning it cannot be assigned null without triggering a compiler warning. If you attempt to assign null to message, the compiler will produce a warning, helping you catch potential issues before they reach runtime.

Nullable Reference Types

To explicitly indicate that a reference type can be null, you use a question mark ? after the type name. This notation tells the compiler that the variable may hold a null value, allowing the assignment of null without warnings. For example:

```
csharp
```

```
string? nullableMessage = null; // Nullable
```

In this code, nullableMessage is a nullable reference type, which means it can safely hold a null value without causing a compiler warning. However, this also means that any code interacting with nullableMessage needs to handle the possibility that it may be null.

Enabling Nullable Reference Types

Nullable reference types are optional and must be explicitly enabled in your project. You can enable them in one of two ways:

Project-Level Enabling: Modify your project file (e.g., .csproj) to enable nullable reference types across the entire project by adding the following line:

```
xml
```

```
<Nullable>enable</Nullable>
```

Code-Level Enabling: Alternatively, you can enable nullable reference types at the code level using a directive at the top of your code file:

```csharp
#nullable enable
```

To disable nullable reference types for specific code sections, you can use #nullable disable:

```csharp
#nullable disable
string legacyString = null; // No warning
```

Benefits of Using Nullable Reference Types

The primary benefit of nullable reference types is that they reduce the risk of NullReferenceExceptions. By catching potential null issues at compile time, you can prevent common errors, increase code clarity, and improve maintainability. Let's explore some key benefits:

1. **Compile-Time Safety**: Nullable reference types bring null-safety checks to the compiler level, allowing you to detect and resolve null-related issues before the application is built and deployed.
2. **Self-Documenting Code**: By marking reference types as nullable or non-nullable, your code communicates the intended usage of each variable, making it easier for other developers (or even your future self) to understand the code's structure and constraints.
3. **Enhanced Code Quality**: Nullable reference types encourage developers to handle nulls explicitly, leading to code that is more robust and less prone to runtime errors. This improvement is particularly beneficial in large applications where null handling might otherwise become inconsistent or difficult to manage.

Working with Nullable Reference Types

When you enable nullable reference types, the compiler starts issuing warnings whenever it detects potential nullability issues. Let's look at some common scenarios and how to handle them.

Nullable Assignment and Warnings

When you declare a non-nullable reference type and attempt to assign a null value, the compiler will issue a warning. For example:

```csharp
string name = null; // Compiler warning: possible null assignment
```

The warning is a reminder to the developer that name is expected to be non-nullable. To resolve the warning, either assign a non-null value or explicitly declare name as nullable:

```csharp
string? name = null; // No warning, since name is nullable
```

Nullability Warnings with Method Parameters

Methods that accept nullable reference types as parameters can use null checks to handle the possibility of a null value being passed in. This practice helps ensure that the method handles nulls gracefully, without causing unexpected behavior. Here's an example:

```csharp
public void Greet(string? name)
{
    if (name == null)
    {
        Console.WriteLine("Hello, guest!");
```

```
    }
    else
    {
        Console.WriteLine($"Hello, {name}!");
    }
}
```

In this example, the Greet method accepts a nullable name parameter and uses a conditional check to determine if it's null. This approach ensures that the method performs correctly regardless of whether a null value is provided.

The Null-Forgiving Operator (!)

In some cases, you may know that a variable cannot be null, even if the compiler issues a warning. To override the compiler's nullability check, you can use the null-forgiving operator (!). This operator tells the compiler to ignore potential null warnings for that specific instance.

csharp

```csharp
string? nullableName = GetName();
Console.WriteLine(nullableName!.Length); // Using null-forgiving
operator
```

Here, nullableName is nullable, but the null-forgiving operator signals to the compiler that nullableName will not be null when accessed. Use this operator sparingly, as it bypasses the safety provided by nullable reference types.

Nullable Reference Types in Method Return Values

Nullable reference types can also be used in method return values to signify that a method may or may not return a valid object. For example:

csharp

```csharp
public string? FindItemById(int id)
{
```

```
    if (itemExists)
        return itemName;
    return null;
}
```

In this example, the method FindItemById returns a string?, indicating that it may return a null value if no item with the specified ID is found. This practice allows calling code to handle the possibility of null results more explicitly.

Using Nullable Reference Types in Collections

Nullable reference types can be used in collections such as arrays and lists, where individual elements may be null. Here's an example:

csharp

```
List<string?> names = new List<string?>() { "Alice", null, "Bob" };
```

In this code, the names list contains nullable strings, allowing each element to either hold a string or be null. When working with nullable collections, ensure that you handle potential null values during iteration and processing.

Best Practices for Nullable Reference Types

To get the most out of nullable reference types, consider the following best practices:

1. **Enable Nullable Reference Types at the Project Level**: Enabling nullable reference types across your entire project ensures consistency in how null values are handled, reducing the risk of null-related errors.
2. **Avoid Excessive Null-Forgiving Operators**: The null-forgiving operator should be used sparingly. Excessive use can undermine the safety that nullable reference types provide, leading to potential runtime errors.
3. **Check Nullability in External APIs**: When working with external

APIs or libraries that may not support nullable reference types, be cautious with null values. Always check the returned values to avoid unexpected nulls from third-party code.

4. **Use Null Checks and ?? Operator**: Use null checks (if (variable == null)) or the null-coalescing operator (??) to handle potential nulls in your code. This practice helps prevent runtime errors and ensures that you're prepared for nullable values.

5. **Review Code for Readability**: Ensure that nullable reference types improve the readability of your code. Using nullable reference types should make code clearer rather than introducing unnecessary complexity.

Nullable reference types in C# 8 are a powerful feature designed to reduce null-related bugs by enforcing a stricter contract around when nulls can or cannot be assigned to variables. By using nullable reference types, you can prevent many common runtime errors, improve code clarity, and build applications that are more robust and easier to maintain.

Understanding Switch Expressions and Their Use Cases

In C# 8, Microsoft introduced switch expressions as an enhancement to the traditional switch statement. Switch expressions streamline code by offering a more concise, expressive syntax, making complex conditional logic easier to read and maintain. While the traditional switch statement remains useful, switch expressions reduce boilerplate code and allow developers to use pattern matching within a functional programming style.

Switch expressions are ideal for scenarios where a value needs to be evaluated against multiple cases, and a corresponding result is returned based on the match. This section will delve into the syntax, usage, and best practices for switch expressions, demonstrating how they enhance readability, efficiency, and flexibility in code.

Traditional switch Statement Recap

Before exploring switch expressions, let's briefly review the traditional switch statement. Typically, a switch statement evaluates an expression and executes the code associated with the matching case. Here's an example:

```csharp
public string GetDayType(string day)
{
    switch (day)
    {
        case "Monday":
        case "Tuesday":
        case "Wednesday":
        case "Thursday":
        case "Friday":
            return "Weekday";
        case "Saturday":
        case "Sunday":
            return "Weekend";
        default:
            return "Invalid day";
    }
}
```

This code checks the value of day and returns "Weekday", "Weekend", or "Invalid day" based on the input. While functional, the traditional switch statement can become verbose, especially when evaluating multiple values or implementing complex patterns. The switch expression addresses this by reducing the amount of code required for similar logic.

Introduction to switch Expressions

Switch expressions in C# 8 allow you to evaluate an expression and return a value based on the matching case, all in a single expression. They are particularly useful for scenarios where you want to return a value directly rather than execute multiple statements. Here's a simple example of a switch expression:

```csharp
public string GetDayType(string day) =>
    day switch
    {
        "Monday" => "Weekday",
        "Tuesday" => "Weekday",
        "Wednesday" => "Weekday",
        "Thursday" => "Weekday",
        "Friday" => "Weekday",
        "Saturday" => "Weekend",
        "Sunday" => "Weekend",
        _ => "Invalid day"
    };
```

Key Features of switch Expressions

1. **Concise Syntax**: Switch expressions eliminate the need for case labels, break statements, and explicit return statements, resulting in cleaner code.
2. **Exhaustive Matching**: The default case (_) is required if there's any possibility that the input value may not match any specified case, ensuring the expression is exhaustive and preventing runtime errors.
3. **Immutable Nature**: Switch expressions return a value rather than modifying a variable, making them ideal for functional-style programming.

Syntax of switch Expressions

The basic syntax of a switch expression involves using the switch keyword after an input expression, followed by a series of cases in the form of pattern-value pairs. Each pair consists of a pattern (such as a constant or type) and a corresponding result or expression. Here's the general form:

```
csharp

result = expression switch
{
    pattern1 => result1,
    pattern2 => result2,
    _ => defaultResult
};
```

In this syntax:

- expression is the value being evaluated.
- Each pattern is a condition to match.
- result is the outcome returned if the pattern is matched.
- _ represents the default or fallback case, which is required if not all cases are covered explicitly.

Using Switch Expressions with Pattern Matching

C# 8 extends switch expressions with pattern matching, enabling more flexible conditions. Patterns can include constant values, type checks, relational patterns, or even property patterns, allowing for complex logic within a single expression. Let's look at some common pattern types.

Constant Pattern Matching

Constant patterns allow matching based on specific values, similar to the example above. Here's another example that uses an integer input:

```
csharp

public string GradeFeedback(int grade) =>
    grade switch
    {
        >= 90 => "Excellent",
        >= 75 => "Good",
```

```
    >= 50 => "Pass",
    < 50 => "Fail",
    _ => "Invalid grade"
};
```

In this example, the GradeFeedback method returns feedback based on the integer value of grade. Relational patterns (>=, <) allow for a range of values within each case, adding flexibility.

Type Pattern Matching

Switch expressions also support type patterns, allowing you to evaluate an object's type at runtime and handle cases accordingly. This approach is helpful in situations involving polymorphism or dynamic objects. Here's an example:

```csharp
public string ProcessData(object data) =>
    data switch
    {
        int i => $"Integer: {i}",
        string s => $"String: {s}",
        bool b => $"Boolean: {b}",
        _ => "Unknown type"
    };
```

In this code, ProcessData checks the runtime type of data and processes it based on whether it's an int, string, or bool. This pattern helps avoid if-else chains and reduces the need for explicit type casting.

Property Pattern Matching

Property patterns allow matching based on the properties of an object, rather than its value or type alone. This is especially useful when dealing with complex objects where decisions depend on specific property values. Here's an example with an Order class:

csharp

```
public string GetOrderStatus(Order order) =>
    order switch
    {
        { Status: "Shipped", IsUrgent: true } => "Urgent shipment
        in progress",
        { Status: "Shipped", IsUrgent: false } => "Shipment in
        progress",
        { Status: "Pending" } => "Order is pending",
        { Status: "Canceled" } => "Order has been canceled",
        _ => "Unknown status"
    };
```

In this example, GetOrderStatus checks multiple properties of an Order object, providing tailored messages based on the combination of Status and IsUrgent. Property patterns streamline complex conditional checks, keeping the code readable and maintainable.

Practical Use Cases for Switch Expressions

Switch expressions can be applied in various real-world scenarios where multiple conditional branches are needed. Here are a few practical use cases:

1. Enum-Based Decision Making

Enums are often used to represent a finite set of values. Switch expressions are ideal for making decisions based on enum values. For example, consider an application that provides different discounts based on membership levels:

csharp

```
public decimal CalculateDiscount(MembershipLevel level) =>
    level switch
    {
        MembershipLevel.Bronze => 0.05m,
```

```csharp
        MembershipLevel.Silver => 0.10m,
        MembershipLevel.Gold => 0.15m,
        MembershipLevel.Platinum => 0.20m,
        _ => 0.0m
    };
```

Using switch expressions with enums provides a clear, concise way to handle each level, ensuring that the code remains easy to read and update if new levels are added.

2. Error Handling and Response Codes

Switch expressions can be used to generate responses based on error codes, simplifying the handling of errors and ensuring consistency in responses:

```csharp
csharp

public string GetErrorMessage(int errorCode) =>
    errorCode switch
    {
        404 => "Not Found",
        500 => "Internal Server Error",
        403 => "Forbidden",
        401 => "Unauthorized",
        _ => "Unknown Error"
    };
```

This approach is particularly useful for API development, where consistent error handling is crucial.

3. Simplifying Complex Decision Trees

For complex conditions that involve a combination of factors, such as eligibility criteria or decision trees, switch expressions with property patterns provide a readable and structured solution. Here's an example:

```csharp
public string DetermineEligibility(Person person) =>
    person switch
    {
        { Age: >= 18, Citizenship: "US" } => "Eligible for voting",
        { Age: >= 18, Citizenship: "Non-US" } => "Not eligible for
        US voting",
        { Age: < 18 } => "Not eligible due to age",
        _ => "Eligibility unknown"
    };
```

This example uses age and citizenship status to determine voting eligibility. By consolidating these checks into a single switch expression, the code is more intuitive and easier to modify if eligibility criteria change.

Best Practices for Using Switch Expressions

1. **Use Switch Expressions for Readability**: Switch expressions improve readability, especially when dealing with simple decisions. Avoid overusing them for highly complex logic, as they may become difficult to maintain.

2. **Leverage Pattern Matching**: Use pattern matching to handle complex conditions and avoid excessive if-else chains. Property and type patterns can make your code cleaner and more efficient.

3. **Handle Exhaustive Cases**: Ensure that switch expressions cover all possible cases, particularly when working with enums or other finite sets. Using a default case (_ =>) helps avoid runtime errors due to unhandled cases.

4. **Prefer Expressions over Statements for Simple Logic**: If the switch operation is straightforward and can return a single result, favor switch expressions over traditional statements. They reduce boilerplate and make code more expressive.

Switch expressions in C# 8 provide a powerful tool for simplifying conditional logic. By allowing for pattern matching, concise syntax, and a functional programming approach, switch expressions make code more readable and maintainable. With applications ranging from enum handling to complex decision trees, switch expressions help developers reduce errors and create more robust applications.

Pattern Matching Enhancements: Simplifying Complex Logic

Pattern matching in C# was first introduced in C# 7, providing a new way to work with conditional logic based on the characteristics of objects and data. In C# 8, pattern matching has been significantly expanded, offering even more powerful constructs that make complex logic simpler and more expressive. These enhancements enable developers to replace verbose if-else chains with clean, declarative code that is easier to read and maintain.

Pattern matching enhancements in C# 8 include new types of patterns: **property patterns**, **positional patterns**, and **recursive patterns**. Each type serves a distinct purpose, helping to streamline code that involves complex data structures, multiple conditions, or nested properties.

Why Pattern Matching Matters

Traditional conditional logic, such as if-else and switch statements, works well for basic scenarios but can become unwieldy when handling complex data or hierarchical structures. Pattern matching allows you to concisely describe conditions and decompose objects without excessive casting, improving both readability and efficiency. For scenarios involving complex business logic, pattern matching significantly reduces boilerplate code, making applications easier to debug and extend.

Pattern Matching Syntax and Types in C# 8

Let's explore the new pattern types introduced in C# 8 and their specific use cases.

1. Property Patterns

Property patterns match values based on the properties of an object, making them particularly useful for objects with multiple properties where different combinations need distinct handling. Instead of using a sequence of nested if conditions, property patterns allow you to evaluate the properties directly within a switch or conditional expression.

Example of Property Patterns

Consider a scenario where we have an Order class with properties Status and IsPriority, and we want to determine the handling process based on these properties:

```csharp
public class Order
{
    public string Status { get; set; }
    public bool IsPriority { get; set; }
}

public string GetOrderStatus(Order order) =>
    order switch
    {
        { Status: "Processing", IsPriority: true } => "Process
        priority order",
        { Status: "Processing", IsPriority: false } => "Process
        regular order",
        { Status: "Completed" } => "Order completed",
        { Status: "Canceled" } => "Order canceled",
        _ => "Unknown status"
    };
```

In this example, each case in the switch expression evaluates a different combination of Status and IsPriority. By directly referencing properties, property patterns provide a succinct alternative to deeply nested if-else conditions.

2. Positional Patterns

Positional patterns are designed for types that follow a specific positional structure, particularly tuples and records, which were introduced in C# 9. While positional patterns are more commonly used with records, they allow you to destructure objects based on positional parameters, making them ideal for types that are defined by a sequence of values.

Positional patterns are often seen in conjunction with deconstruction. Let's consider a hypothetical Point struct:

```csharp
public struct Point
{
    public int X { get; }
    public int Y { get; }

    public Point(int x, int y) => (X, Y) = (x, y);

    public void Deconstruct(out int x, out int y) => (x, y) = (X,
    Y);
}

public string GetPointLocation(Point point) =>
    point switch
    {
        (0, 0) => "Origin",
        (var x, 0) => $"Point on X-axis at {x}",
        (0, var y) => $"Point on Y-axis at {y}",
        _ => $"Point at ({point.X}, {point.Y})"
    };
```

In this code, the Point struct defines a Deconstruct method, enabling it to be used with positional patterns. The GetPointLocation method then matches points based on their positional values for X and Y, which is more compact and readable than manually accessing each property in a nested structure.

3. Recursive Patterns

Recursive patterns allow you to apply pattern matching to nested or hierarchical structures, enabling deep inspection of objects with complex properties. Recursive patterns are particularly useful in scenarios where data structures contain nested objects, such as trees, XML documents, or complex data models.

For instance, consider a scenario with nested data representing a customer's order history:

```csharp
public class Customer
{
    public string Name { get; set; }
    public Order CurrentOrder { get; set; }
}

public class Order
{
    public string Status { get; set; }
    public int TotalItems { get; set; }
}

public string GetCustomerOrderStatus(Customer customer) =>
    customer switch
    {
        { CurrentOrder: { Status: "Processing", TotalItems: > 0 }
        } => $"{customer.Name} has an order in progress",
        { CurrentOrder: { Status: "Completed" } } =>
        $"{customer.Name}'s order is completed",
        { CurrentOrder: null } => $"{customer.Name} has no current
        orders",
        _ => "Unknown order status"
    };
```

In this example, GetCustomerOrderStatus uses a recursive pattern to match CurrentOrder properties within the Customer object. The pattern first matches if CurrentOrder is non-null, then inspects nested properties within CurrentOrder. This approach simplifies complex logic, especially when dealing with nested or hierarchical data structures.

Practical Use Cases for Enhanced Pattern Matching

Pattern matching enhancements in C# 8 allow for versatile applications in real-world scenarios. Let's consider a few common use cases that highlight the advantages of these new patterns.

1. Data Validation and Error Handling

Pattern matching is useful for validating inputs and handling errors more gracefully. By using property patterns, you can check for invalid or unexpected data structures and respond appropriately without excessive code.

```csharp
public string ValidateOrder(Order order) =>
    order switch
    {
        { Status: null } => "Error: Status is missing",
        { Status: "Processing", TotalItems: <= 0 } => "Error:
        Processing order with no items",
        { Status: "Completed", TotalItems: > 0 } => "Order
        completed successfully",
        _ => "Order is valid"
    };
```

This code validates the Order object based on the values of Status and TotalItems. It simplifies error handling by consolidating conditions, making the validation logic concise and easier to extend if new conditions are added.

2. Handling Polymorphic Data

In applications that rely on polymorphism, such as those with interfaces or base classes, pattern matching with type patterns enables more flexible handling of derived types. Here's an example where different types of accounts are processed based on their type:

```csharp
public abstract class Account { }

public class SavingsAccount : Account
{
    public decimal InterestRate { get; set; }
}

public class CheckingAccount : Account
{
    public decimal OverdraftLimit { get; set; }
}

public string GetAccountDetails(Account account) =>
    account switch
    {
        SavingsAccount s => $"Savings Account with interest rate: {s.InterestRate}%",
        CheckingAccount c => $"Checking Account with overdraft limit: {c.OverdraftLimit}",
        _ => "Unknown account type"
    };
```

This example illustrates how pattern matching with type patterns can simplify polymorphic code. By matching Account instances with their specific derived types, this approach avoids manual type-checking and casting, creating more elegant and maintainable code.

3. Complex Conditional Logic

Complex conditional logic that depends on multiple criteria can be simplified with property and recursive patterns, especially when working with business rules or decision trees. For example, let's say we have a program that determines eligibility for a promotion based on several criteria:

```csharp
public class Employee
{
    public string Position { get; set; }
    public int YearsOfService { get; set; }
    public bool HasOutstandingPerformance { get; set; }
}

public string DeterminePromotionEligibility(Employee employee) =>
    employee switch
    {
        { Position: "Manager", YearsOfService: >= 5,
        HasOutstandingPerformance: true } => "Eligible for
        promotion",
        { Position: "Staff", YearsOfService: >= 3,
        HasOutstandingPerformance: true } => "Eligible for
        promotion",
        { HasOutstandingPerformance: false } => "Not eligible due
        to performance",
        _ => "Not eligible"
    };
```

By using property patterns, the code above evaluates multiple conditions (position, years of service, and performance) to determine promotion eligibility. This approach provides a clean and flexible way to handle complex business rules without deeply nested if statements.

Best Practices for Pattern Matching in C# 8

1. **Use Patterns to Replace if-else Chains**: Pattern matching simplifies conditional checks that would otherwise require long if-else chains, making code more readable and maintainable.
2. **Choose the Right Pattern Type**: Select the pattern type that best matches your scenario—use property patterns for object properties, type patterns for polymorphic scenarios, and positional patterns for tuples or records.

3. **Handle Default Cases Carefully**: Always include a default case (_ =>) in switch expressions to cover unexpected scenarios and prevent runtime errors.

4. **Combine Patterns Thoughtfully**: Mixing property, type, and positional patterns within switch expressions can handle complex conditions elegantly but avoid over-complicating logic that could be simplified.

The pattern matching enhancements in C# 8 empower developers to simplify complex conditional logic, offering new ways to match data based on values, types, and properties. By using property, type, and recursive patterns, you can replace verbose if-else constructs with concise, expressive code, improving readability and maintainability.

Hands-On Project: Building a Basic Console Application

In this hands-on project, we'll create a basic console application that applies many of the fundamental C# concepts covered so far. This project will serve as a practical introduction to C# 8, reinforcing the language basics, syntax, and pattern matching techniques while introducing you to structured programming within a real-world context. By the end of this project, you'll have a fully functional application that uses conditional logic, methods, pattern matching, and nullable reference types—all within a simple, interactive console app.

Our goal is to build a console application called **"Simple Student Manager"** that allows users to enter, update, and display student information. This application will handle common tasks such as validating inputs, managing a collection of student data, and interacting with the user through a menu-driven interface.

Project Outline

The **Simple Student Manager** console application will feature the following functions:

1. **Add Student**: Allows the user to add a new student with details such as name, ID, and GPA.
2. **Display Students**: Lists all students with their information.
3. **Find Student**: Searches for a student by ID and displays their details if found.
4. **Update Student GPA**: Updates a student's GPA based on their ID.
5. **Delete Student**: Removes a student from the list by their ID.

Step 1: Setting Up the Project

Create the Project: Open Visual Studio or Visual Studio Code, and create a new console application project called SimpleStudentManager. This will automatically generate a Program.cs file.

```bash
bash
```

```
dotnet new console -o SimpleStudentManager
```

Define the Student Class: Inside the Program.cs file, define a Student class to store information about each student. This class will include properties for ID, Name, and GPA.

```csharp
csharp

public class Student
{
    public int ID { get; set; }
    public string Name { get; set; } = string.Empty;
    public double GPA { get; set; }

    public override string ToString() => $"ID: {ID}, Name: {Name},
    GPA: {GPA:F2}";
}
```

- **Properties**: ID, Name, and GPA represent the student's unique identifier, their name, and their grade point average.

- **ToString Override**: The ToString method provides a formatted string representation of the student's details, useful for displaying information to the console.

Step 2: Creating the Menu System

To create an interactive user interface, we'll implement a menu system. This will allow the user to select different options within the console.

Main Method: Update the Main method to include the primary menu loop, where users can select options and interact with the application.

```csharp
static void Main()
{
    List<Student> students = new List<Student>();
    bool keepRunning = true;

    while (keepRunning)
    {
        Console.WriteLine("\nSimple Student Manager");
        Console.WriteLine("1. Add Student");
        Console.WriteLine("2. Display Students");
        Console.WriteLine("3. Find Student by ID");
        Console.WriteLine("4. Update Student GPA");
        Console.WriteLine("5. Delete Student");
        Console.WriteLine("6. Exit");
        Console.Write("Choose an option: ");

        var choice = Console.ReadLine();

        switch (choice)
        {
            case "1":
                AddStudent(students);
                break;
            case "2":
```

```
                DisplayStudents(students);
                break;
            case "3":
                FindStudentById(students);
                break;
            case "4":
                UpdateStudentGPA(students);
                break;
            case "5":
                DeleteStudent(students);
                break;
            case "6":
                keepRunning = false;
                Console.WriteLine("Exiting program.");
                break;
            default:
                Console.WriteLine("Invalid choice. Please try
                again.");
                break;
        }
    }
}
```

- **Loop Control**: The keepRunning variable controls the loop, allowing the user to continue interacting with the application until they choose to exit.
- **User Choice**: The choice variable captures the user's input and determines which function to execute using a switch statement.

Step 3: Implementing Functionalities

Now, let's implement each of the core functionalities of our **Simple Student Manager**.

Add Student

The AddStudent method will prompt the user to enter a student's details and add them to the list.

csharp

```csharp
static void AddStudent(List<Student> students)
{
    Console.Write("Enter Student ID: ");
    if (int.TryParse(Console.ReadLine(), out int id))
    {
        Console.Write("Enter Student Name: ");
        string name = Console.ReadLine() ?? "Unknown";

        Console.Write("Enter GPA: ");
        if (double.TryParse(Console.ReadLine(), out double gpa))
        {
            students.Add(new Student { ID = id, Name = name, GPA =
            gpa });
            Console.WriteLine("Student added successfully.");
        }
        else
        {
            Console.WriteLine("Invalid GPA.");
        }
    }
    else
    {
        Console.WriteLine("Invalid ID.");
    }
}
```

- **Error Handling**: TryParse methods are used to validate user input for ID and GPA, ensuring that valid numeric values are entered.

Display Students

The DisplayStudents method lists all students in the collection.

csharp

```csharp
static void DisplayStudents(List<Student> students)
{
    if (students.Count == 0)
    {
        Console.WriteLine("No students found.");
    }
    else
    {
        foreach (var student in students)
        {
            Console.WriteLine(student);
        }
    }
}
```

- **Looping Through Students**: A foreach loop iterates through the students list, displaying each student's details using the ToString override.

Find Student by ID

The FindStudentById method searches for a student based on their ID.

csharp

```csharp
static void FindStudentById(List<Student> students)
{
    Console.Write("Enter Student ID to find: ");
    if (int.TryParse(Console.ReadLine(), out int id))
    {
        var student = students.Find(s => s.ID == id);
        Console.WriteLine(student != null ? student.ToString() :
        "Student not found.");
    }
    else
    {
        Console.WriteLine("Invalid ID.");
    }
```

```
}
```

- **Lambda Expression**: Find uses a lambda expression to search for a student with the specified ID, providing a concise and readable way to locate records.

Update Student GPA

The UpdateStudentGPA method allows the user to update a student's GPA by ID.

csharp

```csharp
static void UpdateStudentGPA(List<Student> students)
{
    Console.Write("Enter Student ID to update GPA: ");
    if (int.TryParse(Console.ReadLine(), out int id))
    {
        var student = students.Find(s => s.ID == id);

        if (student != null)
        {
            Console.Write("Enter new GPA: ");
            if (double.TryParse(Console.ReadLine(), out double
            newGpa))
            {
                student.GPA = newGpa;
                Console.WriteLine("GPA updated successfully.");
            }
            else
            {
                Console.WriteLine("Invalid GPA.");
            }
        }
        else
        {
            Console.WriteLine("Student not found.");
```

```
            }
        }
        else
        {
            Console.WriteLine("Invalid ID.");
        }
    }
```

- **Updating Properties**: Once the student is found, the GPA property is updated based on the user's input.

Delete Student

The DeleteStudent method removes a student from the list by their ID.

csharp

```csharp
static void DeleteStudent(List<Student> students)
{
    Console.Write("Enter Student ID to delete: ");
    if (int.TryParse(Console.ReadLine(), out int id))
    {
        var student = students.Find(s => s.ID == id);

        if (student != null)
        {
            students.Remove(student);
            Console.WriteLine("Student deleted successfully.");
        }
        else
        {
            Console.WriteLine("Student not found.");
        }
    }
    else
    {
        Console.WriteLine("Invalid ID.");
    }
```

```
}
```

- **Removing an Item**: If the student is found, they are removed from the students list. If not, an appropriate message is displayed.

Running the Application

With all functions implemented, run the application to ensure it works as expected. Compile and test each function by adding, displaying, updating, finding, and deleting students. Test with valid and invalid inputs to verify the robustness of the application's error handling.

The **Simple Student Manager** console application combines foundational C# 8 concepts with practical pattern matching and data validation. This project introduces the basics of structured programming, user interaction, and error handling, setting a strong foundation for more advanced topics in C# 8 and beyond. As you proceed with this book, the skills developed here will support your understanding of more complex applications and scenarios.

Building Blocks of App Development

Data Types and Structures: Best Practices in C#
Data types and data structures form the foundation of efficient and maintainable applications in C#. They dictate how data is stored, accessed, and manipulated, directly impacting performance, readability, and code reliability. This section will explore the core data types in C#, discuss best practices for working with them, and examine data structures commonly used to organize and manage data efficiently. By adhering to these best practices, developers can produce code that is both high-performing and easy to understand and maintain.

Understanding Data Types in C#

In C#, data types fall into three broad categories: **value types**, **reference types**, and **nullable types**. Each type category has specific behaviors, storage methods, and best-use scenarios. Understanding the distinctions between these types is essential for choosing the correct one for each variable and structuring efficient data processing.

1. Value Types

Value types store their data directly in memory, making them suitable for small, frequently accessed data elements. Common value types include numeric data, bool, and char, as well as structs and enumerations. Since value types store data directly, copying a value type variable creates an independent copy of its data.

Key Value Types in C#:

- **Integral Types**: int, long, short, byte—used for integer values of varying sizes.
- **Floating-Point Types**: float, double—used for decimal numbers but with potential precision trade-offs.
- **Decimal Type**: decimal—used for high-precision financial calculations.
- **Boolean Type**: bool—stores true or false values.
- **Character Type**: char—represents a single character.

Best Practices for Value Types

- **Select the Appropriate Size**: Match the size of the type to the expected range of values. For instance, use byte (0–255) for constrained ranges or long when storing large integers.
- **Use decimal for Financial Calculations**: Avoid float and double for financial calculations due to rounding issues and precision limitations. Instead, use decimal, which is optimized for accuracy.
- **Avoid Unnecessary Casting**: Casting between value types can introduce precision loss. Be explicit with type conversions to avoid unexpected results.

2. Reference Types

Reference types store references (or memory addresses) to data rather than the actual data itself. These include classes, interfaces, arrays, and strings. When a reference type variable is assigned to another variable, they both point to the same data in memory.

Common Reference Types:

- **String**: Represents text and is immutable, meaning any modifications create a new string instance.
- **Arrays**: Collections of elements of the same type with fixed size.
- **Objects and Classes**: User-defined data types for complex data that

require encapsulation and behavior.

Best Practices for Reference Types

- **Use StringBuilder for Frequent String Manipulation**: Since strings are immutable, concatenating strings repeatedly can be inefficient. Use StringBuilder when dealing with multiple string modifications.
- **Leverage Arrays for Fixed-Size Collections**: Arrays are efficient for collections of a fixed size, but avoid them when the size is dynamic.
- **Check for Nulls**: Always validate that reference types are not null before accessing them to avoid NullReferenceException. C# 8's nullable reference types can further reduce this risk.

3. Nullable Types

Nullable types allow value types to hold null, which is useful when representing an undefined or missing value. Nullable types are declared with ?, such as int? or bool?.

```csharp
int? optionalInt = null; // nullable integer
```

Best Practices for Nullable Types

- **Use Nullable Types for Optional Values**: If a value is optional, use nullable types to represent its absence clearly.
- **Simplify with Null-Coalescing Operators**: Use the ?? operator to assign default values if a variable is null. For example:

```csharp
```

```
int value = optionalInt ?? 0; // Sets value to 0 if optionalInt is
null
```

- **Adopt Nullable Reference Types**: In C# 8 or later, enable nullable reference types to enforce null-safety checks in reference types.

Collections and Data Structures in C#

C# provides a rich set of collections for handling data in various forms. Each collection type has specific benefits depending on the data's organization, retrieval needs, and performance constraints. Below are some of the most commonly used collections and best practices for working with each.

1. Arrays

Arrays are fixed-size, strongly-typed collections of elements. They provide fast access to elements due to their contiguous memory allocation but lack flexibility in resizing.

```
csharp

int[] numbers = { 1, 2, 3, 4, 5 };
```

Best Practices for Arrays

- **Use Arrays for Fixed-Size Collections**: Arrays are ideal for collections where the number of elements does not change.
- **Avoid Frequent Resizing**: Since arrays cannot be resized, they are inefficient for collections that grow or shrink dynamically. Use lists instead for variable-sized collections.
- **Leverage Array Methods**: The Array class provides optimized methods like Sort, Find, and BinarySearch that are efficient for array operations.

2. Lists (List<T>)

List<T> is a resizable array, allowing elements to be added or removed dynamically. Lists are generic collections and part of System.Collections.Ge neric.

```csharp
List<string> fruits = new List<string> { "Apple", "Banana",
"Cherry" };
fruits.Add("Date");
```

Best Practices for Lists

- **Prefer Lists for Dynamic Collections**: Lists are efficient for collections where the size changes frequently.
- **Avoid Excessive Additions**: While lists can resize automatically, frequent additions can degrade performance due to internal array resizing.
- **Use LINQ for Complex Operations**: LINQ queries can filter, sort, and transform list data concisely.

3. Dictionaries (Dictionary<TKey, TValue>)

Dictionaries store key-value pairs and provide fast lookups by key, making them suitable for mapping unique identifiers to values.

```csharp
Dictionary<int, string> students = new Dictionary<int, string>
{
    { 1, "Alice" },
    { 2, "Bob" },
    { 3, "Charlie" }
};
```

Best Practices for Dictionaries

- **Ideal for Unique Mappings**: Use dictionaries for data where each element has a unique key, allowing for fast access.
- **Check for Key Existence**: Before accessing elements, use ContainsKey to prevent exceptions for non-existent keys.
- **Minimize Key Collisions**: Choose unique and predictable keys to ensure efficient hashing and minimize collisions.

4. HashSets (HashSet<T>)

HashSet<T> is an unordered collection of unique elements, providing fast lookups and eliminating duplicates.

csharp

```
HashSet<string> uniqueNames = new HashSet<string> { "Alice",
"Bob", "Charlie" };
uniqueNames.Add("Alice"); // Duplicate ignored
```

Best Practices for HashSets

- **Use for Unique Collections**: HashSets are ideal for enforcing uniqueness, such as in user IDs or tags.
- **Leverage Set Operations**: HashSets support operations like union, intersection, and difference, making them suitable for mathematical or comparison-based tasks.

5. Queues (Queue<T>)

Queues are First-In-First-Out (FIFO) structures where elements are added to the end and removed from the front, ideal for sequential processing tasks.

csharp

```
Queue<string> customers = new Queue<string>();
customers.Enqueue("Alice");
customers.Enqueue("Bob");
```

```
string nextCustomer = customers.Dequeue();
```

Best Practices for Queues

- **Use for FIFO Processing**: Queues are suitable for tasks that must be processed in the order of arrival, like message queues or task schedulers.
- **Avoid Random Access**: Queues do not support direct indexing. For random access needs, consider using a list.

6. Stacks (Stack<T>)

Stacks are Last-In-First-Out (LIFO) structures where the most recently added element is the first to be removed. They are useful for tasks like backtracking or undo operations.

```csharp
Stack<string> history = new Stack<string>();
history.Push("Page1");
history.Push("Page2");
string lastPage = history.Pop();
```

Best Practices for Stacks

- **Use for LIFO Processing**: Stacks are suitable for scenarios where the last element added needs to be processed first, such as tracking browser history.
- **Limit Use to Specific Cases**: Stacks are best for applications like backtracking or nested processing, not general-purpose collections.

Advanced Data Structures

Beyond standard collections, C# offers additional data structures in the System.Collections.Generic and System.Collections.Concurrent namespaces that cater to specific needs.

LinkedList (LinkedList<T>)

Linked lists are sequential collections where each element (node) points to the next, allowing efficient insertions and deletions at any position.

Best Practices for Linked Lists

- **Ideal for Frequent Insertions/Deletions**: Use linked lists when elements need to be frequently inserted or removed from any position.
- **Avoid for Random Access**: Linked lists do not support indexing, making random access inefficient.

Concurrent Collections

For applications with multithreaded environments, such as web servers or real-time data processing systems, concurrent collections like Concurrent-Dictionary and BlockingCollection offer thread-safe data management.

Best Practices for Concurrent Collections

- **Use in Multithreaded Scenarios**: For data structures accessed by multiple threads, use concurrent collections to prevent race conditions and ensure thread safety.
- **Choose Based on Requirements**: Each concurrent collection has specific benefits, such as ConcurrentDictionary for concurrent key-value management and BlockingCollection for producer-consumer patterns.

Choosing the Right Data Structure: Best Practices

Choosing the appropriate data structure can greatly impact application performance, readability, and maintainability. Here are some general guidelines:

1. **Consider Access Patterns**: Select structures that best align with data access patterns—use lists for sequential access, dictionaries for key-based lookups, and stacks or queues for specialized ordering needs.
2. **Optimize for Memory Usage**: Certain structures, like dictionaries, consume more memory due to hashing. For memory-sensitive applications, choose leaner structures like arrays or lists where possible.

3. **Leverage LINQ for Data Manipulation**: LINQ offers a concise and readable way to query and transform collections, reducing code complexity.

4. **Avoid Overengineering**: Choose data structures that are sufficient for your needs. Overly complex data structures may add unnecessary overhead.

5. **Evaluate Performance Requirements**: If the application is performance-critical, consider benchmarking different structures to determine the optimal choice.

By following these best practices, developers can leverage C#'s data types and structures to produce efficient, scalable, and maintainable applications. Understanding each data structure's strengths and limitations allows you to make informed choices that align with the requirements of modern app development.

Object-Oriented Principles Refresher: Classes, Inheritance, and Polymorphism

Object-oriented programming (OOP) is a fundamental paradigm in C# that structures code around objects and their interactions. C# leverages OOP principles—encapsulation, inheritance, and polymorphism—to create modular, maintainable, and reusable code. Mastering these principles is essential for building complex applications and understanding modern development practices in C#.

In this section, we'll revisit the core principles of OOP as implemented in C#, focusing on classes, inheritance, and polymorphism. We'll cover best practices for using these principles effectively, explore practical examples, and provide insight into how they contribute to scalable and maintainable code.

1. Classes and Encapsulation

A class is a blueprint for creating objects, encapsulating data and behaviors into a single entity. Encapsulation is the principle of bundling data (fields) and methods (behaviors) within a class, which restricts direct access to an object's internal state and protects it from unintended interference.

Defining a Class

A class in C# is defined with the class keyword. Classes contain fields, properties, methods, and constructors, allowing them to encapsulate both data and functionality.

```csharp
public class Car
{
    // Fields
    private string model;
    private int year;

    // Constructor
    public Car(string model, int year)
    {
        this.model = model;
        this.year = year;
    }

    // Properties
    public string Model
    {
        get => model;
        set => model = value;
    }

    public int Year
    {
        get => year;
        set => year = value;
    }
```

```
// Method
public void StartEngine()
{
    Console.WriteLine("Engine started.");
}
}
```

In this example:

- **Fields** (model, year) are private, meaning they cannot be accessed directly from outside the class, enforcing encapsulation.
- **Properties** (Model, Year) provide controlled access to private fields.
- **Methods** (StartEngine) define behaviors that interact with or manipulate the class's data.

Encapsulation Best Practices

- **Keep Fields Private**: Use private fields to restrict access to an object's internal state. This approach ensures that the object's state can only be modified through well-defined interfaces (such as properties or methods).
- **Use Properties for Controlled Access**: Properties allow controlled access to private fields, enabling validation or additional logic when getting or setting values.
- **Limit Public Exposure**: Minimize the number of public methods and properties to reduce external dependencies and simplify the class's interface.

2. Inheritance: Creating a Class Hierarchy

Inheritance allows classes to inherit properties and methods from other classes, enabling code reuse and the creation of hierarchical relationships. In C#, inheritance is implemented using the : symbol, with a base (or parent) class providing common functionality to derived (or child) classes.

Defining Inheritance

To define inheritance, use the following syntax:

```csharp
public class Vehicle
{
    public int Wheels { get; set; }

    public void Drive()
    {
        Console.WriteLine("Vehicle is driving.");
    }
}

public class Car : Vehicle
{
    public string Model { get; set; }

    public void Honk()
    {
        Console.WriteLine("Car horn sounds.");
    }
}
```

In this example:

- Vehicle is the base class, defining properties and methods that are common across various types of vehicles.
- Car is a derived class, inheriting Wheels and Drive from Vehicle and adding its own properties and behaviors (Model, Honk).

The Car class automatically inherits functionality from Vehicle, allowing code reuse and consistency across classes that share similar characteristics.
Best Practices for Inheritance

- **Use Inheritance for "Is-A" Relationships**: Inheritance should represent an "is-a" relationship, such as a Car "is-a" Vehicle. Avoid using inheritance if the relationship is more accurately described as "has-a" or "uses-a."

- **Avoid Deep Inheritance Chains**: Long inheritance chains can create brittle code that is difficult to maintain. Aim for shallow hierarchies to simplify code and improve readability.
- **Favor Composition Over Inheritance**: In many cases, it's more flexible to use composition (where classes contain other classes) instead of inheritance, especially when functionality needs to be shared without a strict hierarchy.

3. Polymorphism: Extending Functionality

Polymorphism enables classes to be used interchangeably, allowing for flexible and extensible code. In C#, polymorphism is achieved through method overriding and interfaces, which allow derived classes to provide specific implementations of methods declared in base classes or interfaces.

Method Overriding

Method overriding is the most common way to implement polymorphism in C#. When a base class declares a virtual method, derived classes can override it with their own implementations, allowing for customized behavior.

```csharp
public class Animal
{
    public virtual void Speak()
    {
        Console.WriteLine("The animal makes a sound.");
    }
}

public class Dog : Animal
{
    public override void Speak()
    {
        Console.WriteLine("The dog barks.");
```

```
        }
}

public class Cat : Animal
{
    public override void Speak()
    {
        Console.WriteLine("The cat meows.");
    }
}
```

In this example:

- Speak is a virtual method in the Animal base class, which can be overridden by derived classes.
- Dog and Cat override Speak to provide specific behaviors, demonstrating polymorphism.

With polymorphism, we can treat different Animal objects uniformly while allowing each derived class to provide its specific behavior.

Interfaces and Polymorphism

Interfaces define contracts that classes can implement, enabling polymorphic behavior without strict inheritance. An interface specifies what a class must do, but not how it does it, making it ideal for situations where classes need to share functionality but not inherit from the same base.

```
csharp

public interface IMovable
{
    void Move();
}
```

```
public class Car : IMovable
{
    public void Move()
    {
        Console.WriteLine("The car drives.");
    }
}

public class Person : IMovable
{
    public void Move()
    {
        Console.WriteLine("The person walks.");
    }
}
```

In this code:

- IMovable is an interface that requires a Move method.
- Both Car and Person implement IMovable, allowing us to treat them polymorphically as IMovable types, even though they are unrelated by inheritance.

Polymorphism Best Practices

- **Use Virtual Methods with Care**: Mark methods as virtual only when overriding is expected and meaningful. Avoid marking every method as virtual by default.
- **Prefer Interfaces for Shared Behavior**: Use interfaces when multiple classes need to implement similar functionality without sharing a common ancestor.
- **Leverage Abstract Classes for Partial Implementations**: Use abstract classes to define base functionality that some, but not all, derived classes need, offering a mix of implementation and contract.

Practical Applications of OOP Principles in C#

By leveraging OOP principles, developers can create robust, modular applications. Here are a few examples of how these principles apply in practical scenarios:

Example 1: E-Commerce System

In an e-commerce system, different types of Product classes might exist, such as PhysicalProduct and DigitalProduct. Both share common attributes (e.g., name, price) and methods (e.g., CalculateDiscount), which can be encapsulated in a base Product class. Using polymorphism, the system can process products uniformly, regardless of their specific types.

```csharp
public abstract class Product
{
    public string Name { get; set; }
    public decimal Price { get; set; }

    public abstract void CalculateDiscount();
}

public class PhysicalProduct : Product
{
    public override void CalculateDiscount()
    {
        Console.WriteLine("Discount applied to physical product.");
    }
}

public class DigitalProduct : Product
{
    public override void CalculateDiscount()
    {
        Console.WriteLine("Discount applied to digital product.");
    }
}
```

Example 2: User Roles in an Application

Consider an application with multiple user roles, such as Admin, Editor,

81

and Viewer, each with different permissions. By defining a base User class with shared properties (e.g., Username, Email) and using polymorphism, the application can manage different user roles and behaviors cleanly.

```csharp
public abstract class User
{
    public string Username { get; set; }
    public string Email { get; set; }

    public abstract void DisplayRole();
}

public class Admin : User
{
    public override void DisplayRole()
    {
        Console.WriteLine("User is an Admin.");
    }
}

public class Editor : User
{
    public override void DisplayRole()
    {
        Console.WriteLine("User is an Editor.");
    }
}
```

Using these principles, the application can easily manage new roles in the future by creating new classes that extend User without altering existing code.

C#'s OOP model provides powerful tools for creating organized, maintainable, and scalable code. By encapsulating data in classes, leveraging inheritance for code reuse, and applying polymorphism for flexible functionality, developers can structure applications that are modular, easier to test, and adaptable to changing requirements. Understanding these principles is critical for effective C# development, especially as projects grow in complexity.

Handling Errors and Exceptions in Modern Apps

In modern applications, effective error and exception handling is crucial for delivering reliable software, protecting data integrity, and providing a seamless user experience. While exceptions are a standard way to handle unexpected conditions in C#, handling them correctly is essential for maintaining system stability and debugging production issues. This section explores how to handle errors and exceptions with best practices, from structuring try-catch blocks to implementing logging and monitoring for production applications.

Key Principles of Error and Exception Handling

In C#, errors and exceptions are generally managed through a combination of preventive validation, defensive programming, and structured exception handling. Here are some foundational principles:

1. **Prevent Errors Early**: Use validation, type checks, and defensive coding techniques to prevent errors before they occur.
2. **Use Structured Exception Handling**: Exceptions should be handled in try-catch-finally blocks with specific error management logic.
3. **Separate Concerns**: Keep error-handling logic separate from business logic to improve readability and maintainability.
4. **Log Exceptions for Analysis**: Exceptions should be logged with sufficient context to aid in debugging and analysis.
5. **Provide User-Friendly Feedback**: Design applications to inform users gracefully when something goes wrong.

Common Types of Exceptions in C#

Understanding the types of exceptions can help you develop appropriate strategies for handling them. Here are some of the most common types:

- **SystemException**: Base class for exceptions raised by the system, like NullReferenceException, OutOfMemoryException, or StackOverflowException.
- **ApplicationException**: Base class for custom, application-specific exceptions.
- **IOException**: For file and input/output-related exceptions, such as FileNotFoundException and DirectoryNotFoundException.
- **ArgumentException**: Thrown when a method receives an invalid argument; includes ArgumentNullException and ArgumentOutOfRangeException.

Using try-catch-finally for Structured Error Handling

In C#, try-catch-finally blocks are the standard way to handle exceptions, allowing for error-specific responses and resource cleanup. Here's a breakdown:

- **try**: Contains code that might throw an exception.
- **catch**: Handles specific exceptions, allowing for tailored responses based on the exception type.
- **finally**: Executes regardless of whether an exception occurs, often used for cleanup operations.

Example:

```csharp
public void ReadFile(string filePath)
{
    try
    {
```

```
    string content = File.ReadAllText(filePath);
    Console.WriteLine(content);
}
catch (FileNotFoundException ex)
{
    Console.WriteLine("File not found: " + ex.Message);
}
catch (UnauthorizedAccessException ex)
{
    Console.WriteLine("Access denied: " + ex.Message);
}
finally
{
    Console.WriteLine("Operation completed.");
}
}
```

Best Practices for try-catch-finally

- **Catch Specific Exceptions**: Avoid catching generic Exception unless necessary. Instead, catch specific exceptions to handle each case properly.
- **Use Finally for Cleanup**: The finally block is ideal for releasing resources like file handles, even if an exception occurs.
- **Limit the Scope of try-catch Blocks**: Only wrap code that might throw an exception. This approach helps keep try-catch blocks short and focused.

Logging and Monitoring Exceptions

Logging is essential for tracking, analyzing, and diagnosing exceptions, especially in production. Effective logging enables developers to understand the cause of an error without reproducing it. Common logging frameworks include **Serilog**, **NLog**, and **Log4Net**.

Implementing Exception Logging

Using Serilog as an example, here's how to log an exception in a try-catch block:

```csharp
csharp

public void ProcessData()
{
    try
    {
        // Code that may throw an exception
    }
    catch (Exception ex)
    {
        Log.Error(ex, "An error occurred while processing data");
        throw; // Re-throw to preserve the stack trace
    }
}
```

Logging Best Practices

- **Provide Contextual Information**: Log relevant details, such as user ID, operation type, and timestamp, to provide context for the exception.
- **Centralized Logging**: Use centralized logging platforms like **Elastic Stack** or **Azure Application Insights** to collect logs from distributed systems.
- **Monitor Key Exceptions**: Set up real-time monitoring for critical exceptions and alert relevant teams when issues arise.

Creating Custom Exceptions for Business Logic

Custom exceptions allow you to define error conditions specific to your application's domain. They are beneficial for managing errors that standard .NET exceptions don't cover, such as a domain-specific InvalidOrderExcepti on.

```csharp
csharp

public class InvalidOrderException : ApplicationException
{
```

```
    public InvalidOrderException(string message) : base(message) {
    }
}

public void ValidateOrder(Order order)
{
    if (order.Quantity <= 0)
    {
        throw new InvalidOrderException("Order quantity must be
        greater than zero.");
    }
}
```

Best Practices for Custom Exceptions

- **Use Custom Exceptions Sparingly**: Avoid creating unnecessary custom exceptions; use standard .NET exceptions where applicable.
- **Include Clear Messages**: Provide detailed error messages in custom exceptions to simplify debugging.
- **Inherit from ApplicationException**: Use ApplicationException as a base class to distinguish custom exceptions from system exceptions.

Graceful Degradation in Production

Graceful degradation ensures that the application can continue to function or provide a fallback when exceptions occur, enhancing user experience. Here are some strategies:

User-Friendly Error Messages

Instead of displaying technical details, provide a clear message and suggest steps the user can take:

```
csharp

public string GetProductDetails(int productId)
{
    try
```

```
        {
            return FetchProductFromDatabase(productId);
        }
        catch (Exception)
        {
            return "Product details are unavailable. Please try again
            later.";
        }
    }
}
```

Fallback Mechanisms

For errors in critical services, use a fallback mechanism. For instance, if a database query fails, retrieve data from a cached source.

Resilience Patterns for Error Handling

For modern applications, especially those in cloud environments, resilience patterns like **retry**, **circuit breaker**, and **bulkhead** can prevent system failures from propagating and improve fault tolerance.

Retry Pattern

The retry pattern automatically retries an operation when a transient error occurs. Implementing exponential backoff (increasing wait time after each failure) prevents overloading the system.

```csharp
public void ExecuteWithRetry(Action action, int maxRetries = 3)
{
    int attempt = 0;
    while (attempt < maxRetries)
    {
        try
        {
            action();
            return; // Exit on success
```

```
    }
    catch (Exception ex)
    {
        attempt++;
        if (attempt >= maxRetries)
        {
            Log.Error(ex, "Operation failed after multiple
            retries");
            throw; // Re-throw to escalate
        }
        Task.Delay(2000 * attempt).Wait(); // Exponential
        backoff
    }
  }
}
```

Circuit Breaker Pattern

The circuit breaker pattern stops requests to a service after repeated failures, allowing time for recovery. Libraries like **Polly** in .NET simplify circuit breaker implementation.

```csharp

var circuitBreakerPolicy = Policy
    .Handle<Exception>()
    .CircuitBreaker(2, TimeSpan.FromMinutes(1)); // Break for 1
    minute after 2 consecutive failures

circuitBreakerPolicy.Execute(() => ConnectToService());
```

Bulkhead Pattern

The bulkhead pattern isolates parts of a system, preventing failures in one component from affecting others. This pattern is often applied in microservices to limit resources per service.

Effective error handling is vital for building resilient, user-friendly applications. Best practices include catching specific exceptions, logging contextual details, and providing fallback mechanisms for critical functionality. Resilience patterns like retry, circuit breaker, and bulkhead can further enhance fault tolerance in distributed and cloud applications. By implementing these techniques, you can design applications that are robust, recoverable, and capable of gracefully managing unexpected conditions.

Hands-On Project: Creating a Modular and Reusable Codebase

In this hands-on project, we'll design a modular and reusable codebase to demonstrate practical applications of core programming principles, including separation of concerns, modularization, and reusability. This project serves as a blueprint for building scalable applications in C# that are easy to maintain and extend. By creating a well-structured codebase, we can improve code readability, simplify testing, and enhance flexibility.

Our example project, **Task Manager**, is a console-based application that allows users to manage tasks by adding, updating, listing, and removing them. Each part of the application will be divided into modules, emphasizing reusable components and interfaces.

Project Overview: Task Manager

Task Manager is a simple console application with the following features:

1. **Add Task**: Allows users to add new tasks with a title, description, and due date.
2. **List Tasks**: Displays all tasks with their details.
3. **Update Task**: Updates task details by task ID.
4. **Delete Task**: Removes a task by task ID.

We'll achieve modularization by separating the core application logic, data models, and utility services, creating a reusable and scalable structure.

Step 1: Setting Up the Project Structure

1. **Create the Project**: Open Visual Studio or Visual Studio Code and create a new Console App named TaskManager.
2. **Add Project Folders**: Organize your project by creating folders to separate code modules. We'll create three folders:

- **Models**: For data models.
- **Services**: For business logic and utility classes.
- **UI**: For user interaction and console input/output logic.

Your project structure should look like this:

```
TaskManager/ ├───────
  Models/ ├──────
  Services/ └───────
  UI/
```

Step 2: Define Data Models

In the Models folder, define a Task class to represent a task entity in the application. This class will encapsulate data and include properties like ID, Title, Description, and DueDate.

```csharp
namespace TaskManager.Models
{
    public class Task
    {
        public int ID { get; set; }
        public string Title { get; set; } = string.Empty;
        public string Description { get; set; } = string.Empty;
        public DateTime DueDate { get; set; }

        public override string ToString() =>
            $"ID: {ID}, Title: {Title}, Due:
```

```
                    {DueDate.ToShortDateString()}";
    }
}
```

Model Best Practices

- **Keep Models Simple**: Only include properties and basic validation or formatting.
- **Encapsulate Data**: Models should represent the data but avoid containing business logic.

Step 3: Create the Service Layer

The service layer contains business logic, responsible for adding, updating, retrieving, and deleting tasks. This code is reusable, making it easy to implement in other applications.

Define ITaskService Interface: Interfaces provide contracts for services, ensuring that the implementation meets specific requirements and promoting code reusability.

```csharp
using TaskManager.Models;
using System.Collections.Generic;

namespace TaskManager.Services
{
    public interface ITaskService
    {
        void AddTask(Task task);
        List<Task> GetTasks();
        Task? GetTaskById(int id);
        void UpdateTask(Task task);
        void DeleteTask(int id);
    }
}
```

Implement TaskService: Create the TaskService class to implement the ITaskService interface, managing the application's task-related operations.

```csharp
using TaskManager.Models;
using System;
using System.Collections.Generic;
using System.Linq;

namespace TaskManager.Services
{
    public class TaskService : ITaskService
    {
        private readonly List<Task> _tasks = new();
        private int _nextId = 1;

        public void AddTask(Task task)
        {
            task.ID = _nextId++;
            _tasks.Add(task);
        }

        public List<Task> GetTasks() => _tasks;

        public Task? GetTaskById(int id) =>
        _tasks.FirstOrDefault(t => t.ID == id);

        public void UpdateTask(Task task)
        {
            var existingTask = GetTaskById(task.ID);
            if (existingTask != null)
            {
                existingTask.Title = task.Title;
                existingTask.Description = task.Description;
                existingTask.DueDate = task.DueDate;
            }
        }

        public void DeleteTask(int id)
```

```
        {
            var task = GetTaskById(id);
            if (task != null) _tasks.Remove(task);
        }
    }
}
```

Service Layer Best Practices

- **Interface-Driven Design**: Use interfaces for defining services, making it easier to swap implementations (e.g., for unit testing or dependency injection).
- **Single Responsibility Principle**: Keep services focused on specific business logic. Avoid mixing unrelated functionality.

Step 4: Building the User Interface Layer

The UI layer handles console input and output, interacting with the user. We'll create a Menu class to present options and call methods from the TaskService for each operation.

Implement Menu Class: The Menu class should handle displaying the menu options, collecting user input, and managing interactions with TaskService.

```csharp
using TaskManager.Models;
using TaskManager.Services;
using System;

namespace TaskManager.UI
{
    public class Menu
    {
        private readonly ITaskService _taskService;

        public Menu(ITaskService taskService)
```

```
{
    _taskService = taskService;
}

public void Display()
{
    bool running = true;

    while (running)
    {
        Console.WriteLine("\nTask Manager");
        Console.WriteLine("1. Add Task");
        Console.WriteLine("2. List Tasks");
        Console.WriteLine("3. Update Task");
        Console.WriteLine("4. Delete Task");
        Console.WriteLine("5. Exit");
        Console.Write("Choose an option: ");

        var choice = Console.ReadLine();

        switch (choice)
        {
            case "1":
                AddTask();
                break;
            case "2":
                ListTasks();
                break;
            case "3":
                UpdateTask();
                break;
            case "4":
                DeleteTask();
                break;
            case "5":
                running = false;
                break;
            default:
                Console.WriteLine("Invalid option, please
                try again.");
```

```csharp
            break;
        }
    }
}

private void AddTask()
{
    Console.Write("Enter Title: ");
    var title = Console.ReadLine();
    Console.Write("Enter Description: ");
    var description = Console.ReadLine();
    Console.Write("Enter Due Date (yyyy-mm-dd): ");
    var dueDate = DateTime.Parse(Console.ReadLine() ??
    DateTime.Now.ToString());

    _taskService.AddTask(new Task
    {
        Title = title ?? string.Empty,
        Description = description ?? string.Empty,
        DueDate = dueDate
    });

    Console.WriteLine("Task added successfully.");
}

private void ListTasks()
{
    var tasks = _taskService.GetTasks();
    if (tasks.Count == 0)
    {
        Console.WriteLine("No tasks available.");
        return;
    }

    foreach (var task in tasks)
    {
        Console.WriteLine(task);
    }
}
```

```
private void UpdateTask()
{
    Console.Write("Enter Task ID to update: ");
    if (int.TryParse(Console.ReadLine(), out int id))
    {
        var task = _taskService.GetTaskById(id);
        if (task != null)
        {
            Console.Write("Enter New Title: ");
            task.Title = Console.ReadLine() ?? task.Title;
            Console.Write("Enter New Description: ");
            task.Description = Console.ReadLine() ??
            task.Description;
            Console.Write("Enter New Due Date
            (yyyy-mm-dd): ");
            task.DueDate =
            DateTime.Parse(Console.ReadLine() ??
            task.DueDate.ToString());

            _taskService.UpdateTask(task);
            Console.WriteLine("Task updated
            successfully.");
        }
        else
        {
            Console.WriteLine("Task not found.");
        }
    }
}

private void DeleteTask()
{
    Console.Write("Enter Task ID to delete: ");
    if (int.TryParse(Console.ReadLine(), out int id))
    {
        _taskService.DeleteTask(id);
        Console.WriteLine("Task deleted successfully.");
    }
}
}
```

```
}
```

UI Layer Best Practices

- **Separate Concerns**: Keep the UI focused on input and output. Avoid embedding business logic within the UI.
- **Reusable UI Components**: The UI layer should be modular, making it easy to adapt for other interfaces (e.g., web or mobile).

Step 5: Integrating and Running the Application

Main Program File: In Program.cs, instantiate the TaskService and pass it to the Menu class.

```csharp
using TaskManager.Services;
using TaskManager.UI;

namespace TaskManager
{
    class Program
    {
        static void Main(string[] args)
        {
            ITaskService taskService = new TaskService();
            Menu menu = new Menu(taskService);
            menu.Display();
        }
    }
}
```

Run the Application: Run the program and test each option in the menu. Verify that tasks can be added, listed, updated, and deleted as expected.

By modularizing the Task Manager codebase, we've created a structure that separates concerns, promotes reusability, and supports scalability. Using interfaces, services, and models, we ensure that each layer in the application is cohesive and focused on specific responsibilities. This modular approach not only simplifies code maintenance but also makes it easy to extend the application with new features or adapt it to different platforms in the future.

Leveraging Asynchronous Programming with Async Streams

The Need for Async Programming in Modern Applications
Modern applications demand high performance, responsiveness, and efficiency, especially as they handle increasingly complex tasks, larger datasets, and more user interactions. Asynchronous programming addresses these needs by allowing applications to manage time-consuming operations, such as I/O-bound tasks, without blocking the main thread. In this section, we'll explore why asynchronous programming is essential in modern development, its key benefits, and the types of applications where asynchronous code is invaluable.

Why Asynchronous Programming is Necessary

At its core, asynchronous programming allows an application to perform tasks concurrently. In a synchronous model, tasks are executed one after the other, causing bottlenecks when a task requires significant time to complete— such as waiting for a network response, reading from disk, or performing complex computations. When tasks block the main execution thread, the application may become unresponsive, leading to poor user experiences and system inefficiencies.

Asynchronous programming solves this problem by allowing the main thread to remain available for other operations while a task completes in the background. This approach is especially critical in the following contexts:

1. **Improved User Responsiveness**: For user interfaces, async programming keeps applications responsive by preventing the main UI thread from freezing. Users can interact with the app without experiencing delays, regardless of what's happening in the background.

2. **Efficient Resource Utilization**: Async programming maximizes system resources by allowing multiple tasks to run in parallel without waiting on one another. This is ideal for applications that require frequent network access, I/O operations, or data processing.

3. **Scalability in Web and Cloud Applications**: In web and cloud applications, async programming enables services to handle many requests simultaneously. This scalability improves performance, minimizes downtime, and enhances the user experience.

Key Scenarios for Asynchronous Programming

Asynchronous programming is especially valuable for applications with the following characteristics:

1. I/O-Bound Operations

I/O-bound operations are tasks that rely on external systems, such as file systems, databases, or network resources. These tasks can cause long wait times as they depend on factors outside the application's control, such as network latency or disk speed. Asynchronous programming enables these tasks to run without blocking other code, improving the application's overall responsiveness and efficiency.

Examples of I/O-bound tasks:

- Database queries
- File reading and writing
- Web service calls (e.g., RESTful APIs)
- Message queuing and processing

In applications where I/O operations are frequent, asynchronous programming prevents bottlenecks and improves throughput.

2. Network-Bound Operations

Network latency, bandwidth, and remote server response times are all factors that make network-bound operations particularly unpredictable and time-consuming. Async programming allows an application to send network requests, receive responses, or wait on data without blocking other code, which is crucial for web applications and services that rely heavily on API calls or real-time data updates.

Examples of network-bound operations:

- Fetching data from APIs (REST, GraphQL)
- Uploading and downloading files
- Streaming media (e.g., video or audio)
- Real-time communication (e.g., WebSocket connections)

Async programming in network-bound tasks minimizes the waiting time users experience and allows the system to handle other requests concurrently.

3. Real-Time and Event-Driven Applications

Modern applications, especially those with real-time requirements, benefit from async programming as it allows the system to handle events and respond to them immediately without blocking other operations. Real-time applications, such as chat apps, financial tickers, or gaming systems, need to process inputs, updates, or events as they occur to provide a seamless user experience.

Examples of real-time and event-driven applications:

- Chat applications
- Real-time dashboards (e.g., stock market tickers)
- Multiplayer online games
- Event-based systems (e.g., event processing in IoT devices)

Async programming ensures that these applications remain responsive and capable of handling incoming data streams efficiently.

4. High-Concurrency Applications

Concurrency is essential in applications that handle many tasks simultaneously, such as web servers processing multiple HTTP requests. Async programming enables these applications to scale effectively, handling numerous tasks without requiring each task to have its dedicated thread. This approach reduces memory overhead and enhances scalability, allowing the system to manage high traffic loads.

Examples of high-concurrency applications:

- Web servers (e.g., handling multiple client requests)
- Microservices architectures
- Distributed systems with high workloads

High-concurrency applications use asynchronous programming to handle multiple requests concurrently, maximizing resource usage without sacrificing performance.

Advantages of Asynchronous Programming in C#

C# offers built-in support for asynchronous programming through the async and await keywords. These constructs make async programming straightforward, providing several benefits for modern applications:

1. **Enhanced Responsiveness and User Experience**
2. In desktop and mobile applications, a responsive UI is critical for user satisfaction. Async programming ensures that the UI remains active and interactive while background tasks are processed. For example, in a data-heavy application, fetching data asynchronously allows users to interact with the interface while waiting for data to load.
3. **Improved Application Performance**
4. Async programming enables applications to perform time-consuming operations without occupying the main thread. This approach leads to more efficient use of system resources, as tasks are processed in parallel, reducing wait times and improving throughput.

5. **Simplified Code for Concurrent Tasks**
6. In C#, async and await simplify the code for handling concurrent tasks, reducing the need for complex threading logic. This approach results in cleaner, more readable code while avoiding common pitfalls like deadlocks or race conditions.
7. **Reduced Resource Consumption**
8. Unlike synchronous programming, which may require creating multiple threads to handle concurrent operations, asynchronous programming allows tasks to run without occupying system threads. This feature reduces memory consumption and increases the application's capacity to handle multiple operations simultaneously.
9. **Scalability for Cloud and Web Applications**
10. Async programming is essential for cloud applications, where scalability and cost-efficiency are critical. By processing requests asynchronously, cloud-based systems can handle large volumes of requests with minimal resource use, making it easier to scale up or down based on demand.

Asynchronous Patterns and Tools in C#

C# provides a range of constructs for implementing asynchronous programming effectively. Here's a quick overview of common async patterns and tools used in C#:

1. **async and await**: These keywords simplify asynchronous code by allowing developers to write async methods that perform non-blocking operations. async methods return Task or Task<T> objects, enabling tasks to run in the background.
2. **Tasks (Task and Task<T>)**: Tasks represent operations that run asynchronously. The Task type is used for async methods that return no result, while Task<T> is for methods that return a value.
3. **Parallel Processing with PLINQ**: The Parallel LINQ (PLINQ) library allows developers to process data in parallel. PLINQ is useful for CPU-bound tasks that can be broken down into smaller, concurrent operations.

4. **Async Streams**: Introduced in C# 8, async streams allow developers to work with data streams asynchronously, enabling applications to retrieve data elements one at a time as they become available. This feature is especially useful for applications that process large datasets or real-time data sources.

5. **Cancellation Tokens**: Asynchronous operations sometimes need to be canceled. CancellationToken allows developers to cancel a task mid-execution, improving control over resource-intensive tasks.

6. **Exception Handling in Async Code**: Async methods require special exception handling practices. In async methods, exceptions are propagated through the await statement and can be caught in a try-catch block around await.

Common Challenges and Best Practices in Async Programming

While async programming is powerful, it also comes with unique challenges. Here are some best practices for managing these complexities:

1. Avoid Blocking the Main Thread

Even with async programming, avoid blocking calls (such as Thread.Sleep or Task.Wait) on the main thread. Blocking the main thread can defeat the purpose of async programming, leading to unresponsive applications.

2. Use ConfigureAwait(false) in Library Code

When creating libraries or reusable code, consider using ConfigureAwait(false) to prevent async code from capturing the synchronization context. This approach reduces deadlock risk in environments with specific threading requirements, such as UI applications.

3. Manage Resources with Cancellation Tokens

Cancellation tokens allow for graceful task termination, helping manage resources effectively and preventing runaway tasks. Use cancellation tokens in scenarios where the user may need to stop a task or operation.

4. Be Cautious with Long-Running Operations

Async programming does not always equate to performance gains, especially in CPU-bound tasks. For CPU-intensive tasks, consider using Task.Run to run them on separate threads, avoiding bottlenecks in the async flow.

5. Structure Async Code for Readability

Async programming can lead to complex code if not structured carefully. Use meaningful method names, break down complex operations into smaller functions, and avoid nesting async calls whenever possible. Clear structure helps prevent issues like deadlocks, unhandled exceptions, or incorrect state management.

Asynchronous programming is essential for modern applications to ensure responsiveness, maximize resource utilization, and handle concurrent operations effectively. From network-bound tasks to real-time applications and cloud services, async programming helps applications scale efficiently while providing a seamless user experience. C#'s async features, including async and await, async streams, and cancellation tokens, make it easy to write readable and efficient asynchronous code. In the next section, we'll delve deeper into the technical aspects of implementing async programming in C#, focusing on async streams and real-world examples.

Deep Dive into Async Streams and IAsyncEnumerable

With the release of C# 8, async streams and the IAsyncEnumerable<T> interface have transformed how developers handle asynchronous sequences of data. Async streams allow applications to process data incrementally as it becomes available, without waiting for the entire dataset to load. This capability is particularly useful in scenarios involving real-time data, large data sets, and network streams, as it minimizes memory consumption and improves responsiveness.

In this section, we'll explore async streams, IAsyncEnumerable<T>, and their use cases in detail, covering the benefits of async streaming, how to implement async streams in C#, and best practices for handling asynchronous data.

What are Async Streams?

Async streams enable you to asynchronously iterate over a sequence of data elements as they arrive, rather than waiting for the complete data to become available before starting to process it. The await foreach syntax in C# 8 allows you to retrieve elements from an async stream one at a time, making it easier to handle scenarios where data is retrieved from external sources, such as APIs, databases, or file streams, in a non-blocking manner.

Use Cases for Async Streams

Async streams and IAsyncEnumerable<T> are ideal for applications where:

1. **Data is retrieved incrementally**: Data can be processed one element at a time as it becomes available (e.g., database or network streams).
2. **Real-time data processing is required**: Applications like financial tickers, social media feeds, and IoT data streams benefit from async streams.
3. **Large data sets need efficient memory handling**: Async streams help conserve memory by loading data in small chunks instead of all at once.

Introduction to IAsyncEnumerable<T>

The IAsyncEnumerable<T> interface, introduced in C# 8, provides asynchronous iteration over a collection. It works similarly to the IEnumerable<T> interface but allows data to be retrieved asynchronously. Instead of foreach, which iterates synchronously, await foreach is used with async streams to handle data elements asynchronously.

```
csharp

public async IAsyncEnumerable<int> GenerateNumbersAsync()
{
    for (int i = 1; i <= 5; i++)
```

```
    {
        await Task.Delay(1000); // Simulate async work
        yield return i;
    }
}

public async Task ProcessNumbersAsync()
{
    await foreach (var number in GenerateNumbersAsync())
    {
        Console.WriteLine($"Received number: {number}");
    }
}
```

In this example:

- **GenerateNumbersAsync**: This method produces a series of numbers asynchronously, simulating a data source that provides one element at a time with a delay.
- **ProcessNumbersAsync**: The await foreach loop retrieves each number as it becomes available, allowing the program to process numbers incrementally without blocking.

Implementing Async Streams in C#

To implement async streams, follow these steps:

1. **Define an Async Stream Method**: The method must return IAsyncEnumerable<T> and use the async keyword.
2. **Yield Data Asynchronously**: Use yield return to emit values as they become available. If there's a delay or dependency, use await to asynchronously wait before yielding each element.
3. **Consume the Async Stream with await foreach**: Use await foreach in the calling code to retrieve elements asynchronously, allowing the application to continue processing data as it arrives.

Example: Fetching Data from an API Using Async Streams

Let's look at a practical example where async streams retrieve data from an API incrementally. Suppose you are fetching large datasets from a paginated API. Async streams allow you to process each page as it arrives, rather than waiting for all pages to load.

```csharp
public async IAsyncEnumerable<string> FetchDataFromApiAsync(string
apiUrl)
{
    int page = 1;
    while (true)
    {
        var response = await GetApiPageAsync(apiUrl, page);
        if (response == null) yield break; // End if no more data

        yield return response;
        page++;
    }
}

private async Task<string?> GetApiPageAsync(string apiUrl, int
page)
{
    // Simulate API call for a specific page
    await Task.Delay(1000); // Simulate network delay
    return page > 5 ? null : $"Data from page {page}";
}

public async Task ProcessApiDataAsync()
{
    await foreach (var pageData in
    FetchDataFromApiAsync("https://api.example.com/data"))
    {
        Console.WriteLine(pageData);
    }
}
```

In this example:

- **FetchDataFromApiAsync**: Uses async streams to fetch pages incrementally from an API. When no more data is available, the stream ends.
- **await foreach**: Consumes the data incrementally, processing each page as it arrives without blocking the main thread.

Working with Cancellation in Async Streams

Handling cancellation in async streams is essential, especially in applications where users may wish to stop data retrieval before completion. IAsyncEnumerable<T> methods can accept CancellationToken parameters to support cancellation requests. This allows an async stream to stop processing when a cancellation is requested.

```csharp
public async IAsyncEnumerable<int>
GenerateNumbersWithCancellationAsync([EnumeratorCancellation]
CancellationToken cancellationToken = default)
{
    for (int i = 1; i <= 10; i++)
    {
        await Task.Delay(500, cancellationToken); // Supports
        cancellation
        yield return i;
    }
}

public async Task ProcessWithCancellationAsync(CancellationToken
cancellationToken)
{
    await foreach (var number in
    GenerateNumbersWithCancellationAsync(cancellationToken))
    {
        Console.WriteLine($"Received: {number}");
    }
}
```

In this example:

- The cancellationToken is passed to the Task.Delay method. If cancellation is requested, the async operation will throw a TaskCanceledException and exit the loop.

Handling Exceptions in Async Streams

Error handling in async streams requires try-catch blocks. Errors occurring within an async stream can be caught either in the stream-producing method or in the consuming code.

```csharp
public async IAsyncEnumerable<int> GenerateNumbersWithErrorAsync()
{
    for (int i = 1; i <= 5; i++)
    {
        if (i == 3) throw new InvalidOperationException("An error
        occurred.");
        await Task.Delay(1000);
        yield return i;
    }
}

public async Task ProcessNumbersWithErrorHandlingAsync()
{
    try
    {
        await foreach (var number in
        GenerateNumbersWithErrorAsync())
        {
            Console.WriteLine($"Received number: {number}");
        }
    }
    catch (InvalidOperationException ex)
    {
        Console.WriteLine($"Error: {ex.Message}");
    }
}
```

In this example:

- **Exception Handling**: The ProcessNumbersWithErrorHandlingAsync method wraps the await foreach loop in a try-catch block, catching exceptions that occur in the async stream.

Best Practices for Using Async Streams

1. **Use Async Streams for Large Data Sets**: Async streams work best with large datasets or scenarios where data arrives incrementally, allowing for improved memory usage and responsiveness.
2. **Combine with Cancellation Tokens**: Always offer cancellation options for async streams to provide users with control over lengthy or complex data operations.
3. **Handle Exceptions Gracefully**: Place try-catch blocks around await foreach loops to manage errors, logging or handling exceptions without crashing the application.
4. **Avoid Blocking Operations in Async Streams**: Do not use blocking calls within async streams, as this negates the benefits of asynchronous processing. Use await for all time-consuming tasks.

Practical Applications of Async Streams in Real-World Scenarios

Async streams are ideal for a range of real-world applications where data needs to be processed in an incremental, non-blocking fashion. Here are a few scenarios where async streams add significant value:

1. Real-Time Data Processing

Applications like financial dashboards or live feeds benefit from async streams, as they can process data incrementally as updates arrive, keeping the user informed without delay.

2. Streaming APIs

APIs that deliver data over time, such as weather services, social media feeds, or news aggregators, can use async streams to handle incoming data efficiently, displaying updates to users without blocking the main UI.

3. Database and File Processing

When handling large databases or reading large files, async streams allow you to retrieve and process data in smaller chunks, conserving memory and providing a responsive interface.

4. IoT Device Data Collection

Async streams are well-suited for IoT applications, where devices continuously send data. With async streams, applications can collect and process data from multiple devices concurrently, handling each data stream independently.

Async streams and IAsyncEnumerable<T> enable developers to process data incrementally and asynchronously, which is invaluable in scenarios involving large datasets, real-time data, or networked applications. By leveraging async streams, applications achieve greater efficiency, enhanced responsiveness, and improved memory usage. C#'s await foreach and yield return syntax simplify the implementation of async streams, while support for cancellation and exception handling makes them robust and adaptable to a wide variety of use cases.

Best Practices for Managing Asynchronous Code

Writing asynchronous code effectively requires a strong understanding of best practices to ensure your application remains responsive, efficient, and free from common pitfalls. Properly managed async code not only enhances user experience but also minimizes resource usage and helps prevent hard-to-debug issues like deadlocks and memory leaks. In this section, we'll cover essential best practices for managing asynchronous code in C#.

1. Avoid Blocking Calls on the Main Thread

Blocking calls (e.g., Thread.Sleep, Task.Wait, Result) within asynchronous code can negate the benefits of async programming, especially when executed on the main thread. These calls block the thread, causing delays and potentially freezing the application, particularly in UI-based applications like WPF or Windows Forms.

Example of Blocking Calls to Avoid

csharp

```
public async Task PerformAsyncOperation()
{
    var resultTask = SomeAsyncMethod();
    // Avoid calling .Result or .Wait() on async operations
    var result = resultTask.Result; // Blocks the main thread
    Console.WriteLine(result);
}
```

Solution

Use await instead of blocking calls:

csharp

```
public async Task PerformAsyncOperation()
{
    var result = await SomeAsyncMethod();
    Console.WriteLine(result);
}
```

By using await, you allow the operation to run asynchronously, freeing up the main thread and preventing UI or application freezes.

2. Use ConfigureAwait(false) in Library Code

When writing library code or general-purpose components, it's best to use ConfigureAwait(false) on awaited tasks. This practice prevents the code from capturing the caller's synchronization context, which can help avoid deadlocks, particularly in UI applications.

Example of ConfigureAwait(false)

```csharp
public async Task PerformLibraryOperation()
{
    await Task.Delay(1000).ConfigureAwait(false);
    // This prevents the continuation from capturing the caller's
    context
}
```

When to Avoid ConfigureAwait(false)

In UI applications, avoid ConfigureAwait(false) if the continuation needs to update the UI, as it may not return to the main thread. However, for background or non-UI code, ConfigureAwait(false) helps improve performance and avoid deadlocks.

3. Handle Exceptions Properly in Async Methods

In async methods, exceptions do not immediately propagate to the calling code; instead, they are wrapped in the Task object. Therefore, it's essential to catch exceptions using try-catch blocks around await statements to prevent unhandled exceptions.

Example of Exception Handling in Async Methods

```csharp
public async Task PerformOperationWithExceptionHandling()
{
    try
    {
        await SomeAsyncMethod();
    }
    catch (Exception ex)
    {
        Console.WriteLine($"Error occurred: {ex.Message}");
        // Handle the exception or log it
    }
}
```

This approach ensures that exceptions are managed gracefully, either by logging, notifying the user, or applying fallback logic as needed.

4. Use Cancellation Tokens for Canceling Async Operations

Asynchronous tasks can sometimes run longer than expected, or users may want to stop an operation before it completes. Cancellation tokens provide a way to signal that a task should be canceled, allowing for responsive and user-friendly applications.

Example of Using Cancellation Tokens

```csharp
public async Task PerformCancellableOperation(CancellationToken
cancellationToken)
{
    try
    {
        await Task.Delay(5000, cancellationToken); // This will
        throw if canceled
        Console.WriteLine("Operation completed.");
    }
    catch (OperationCanceledException)
    {
        Console.WriteLine("Operation was canceled.");
    }
}
```

Best Practices with Cancellation Tokens

- Always pass CancellationToken to async methods that may require cancellation.
- Check for IsCancellationRequested within long-running loops to exit promptly if cancellation is signaled.

5. Avoid Fire-and-Forget Async Methods

Fire-and-forget methods (async methods that are not awaited) can lead to unhandled exceptions, memory leaks, and unpredictable behavior, as the caller does not track or manage the task's lifecycle.

Example of Fire-and-Forget Issue

```csharp
public void StartOperation()
{
    SomeAsyncMethod(); // Not awaited
}
```

Solution

Make sure to await async methods or explicitly handle them with Task.Run if true parallel execution is required.

```csharp
public async Task StartOperation()
{
    await SomeAsyncMethod();
    Console.WriteLine("Operation finished.");
}
```

6. Use Task.WhenAll and Task.WhenAny for Concurrent Async Operations

When running multiple tasks concurrently, Task.WhenAll and Task.WhenAny are effective ways to manage them. Task.WhenAll waits until all tasks are complete, while Task.WhenAny returns as soon as any one of the tasks completes.

Example of Using Task.WhenAll

```csharp
public async Task RunMultipleOperationsAsync()
{
```

```csharp
var task1 = SomeAsyncMethod();
var task2 = AnotherAsyncMethod();

await Task.WhenAll(task1, task2); // Runs tasks concurrently
Console.WriteLine("All tasks completed.");
}
```

This approach is particularly useful for scenarios like parallel data fetching, where tasks are independent and can run in parallel.

7. Limit Concurrent Operations with SemaphoreSlim

Running too many concurrent operations can overwhelm resources or degrade performance. Use SemaphoreSlim to limit the number of concurrent tasks.

Example of Using SemaphoreSlim

csharp

```csharp
private readonly SemaphoreSlim _semaphore = new SemaphoreSlim(3);
// Limit to 3 tasks

public async Task ProcessDataAsync()
{
    await _semaphore.WaitAsync();
    try
    {
        await SomeAsyncMethod();
    }
    finally
    {
        _semaphore.Release();
    }
}
```

This method prevents the application from running more than the specified number of tasks concurrently, controlling resource usage and improving performance.

8. Avoid Mixing async and void

Async methods should return Task or Task<T>, not void, as returning void can lead to unhandled exceptions and makes it difficult to await the method. Use void only for async event handlers.

Example of Avoiding async void

```csharp
public async Task PerformOperationAsync()
{
    await SomeAsyncMethod();
}
```

For event handlers, which require void, ensure to handle exceptions carefully:

```csharp
private async void OnButtonClick(object sender, EventArgs e)
{
    try
    {
        await SomeAsyncMethod();
    }
    catch (Exception ex)
    {
        Console.WriteLine($"Error: {ex.Message}");
    }
}
```

9. Avoid Deep Async Call Stacks

Deep async call stacks with nested await statements can lead to performance issues due to excessive context-switching. Instead, structure your code to flatten async calls and minimize nested await statements.

Example of Avoiding Deep Call Stacks

```csharp
public async Task PerformOperationsAsync()
{
    var task1 = Task1();
    var task2 = Task2();
    await Task.WhenAll(task1, task2); // Run tasks concurrently,
    reducing depth
}
```

Flattened async calls improve readability and minimize overhead, especially in scenarios involving multiple async operations.

10. Structure Asynchronous Code for Readability

Async code can become complex, especially when handling multiple tasks, error handling, and cancellation. Break down long methods into smaller, reusable methods and name methods meaningfully to improve readability and maintainability.

Example of Structured Async Code

Instead of a long async method:

```csharp
public async Task ProcessData()
{
    // Multiple lines of code with async calls
}
```

Break it down into smaller methods:

```csharp
public async Task ProcessData()
{
    await FetchDataAsync();
```

```
    await TransformDataAsync();
    await SaveDataAsync();
}

private async Task FetchDataAsync() { /* Code */ }
private async Task TransformDataAsync() { /* Code */ }
private async Task SaveDataAsync() { /* Code */ }
```

This approach enhances code organization, making it easier to maintain, debug, and extend.

Asynchronous programming is a powerful tool in modern applications, enabling responsiveness, efficient resource usage, and scalability. By following these best practices, developers can write robust, maintainable async code:

1. Avoid blocking calls on the main thread to prevent freezing.
2. Use ConfigureAwait(false) in non-UI code to improve performance.
3. Catch exceptions in async methods to handle errors gracefully.
4. Use cancellation tokens for responsive user experiences.
5. Avoid fire-and-forget methods unless truly necessary.
6. Run multiple tasks concurrently with Task.WhenAll or Task.WhenAny.
7. Control concurrency with SemaphoreSlim to avoid resource exhaustion.
8. Avoid mixing async and void, except for event handlers.
9. Minimize deep async call stacks to reduce context-switching overhead.
10. Structure async code for readability and modularity.

By applying these techniques, developers can harness the full power of asynchronous programming, ensuring that applications remain responsive, scalable, and easy to maintain. In the next section, we'll look at advanced async patterns and tools in C#, exploring how to optimize and expand async operations in real-world scenarios.

Handling Concurrency Safely

Concurrency is essential for applications to handle multiple tasks at once, improving responsiveness and resource utilization. However, concurrent operations introduce risks such as race conditions, deadlocks, and data inconsistencies if shared resources are accessed unsafely. This section covers strategies and best practices for handling concurrency safely in C#, focusing on managing access to shared resources, preventing race conditions, and using synchronization mechanisms effectively.

Common Concurrency Challenges

When multiple tasks attempt to access or modify shared data simultaneously, various concurrency issues can arise:

1. **Race Conditions**: Occur when two or more threads or tasks access shared data simultaneously, potentially leading to unexpected or incorrect results.
2. **Deadlocks**: Happen when two or more threads are waiting on each other to release resources, leading to a state where no task can proceed.
3. **Data Inconsistencies**: Arise when concurrent tasks modify shared data without proper synchronization, resulting in an inconsistent or corrupted state.

Techniques for Safe Concurrency Management

C# provides a range of tools and techniques to handle concurrency safely. Each technique addresses specific challenges, from basic locking mechanisms to more sophisticated concurrency controls for complex applications.

1. Using lock Statements for Critical Sections

The lock statement is one of the simplest ways to prevent race conditions by restricting access to a critical section of code, ensuring only one thread can execute it at a time.

Example of lock Statement

```csharp
private readonly object _lockObject = new object();
private int _counter = 0;

public void IncrementCounter()
{
    lock (_lockObject)
    {
        _counter++;
    }
}
```

In this example:

- **Critical Section**: The lock statement ensures that _counter is incremented by only one thread at a time.
- **Lock Object**: _lockObject is a private object used as a synchronization primitive, avoiding the risks of locking on this or a type, which could lead to unintended locking in other parts of the code.

Best Practices for lock Statements

- **Keep Locked Code Short**: Minimize the amount of code within a lock statement to reduce contention and avoid performance bottlenecks.
- **Avoid Nested Locks**: Nesting locks can lead to deadlocks, as the order of acquiring locks becomes critical. Aim for a lock-free or lock-minimal design whenever possible.

2. Using Synchronization Primitives: SemaphoreSlim and Mutex

In addition to lock, C# provides synchronization primitives for more advanced concurrency scenarios:

- **SemaphoreSlim**: Controls the number of threads that can access a resource at once. It's ideal for limiting concurrent access to a resource (e.g., allowing only a fixed number of tasks to access a database).

- **Mutex**: Similar to lock, but can be used across processes. It's typically slower than lock or SemaphoreSlim due to its cross-process capability.

Example of Using SemaphoreSlim for Throttling Concurrent Access

csharp

```
private static readonly SemaphoreSlim _semaphore = new
SemaphoreSlim(3); // Limit to 3 concurrent threads

public async Task ProcessDataAsync()
{
    await _semaphore.WaitAsync();
    try
    {
        // Perform data processing
    }
    finally
    {
        _semaphore.Release();
    }
}
```

In this example:

- The SemaphoreSlim restricts concurrent access to a maximum of three tasks, making it ideal for scenarios where you need to control the number of simultaneous operations (e.g., limiting database connections).

Best Practices for Synchronization Primitives

- **Use SemaphoreSlim for Async Scenarios**: Prefer SemaphoreSlim over Mutex for async operations, as it's optimized for asynchronous workflows.
- **Always Release in finally Blocks**: Ensure resources are released even

if an exception occurs by placing Release calls in a finally block.

3. Using Thread-Safe Collections in System.Collections.Concurrent

For scenarios where multiple threads need to read and write data concurrently, C# offers several thread-safe collections in the System.Collections.Concurrent namespace, eliminating the need for explicit locks.

Popular Concurrent Collections

- **ConcurrentDictionary<TKey, TValue>**: A thread-safe dictionary for concurrent read and write access.
- **ConcurrentQueue<T>**: A thread-safe FIFO (first-in, first-out) collection.
- **BlockingCollection<T>**: Provides a thread-safe collection with blocking and bounding capabilities, ideal for producer-consumer scenarios.

Example of Using ConcurrentDictionary

```csharp
private readonly ConcurrentDictionary<int, string> _dataCache =
new ConcurrentDictionary<int, string>();

public void AddOrUpdateData(int key, string value)
{
    _dataCache.AddOrUpdate(key, value, (existingKey,
    existingValue) => value);
}
```

In this example:

- ConcurrentDictionary provides a thread-safe way to add or update data without locks, simplifying concurrent access to shared data.

Best Practices for Concurrent Collections

- **Use Concurrent Collections for Shared Data Access**: When tasks or threads access shared data frequently, concurrent collections handle synchronization internally, simplifying code.
- **Avoid Adding Locks to Concurrent Collections**: These collections are already thread-safe. Adding explicit locks can lead to performance degradation and negate their benefits.

4. Async-Friendly Locking: SemaphoreSlim for Async Code

Asynchronous workflows can complicate concurrency control because traditional locks (e.g., lock) are not compatible with await. SemaphoreSlim can function as an async lock, allowing safe access to resources in async methods.

Example of Using SemaphoreSlim for Async Locking

```csharp
private readonly SemaphoreSlim _asyncLock = new SemaphoreSlim(1,
1);

public async Task PerformAsyncWorkSafely()
{
    await _asyncLock.WaitAsync();
    try
    {
        // Perform async work here
    }
    finally
    {
        _asyncLock.Release();
    }
}
```

In this example:

- SemaphoreSlim acts as an async-friendly lock, allowing only one task to access the critical section at a time while still supporting await.

Best Practices for Async Locking

- **Minimize Code Inside Async Locks**: Keep the async lock scope minimal to avoid long waits for other tasks.
- **Use SemaphoreSlim for async/await**: SemaphoreSlim is optimized for async workflows, making it ideal for locking in async methods.

5. Avoid Shared State and Embrace Immutability

Avoiding shared mutable state is one of the most effective ways to handle concurrency safely. By keeping data local to each task or making it immutable, you reduce the need for synchronization.

Example of Using Immutable State

```csharp
public async Task<int> CalculateSumAsync(int[] numbers)
{
    int sum = 0;
    foreach (var number in numbers)
    {
        sum += number;
    }
    return sum;
}
```

In this example:

- By using local variables (e.g., sum), there's no risk of concurrent modifications, and no locks are needed.

Best Practices for Immutability

- **Favor Local Variables and Parameters**: Where possible, keep variables local to avoid shared access across threads.
- **Use Immutable Data Structures**: For complex data, consider using

immutable collections or readonly fields to prevent accidental modification.

6. Parallelism for CPU-Bound Tasks with Parallel.For and Parallel.ForEach

Parallel.For and Parallel.ForEach are useful for parallelizing CPU-bound tasks, maximizing CPU usage while keeping each task independent. However, these constructs can lead to contention if shared data is accessed frequently.

Example of Using Parallel.ForEach for Independent Tasks

csharp

```csharp
public void ProcessItemsConcurrently(List<int> items)
{
    Parallel.ForEach(items, item =>
    {
        Console.WriteLine($"Processing item {item}");
    });
}
```

In this example:

- **Parallel.ForEach** runs the loop concurrently, providing speedup for CPU-intensive work where tasks are independent.

Best Practices for Parallel Loops

- **Avoid Shared State in Parallel Loops**: Minimize the use of shared variables within parallel loops.
- **Use for CPU-Bound Tasks Only**: Parallel loops are best for compute-intensive operations where each task is isolated.

Summary of Safe Concurrency Practices in C#

Handling concurrency safely is essential for building robust and scalable applications. Here are the main best practices to consider:

1. **Use lock for Simple Critical Sections**: Prevent race conditions by using lock statements in small, focused critical sections.
2. **Employ Synchronization Primitives**: Use SemaphoreSlim and Mutex for more complex scenarios that require controlled access to resources.
3. **Utilize Concurrent Collections**: Simplify concurrent data access with thread-safe collections from System.Collections.Concurrent.
4. **Implement Async-Aware Locking**: Use SemaphoreSlim as an async-friendly lock to support await without blocking.
5. **Avoid Shared State When Possible**: Embrace immutability and isolate state within each task or thread to minimize the need for locks.
6. **Use Parallelism for Independent CPU-Bound Work**: For computationally heavy, independent tasks, leverage Parallel.For and Parallel.ForEach.

By following these practices, developers can mitigate concurrency issues, making their applications more resilient, responsive, and efficient. In the next section, we'll look at advanced patterns for concurrency control, including the use of dataflow and reactive programming, to further enhance your concurrency strategy in C#.

Hands-On Project: Developing an Asynchronous Data Fetching Service

In this project, we'll develop an asynchronous data fetching service in C# that simulates retrieving paginated data from an API. This example will demonstrate how to structure asynchronous services effectively using async streams and IAsyncEnumerable<T>. The service will support advanced features like cancellation, error handling, and concurrency management, making it flexible for various applications that require efficient, non-blocking data retrieval.

Project Overview: Asynchronous Data Fetching Service

The **Async Data Fetching Service** will:

1. **Simulate fetching paginated data** from a mock API using async methods.
2. **Stream data using async streams** with IAsyncEnumerable<T>, allowing for incremental processing.
3. **Support cancellation tokens** to allow users to cancel the fetching process mid-operation.
4. **Implement error handling** to catch and log errors without disrupting the service.
5. **Control concurrency**, making the service efficient and responsive.

Step 1: Setting Up the Project Structure

1. **Create a New Project**: Start a Console App in Visual Studio or Visual Studio Code named AsyncDataFetchingService.
2. **Organize Folders**:

- **Models**: Contains data models used in the service.
- **Services**: Implements the core data fetching functionality.
- **UI**: Manages user interaction, including starting, monitoring, and canceling the data fetching process.

Step 2: Designing the Data Model

In the Models folder, create a DataRecord class to represent an individual data item from the API. This model will hold basic information for each record, making it easy to structure and manipulate data.

```csharp
namespace AsyncDataFetchingService.Models
{
    public class DataRecord
```

```
{
    public int Id { get; set; }
    public string Content { get; set; } = string.Empty;

    public override string ToString() => $"ID: {Id}, Content:
    {Content}";
}
}
```

The model includes:

- **Id**: A unique identifier for each data record.
- **Content**: Represents the content of the data record.

Step 3: Creating the Data Fetching Service

In the Services folder, create a DataFetchingService class. This class will simulate an API that fetches data in pages. It will expose an async stream method, FetchDataAsync, that returns records one by one.

Define the IDataFetchingService Interface: Start by defining an interface for the service.

csharp

```
using AsyncDataFetchingService.Models;
using System.Collections.Generic;
using System.Threading;

namespace AsyncDataFetchingService.Services
{
    public interface IDataFetchingService
    {
        IAsyncEnumerable<DataRecord> FetchDataAsync(int pageSize,
        CancellationToken cancellationToken);
    }
}
```

Implement the DataFetchingService Class: Implement IDataFetchingSer

131

vice, simulating a paginated API by creating async streams.

```csharp
using AsyncDataFetchingService.Models;
using System;
using System.Collections.Generic;
using System.Threading;
using System.Threading.Tasks;

namespace AsyncDataFetchingService.Services
{
    public class DataFetchingService : IDataFetchingService
    {
        public async IAsyncEnumerable<DataRecord>
        FetchDataAsync(int pageSize, [EnumeratorCancellation]
        CancellationToken cancellationToken)
        {
            int page = 1;
            while (true)
            {
                // Fetch data for the current page
                var records = await GetDataPageAsync(page,
                pageSize, cancellationToken);
                if (records == null || records.Count == 0) yield
                break;

                foreach (var record in records)
                {
                    yield return record;
                }

                page++;
            }
        }

        private async Task<List<DataRecord>> GetDataPageAsync(int
        page, int pageSize, CancellationToken cancellationToken)
        {
            // Simulate network delay
```

```csharp
        await Task.Delay(500, cancellationToken);

        // Generate mock data
        var records = new List<DataRecord>();
        for (int i = 0; i < pageSize; i++)
        {
            records.Add(new DataRecord
            {
                Id = (page - 1) * pageSize + i + 1,
                Content = $"Record {(page - 1) * pageSize + i
                + 1}"
            });
        }

        return page > 5 ? new List<DataRecord>() : records;
    }
  }
}
```

In this service:

- **FetchDataAsync**: Provides an async stream of data, yielding each record incrementally.
- **GetDataPageAsync**: Simulates data retrieval with a delay and returns mock data.

Step 4: Implementing the UI Layer for Data Retrieval

Create a DataFetcherUI class in the UI folder to interact with DataFetch-ingService, manage user input, and handle data display.

Create the DataFetcherUI Class: This class will interact with the user, start data retrieval, and display each record as it arrives.

```csharp
csharp

using AsyncDataFetchingService.Models;
using AsyncDataFetchingService.Services;
```

```csharp
using System;
using System.Threading;
using System.Threading.Tasks;

namespace AsyncDataFetchingService.UI
{
    public class DataFetcherUI
    {
        private readonly IDataFetchingService _dataService;

        public DataFetcherUI(IDataFetchingService dataService)
        {
            _dataService = dataService;
        }

        public async Task RunAsync(CancellationToken
        cancellationToken)
        {
            Console.WriteLine("Fetching data...");

            await foreach (var record in
            _dataService.FetchDataAsync(5, cancellationToken))
            {
                Console.WriteLine(record);

                if (cancellationToken.IsCancellationRequested)
                {
                    Console.WriteLine("Data fetching canceled.");
                    break;
                }
            }

            Console.WriteLine("Data fetching completed.");
        }
    }
}
```

In this UI class:

- **RunAsync**: Starts data fetching and prints each record as it becomes available, supporting real-time data streaming.

Step 5: Putting It All Together in Program.cs

In Program.cs, set up the application, initialize services, and configure cancellation handling.

```csharp
using AsyncDataFetchingService.Services;
using AsyncDataFetchingService.UI;
using System;
using System.Threading;
using System.Threading.Tasks;

namespace AsyncDataFetchingService
{
    class Program
    {
        static async Task Main(string[] args)
        {
            var dataService = new DataFetchingService();
            var ui = new DataFetcherUI(dataService);

            using var cancellationTokenSource = new
            CancellationTokenSource();

            // Handle user cancellation (Ctrl+C)
            Console.CancelKeyPress += (sender, eventArgs) =>
            {
                eventArgs.Cancel = true;
                cancellationTokenSource.Cancel();
                Console.WriteLine("Cancellation requested...");
            };

            try
            {
                await ui.RunAsync(cancellationTokenSource.Token);
            }
            catch (OperationCanceledException)
```

```
        {
            Console.WriteLine("Operation was canceled.");
        }

        Console.WriteLine("Program finished.");
    }
  }
}
```

In this setup:

- **CancellationTokenSource**: Allows users to cancel the operation with Ctrl+C.
- **RunAsync**: Initiates data fetching and respects user-triggered cancellation.

Step 6: Running and Testing the Application

To test:

1. Start the application to observe data being fetched page by page.
2. Press Ctrl+C to simulate user cancellation.
3. Verify that the application exits gracefully, logging a cancellation message.

Step 7: Enhancing the Service with Error Handling

Add error handling in FetchDataAsync within DataFetchingService to manage errors gracefully and log issues without crashing the application.

```csharp
csharp

public async IAsyncEnumerable<DataRecord> FetchDataAsync(int
pageSize, [EnumeratorCancellation] CancellationToken
cancellationToken)
{
```

```
int page = 1;
while (true)
{
    try
    {
        var records = await GetDataPageAsync(page, pageSize,
        cancellationToken);
        if (records == null || records.Count == 0) yield break;

        foreach (var record in records)
        {
            yield return record;
        }

        page++;
    }
    catch (Exception ex)
    {
        Console.WriteLine($"Error fetching data on page
        {page}: {ex.Message}");
        yield break;
    }
}
}
```

This implementation:

- **Logs exceptions** without terminating the program, ensuring smoother error handling and logging issues when they occur.

Summary of the Asynchronous Data Fetching Service Project

This hands-on project has demonstrated how to build a robust asynchronous data fetching service in C#. Key highlights include:

1. **Incremental Data Streaming**: Using async streams to fetch and process data as it becomes available, optimizing memory usage.
2. **Support for Cancellation**: Allowing users to cancel operations for

enhanced control.

3. **Error Handling**: Handling and logging exceptions, making the service more resilient.

4. **Concurrency Management**: Designing a responsive, scalable service that can handle real-world demands.

This project serves as a foundation for applications requiring efficient data fetching and processing, such as real-time dashboards, streaming applications, and data processing pipelines.

Advanced Language Features in C# 8

Recursive Patterns: Applying Advanced Pattern Matching
In C# 8, pattern matching was significantly enhanced with the introduction of recursive patterns. Recursive patterns extend the capabilities of pattern matching by allowing patterns to be applied within other patterns, enabling more expressive and concise code. This feature is especially useful for complex data structures like tuples, arrays, or custom object hierarchies where nested pattern matching helps streamline logic by reducing the need for multiple conditional statements.

This section explores the types of recursive patterns in C# 8, their applications, and best practices for writing clear and efficient pattern-matching code.

Overview of Recursive Patterns in C#

Recursive patterns in C# 8 include:

1. **Positional Patterns**: Extract data based on the structure of a type, like tuples and positional records.
2. **Property Patterns**: Match specific properties within an object.
3. **Tuple and List Patterns**: Match tuples or lists by their structure and contents.
4. **Combining Patterns**: Combine recursive patterns with logical patterns (and, or, not) to form complex matching criteria.

These patterns make it easy to match and extract nested data in a way that would otherwise require verbose code with multiple if-else statements and type checks.

1. Positional Patterns

Positional patterns match the components of an object in a specific order, which is particularly useful for deconstructing types that support deconstruction (like tuples or positional records). With positional patterns, you can extract values directly from a type's deconstructor method, simplifying how you access its data.

Example of Positional Pattern with Tuples

csharp

```
public string AnalyzePoint((int X, int Y) point) =>
    point switch
    {
        (0, 0) => "Origin",
        (0, _) => "On the Y-axis",
        (_, 0) => "On the X-axis",
        (_, _) => "Somewhere else"
    };
```

In this example:

- **Tuple Pattern Matching**: (int X, int Y) is matched with specific values for X and Y. Each pattern checks the values of X and Y to determine the location of the point.
- **Underscore _ as a Wildcard**: The underscore _ acts as a wildcard, indicating that we don't care about the value in that position, only the overall structure of the pattern.

Example of Positional Pattern with Custom Types

Positional patterns can also be used with custom types that have deconstructors defined. Let's create a custom Point class with a deconstructor:

```csharp
csharp

public class Point
{
    public int X { get; }
    public int Y { get; }

    public Point(int x, int y) => (X, Y) = (x, y);

    public void Deconstruct(out int x, out int y) => (x, y) = (X,
    Y);
}

public string DescribePoint(Point point) =>
    point switch
    {
        (0, 0) => "At the origin",
        (0, _) => "On the Y-axis",
        (_, 0) => "On the X-axis",
        _ => "Somewhere else"
    };
```

Here:

- **Deconstructor Method**: The Deconstruct method in Point allows Point objects to be deconstructed, enabling the use of positional patterns.
- **Pattern Matching with Custom Types**: The switch expression matches Point based on its X and Y values, using tuples to simplify the logic.

2. Property Patterns

Property patterns allow you to match objects based on specific property values, making it easy to evaluate complex objects without manually accessing properties. This feature is useful when working with nested data structures or when you want to match only certain properties within a larger object.

Example of Property Pattern

Suppose we have a Person class with properties Name, Age, and Address:

```csharp
public class Person
{
    public string Name { get; set; }
    public int Age { get; set; }
    public Address Address { get; set; }
}

public class Address
{
    public string City { get; set; }
    public string Country { get; set; }
}
```

Using a property pattern, we can match a Person based on specific values within the nested Address property.

```csharp
public string DescribePerson(Person person) =>
    person switch
    {
        { Age: > 18, Address: { Country: "USA" } } =>
        $"{person.Name} is an adult living in the USA.",
        { Age: <= 18 } => $"{person.Name} is a minor.",
        _ => "Unknown category"
    };
```

In this example:

- **Nested Property Pattern**: { Age: > 18, Address: { Country: "USA" } } matches Person instances where Age is greater than 18 and Country is "USA".
- **Default Case**: The final pattern (_ => "Unknown category") acts as a catch-all for cases that don't match any prior patterns.

3. Tuple and List Patterns

C# 8 supports pattern matching for tuples and lists, allowing you to match elements based on their order and values.

Example of Tuple Pattern

Tuples can be matched directly in switch expressions, simplifying logic when you need to evaluate a combination of values.

```csharp
public string ClassifyCoordinates((int x, int y) coordinates) =>
    coordinates switch
    {
        (0, 0) => "Origin",
        ( > 0, > 0) => "In Quadrant I",
        ( < 0, > 0) => "In Quadrant II",
        ( < 0, < 0) => "In Quadrant III",
        ( > 0, < 0) => "In Quadrant IV",
        _ => "On an axis"
    };
```

In this example:

- **Tuple Deconstruction and Matching**: The tuple (int x, int y) is decomposed and matched according to specific coordinate values, identifying where the point lies on a 2D grid.

Example of List Pattern Matching

With list patterns, we can check collections based on the number of elements or their values.

```csharp
public string AnalyzeList(List<int> numbers) =>
    numbers switch
    {
```

143

```
    [1, 2, 3] => "Exact match for [1, 2, 3]",
    [1, 2, _] => "Starts with [1, 2]",
    [_, _, _] => "Has exactly 3 elements",
    _ => "Does not match any pattern"
};
```

In this example:

- **Specific Patterns for Lists**: Each pattern checks specific elements within the list. [1, 2, 3] matches an exact list, [1, 2, _] matches lists starting with 1 and 2, and [_, _, _] matches any list with exactly three elements.

4. Combining Recursive Patterns with Logical Patterns

Combining recursive patterns with logical patterns (and, or, not) enhances their flexibility, allowing complex conditions to be expressed concisely.

Example of Logical and Recursive Pattern Matching

Let's say we want to classify Person objects with additional logical conditions.

```csharp
public string EvaluatePerson(Person person) =>
    person switch
    {
        { Age: >= 65 } and { Address: { Country: "Canada" } } =>
        "Senior in Canada",
        { Age: < 18 } or { Name: "Alice" } => "Minor or Alice",
        { Age: not 30 } => "Not 30 years old",
        _ => "Unclassified"
    };
```

In this example:

- **and Pattern**: Matches Person instances that are seniors (Age >= 65) and reside in Canada.

- **or Pattern**: Matches either minors (Age < 18) or individuals named "Alice."
- **not Pattern**: Excludes individuals aged exactly 30.

Benefits and Best Practices for Recursive Patterns

Recursive patterns provide a clean, readable alternative to deeply nested if-else logic, making your code easier to understand and maintain. Here are some best practices:

1. **Use Patterns for Readability**: When possible, use patterns to make conditions more readable, especially for nested data structures.
2. **Take Advantage of switch Expressions**: Combining recursive patterns with switch expressions makes code more concise and expressive.
3. **Use Default Cases to Handle Unmatched Scenarios**: Always include a default case (_) to handle unexpected values, ensuring robustness.
4. **Leverage Logical Patterns for Complex Conditions**: Combine and, or, and not with recursive patterns to express complex matching conditions without overly verbose code.

Recursive patterns in C# 8 elevate pattern matching by enabling concise handling of complex data structures. By using positional patterns, property patterns, tuple and list patterns, and combining these with logical operators, developers can write clear, maintainable code that efficiently handles sophisticated data structures. This approach simplifies conditional logic, reduces code complexity, and enhances readability—particularly valuable in applications where data structures are complex or deeply nested. As a best practice, take advantage of recursive patterns to simplify your code while keeping it expressive and precise.

Indices and Ranges: Streamlining Data Access

Indices and ranges in C# 8 provide a streamlined approach to accessing subsets of data in arrays, strings, and collections. With the ^ operator for indices and the .. operator for ranges, developers can slice and access data efficiently, improving both readability and performance. These features are particularly beneficial in applications requiring frequent data manipulation or selective access to parts of larger data structures.

This section covers how to use indices and ranges, their applications, and best practices to make data handling in C# more intuitive and concise.

Understanding Indices in C# 8

An index in C# 8 can be represented using the ^ operator, which simplifies access to elements from the end of an array or collection. This complements traditional zero-based indexing by providing a straightforward way to retrieve elements from the end of the collection without needing to calculate offsets manually.

Using the ^ Operator for Reverse Indexing

The ^ symbol signifies "from the end," allowing you to specify elements relative to the collection's last element. For example, ^1 represents the last element, ^2 the second-to-last element, and so on.

Example of Using the ^ Operator with Arrays

csharp

```
int[] numbers = { 10, 20, 30, 40, 50 };
Console.WriteLine(numbers[^1]); // Outputs: 50 (last element)
Console.WriteLine(numbers[^2]); // Outputs: 40 (second-to-last
element)
```

In this example:

- **numbers[^1]** accesses the last element directly, eliminating the need to calculate numbers.Length - 1.
- **numbers[^2]** provides access to the second-to-last element, streamlining code readability and reducing errors in accessing elements from the end.

Use Case: Reverse indexing is particularly useful when working with collections where the last few elements hold special significance, such as retrieving recent entries in a log file or the latest values in a data series.

Introducing Ranges in C# 8

Ranges allow developers to retrieve contiguous segments of an array or collection using the .. operator. A range specifies a starting and ending point, providing a concise syntax for slicing arrays and other data structures.

Using the .. Operator for Data Slicing

With the .. operator, you can define a range within the bounds of a collection. The expression x..y creates a range starting at x and ending before y. If omitted, the start or end defaults to the beginning or end of the collection.

Example of Using the .. Operator with Arrays

```csharp
int[] numbers = { 10, 20, 30, 40, 50 };

// Using ranges to access subsets
int[] firstTwo = numbers[..2]; // {10, 20}
int[] middle = numbers[1..4]; // {20, 30, 40}
int[] lastTwo = numbers[^2..]; // {40, 50}
```

In this example:

- **numbers[..2]** retrieves the first two elements.
- **numbers[1..4]** extracts elements from index 1 to 3 (not including 4), allowing precise control over the segment of the array.
- **numbers[^2..]** returns the last two elements, utilizing the ^ operator in combination with ranges.

Use Case: Ranges are valuable in scenarios where you need to access specific slices of data, such as pagination, segmenting a large dataset, or working with subarrays.

Combining Indices and Ranges for Complex Data Access

Indices and ranges can be combined for more complex data access needs, providing flexibility in slicing and manipulating data. These combinations allow developers to write concise, expressive code that targets specific parts of data structures efficiently.

Example of Combining Indices and Ranges

Let's consider a scenario where we need the first half, the middle elements, and the last half of an array:

```csharp
int[] data = { 5, 10, 15, 20, 25, 30, 35, 40, 45, 50 };

int[] firstHalf = data[..^5]; // First half of the array
int[] middleSegment = data[3..7]; // Middle elements from index 3
to 6
int[] lastHalf = data[^5..]; // Last half of the array
```

In this example:

- **data[..^5]** selects elements from the start up to the fifth-to-last element.
- **data[3..7]** retrieves a middle segment, from index 3 up to but not including index 7.
- **data[^5..]** returns the last five elements.

Working with Strings and Collections Using Indices and Ranges

Indices and ranges are also compatible with strings, making substring extraction more intuitive and concise. This feature provides an alternative to Substring with clearer syntax.

Example of Using Ranges with Strings

```csharp
string message = "Hello, World!";
string greeting = message[..5]; // "Hello"
string remainder = message[7..^1]; // "World"
```

In this example:

- **message[..5]** extracts the first five characters, "Hello."
- **message[7..^1]** removes the first seven characters and the last character, extracting "World" from the original string.

Ranges with List<T> and Other Collections

While indices and ranges work natively with arrays and strings, they can also be applied to List<T> and other collections using the .ToArray() method or by implementing custom indexers. For instance:

```csharp
List<int> numbers = new List<int> { 1, 2, 3, 4, 5, 6 };
int[] rangeFromList = numbers.GetRange(2, 3).ToArray(); // {3, 4, 5}
```

Best Practices for Using Indices and Ranges

1. **Use Ranges for Readability**: Ranges simplify the code and improve readability when accessing contiguous elements, making your intentions clear.
2. **Combine with Reverse Indexing**: Use the ^ operator with ranges to access data from the end of a collection, avoiding length calculations and reducing errors.
3. **Avoid Overusing Ranges for Small Slices**: While ranges are powerful, they are most effective when accessing larger segments of data. For small slices, traditional indexing may be clearer.

4. **Use Caution with Large Data Sets**: Ranges create a new array, so using them with large data sets may have performance implications. Consider alternatives like lazy evaluation or iterators for large-scale data manipulation.

Indices and ranges in C# 8 add flexibility and precision to data access, allowing developers to manipulate arrays, strings, and collections efficiently. By using the ^ operator for reverse indexing and the .. operator for ranges, you can create readable, concise code that improves data-handling workflows. These features make code easier to write, understand, and maintain, especially in applications that require frequent data slicing or selective access. In practice, indices and ranges help streamline operations across a wide range of scenarios, from data manipulation in algorithms to user-facing features like pagination.

Static Local Functions: Optimizing Code Structure and Memory Usage

Introduced in C# 8, static local functions enhance code structure and efficiency by allowing local functions to be marked as static. Static local functions, unlike regular local functions, do not capture or access any variables from their surrounding scope. This restriction brings performance advantages by reducing memory usage and improving the predictability of local function behavior.

In this section, we'll explore static local functions, their benefits, practical use cases, and best practices for using them to create optimized and maintainable code.

Understanding Static Local Functions in C#

A static local function is a nested function defined inside another method and declared as static. Unlike regular local functions, static local functions do not have access to instance variables, this, or any variables in the enclosing scope. This restriction means static local functions can only use parameters and local variables declared within the function itself, making them more memory-efficient and faster.

Syntax of Static Local Functions

The syntax for defining a static local function is similar to a regular local function, with the addition of the static keyword:

```csharp
void MainFunction()
{
    static int StaticLocalFunction(int x, int y)
    {
        return x + y;
    }
}
```

In this example:

- **StaticLocalFunction** is a static local function within MainFunction, and it can only access parameters x and y passed directly to it.

Benefits of Static Local Functions

Static local functions provide several benefits over regular local functions, particularly in terms of memory management, performance, and code organization:

1. **Reduced Memory Usage**: Because static local functions don't capture any variables from their enclosing scope, they avoid allocating additional memory for closures, reducing heap usage.
2. **Improved Performance**: Static local functions eliminate the overhead of closure allocation, making function calls faster and reducing garbage collection pressure.
3. **Enhanced Code Clarity**: Static local functions make it clear that no external dependencies are used, simplifying the code structure and reducing potential side effects.
4. **Greater Predictability**: By limiting access to external variables, static

local functions reduce the chances of unintended side effects, leading to safer, more predictable code.

When to Use Static Local Functions

Static local functions are particularly useful in scenarios where local functions don't need access to external variables and where performance is critical. Here are some common use cases:

1. **Helper Functions with Limited Scope**: Use static local functions to encapsulate helper logic within a method without cluttering the main codebase. Static local functions are ideal when the helper function doesn't rely on any instance-specific data.
2. **Optimizing Recursive Algorithms**: Recursive algorithms often benefit from static local functions, especially if they don't require access to the outer method's variables. The static keyword helps avoid closure creation for each recursive call.
3. **Mathematical and Pure Functions**: Static local functions work well for mathematical computations or other pure functions, as they don't depend on mutable external state.
4. **Data Processing Pipelines**: When creating functions that operate on collections or data transformations, static local functions reduce overhead and improve efficiency by preventing external dependencies.

Example of Static Local Functions in Practice

Let's look at examples demonstrating static local functions in various contexts.

Example 1: Mathematical Helper Function

Here's an example where a static local function is used within a method to encapsulate a helper function for factorial calculations:

```
csharp
```

ADVANCED LANGUAGE FEATURES IN C# 8

```csharp
public int CalculateFactorial(int number)
{
    if (number < 0)
    {
        throw new ArgumentException("Number must be
        non-negative.");
    }

    static int Factorial(int n)
    {
        return n <= 1 ? 1 : n * Factorial(n - 1);
    }

    return Factorial(number);
}
```

In this example:

- **Static Local Function Factorial**: Declared as static within Calculate-Factorial, Factorial is a recursive helper that calculates the factorial of n.
- **No Closure Overhead**: Since Factorial doesn't depend on any external variables, marking it as static prevents unnecessary memory allocation.

Example 2: Optimizing Recursive Algorithms

Consider a method that calculates the Fibonacci sequence, where a static local function optimizes the recursive calls:

```csharp
csharp

public int Fibonacci(int n)
{
    if (n < 0)
    {
        throw new ArgumentException("n must be non-negative.");
    }
```

```
static int Fib(int current, int next, int count)
{
    return count == 0 ? current : Fib(next, current + next,
    count - 1);
}

return Fib(0, 1, n);
}
```

In this example:

- **Static Local Function Fib**: The Fib function performs a tail-recursive Fibonacci calculation.
- **Performance Optimization**: By making Fib static, the function avoids unnecessary memory allocation, making it more efficient for large values of n.

Differences Between Regular and Static Local Functions

It's important to understand how static local functions differ from regular local functions:

1. **Access to Enclosing Scope**: Regular local functions can access variables from the outer scope, while static local functions cannot.
2. **Closure Creation**: Regular local functions that capture variables from the outer scope create closures, increasing memory usage. Static local functions don't create closures, which improves performance.
3. **Error Prevention**: Static local functions reduce the risk of accidental modifications to external variables, leading to safer, more predictable code.

Example of Error Prevention with Static Local Functions

Consider a scenario where a regular local function unintentionally modifies an external variable:

```csharp
public void CalculateSquares(int limit)
{
    int totalSum = 0;

    void RegularLocalFunction(int number)
    {
        totalSum += number * number; // Modifies external variable
    }

    for (int i = 1; i <= limit; i++)
    {
        RegularLocalFunction(i);
    }

    Console.WriteLine($"Total Sum: {totalSum}");
}
```

In this example:

- **Unintentional Modification**: The regular local function RegularLocal-Function modifies totalSum, an external variable. This modification could be unintended, especially in larger codebases.
- **Solution**: Converting this to a static local function would prevent the function from modifying totalSum, encouraging a design that passes totalSum as a parameter if needed.

Static Local Functions in Asynchronous Code

Static local functions can also be useful in asynchronous methods, helping to avoid memory leaks or performance issues associated with capturing async state machines.

Example of Static Local Function in an Asynchronous Method

csharp

```
public async Task ProcessDataAsync(List<int> data)
{
    static async Task<int> ProcessItemAsync(int item)
    {
        await Task.Delay(100); // Simulate async work
        return item * item;
    }

    foreach (var item in data)
    {
        int result = await ProcessItemAsync(item);
        Console.WriteLine($"Processed item: {result}");
    }
}
```

In this example:

- **Asynchronous Static Local Function**: ProcessItemAsync is defined as an async static local function within ProcessDataAsync. Since it's static, it doesn't capture any external variables, reducing overhead.

Best Practices for Static Local Functions

1. **Use Static Local Functions for Isolation**: When writing helper functions that don't need access to the enclosing method's variables, use static to avoid accidental dependencies and make the function self-contained.
2. **Pass Dependencies as Parameters**: If a static local function requires external data, pass it as a parameter rather than relying on external scope. This approach improves function reusability and avoids hidden dependencies.
3. **Limit Use to Performance-Critical Code**: While static local functions improve memory usage, they are most beneficial in performance-critical scenarios. For general-purpose code, regular local functions may suffice.

4. **Use for Recursive Functions and Complex Computations**: Recursive algorithms and computational tasks benefit most from static local functions due to the lack of closure overhead, improving performance in nested or recursive calls.

Static local functions in C# 8 provide a powerful way to write optimized, efficient code. By avoiding closure allocations and limiting access to external variables, static local functions reduce memory usage and improve performance. They're especially useful for helper functions, recursive algorithms, and asynchronous code where efficiency is critical. By following best practices, developers can use static local functions to create more predictable, maintainable, and high-performing applications.

Default Interface Methods: Simplifying Interface Management

With C# 8, default interface methods allow developers to define method implementations directly within interfaces. This feature enables interfaces to include functionality while preserving backward compatibility. Default interface methods make it easier to evolve and extend interfaces without requiring changes to all implementing classes, which can be especially helpful in large, complex codebases or API design. By defining default behavior in an interface, you can reduce boilerplate code, simplify interface evolution, and improve the maintainability of your code.

This section explores default interface methods, their benefits, common use cases, and best practices for using them effectively in C#.

What Are Default Interface Methods?

In traditional C# interfaces, only method signatures could be defined, while implementation had to be provided by each implementing class. Default interface methods change this by allowing methods with full implementations to be included in an interface, which implementing classes inherit automatically unless they choose to override.

Syntax for Default Interface Methods

The syntax for defining a default interface method is similar to a regular method, with the method defined directly in the interface:

```csharp
public interface IDisplayable
{
    void Display();

    // Default interface method with implementation
    void Print()
    {
        Console.WriteLine("Default print method");
    }
}
```

In this example:

- **Print Method**: A default interface method, providing a default implementation that all implementing classes will inherit unless they override it.

Key Benefits of Default Interface Methods

Default interface methods provide several advantages, particularly in large or evolving codebases where backward compatibility is important:

1. **Easier Interface Evolution**: Adding new methods to interfaces can be challenging, as all implementing classes need to be updated. Default methods enable you to add functionality without breaking existing implementations.
2. **Reduction in Boilerplate Code**: Default methods allow common functionality to be defined once, reducing repetitive code across multiple classes.
3. **Improved Maintainability**: Since default implementations reside

within the interface, maintaining or updating shared functionality is easier and centralized.

4. **Enhanced Extensibility**: Default methods support the introduction of optional functionality, giving implementing classes the choice to override as needed.

Implementing Default Interface Methods

To illustrate how default interface methods work, let's explore a few examples where default behavior is defined directly in the interface.

Example 1: Providing a Default Method Implementation

Consider an interface for logging messages. By including a default method, we can provide common logging behavior for all implementing classes.

```csharp
public interface ILogger
{
    void Log(string message);

    // Default interface method
    void LogInfo(string message)
    {
        Log($"INFO: {message}");
    }
}
```

In this example:

- **LogInfo Method**: Implements a default behavior for logging informational messages. Any class implementing ILogger can use LogInfo without explicitly defining it, or it can override this method to provide a custom implementation.

Example 2: Using Default Interface Methods with Existing Implementations
Let's consider a scenario where we have several classes implementing

an interface. Adding a default method allows new functionality without modifying each class.

```csharp
public interface IDevice
{
    void Start();

    // Adding a default method
    void Restart()
    {
        Console.WriteLine("Restarting device...");
        Stop();
        Start();
    }

    void Stop();
}

public class Printer : IDevice
{
    public void Start() => Console.WriteLine("Printer
    starting...");
    public void Stop() => Console.WriteLine("Printer stopping...");
}

public class Scanner : IDevice
{
    public void Start() => Console.WriteLine("Scanner
    starting...");
    public void Stop() => Console.WriteLine("Scanner stopping...");
}
```

In this example:

- **Restart Method**: The default Restart method provides a standardized way to restart a device by stopping and then starting it.
- **Automatic Inheritance**: Printer and Scanner classes inherit the Restart

method, providing them with restart functionality without additional code. Each class is free to override Restart if a custom behavior is needed.

Overriding Default Interface Methods

Implementing classes can override default methods to provide specific behavior, which is especially useful when the default implementation doesn't fully meet a class's needs.

Example of Overriding a Default Method

```csharp
public class AdvancedPrinter : Printer
{
    public override void Restart()
    {
        Console.WriteLine("Performing advanced restart
        sequence...");
        base.Stop();
        InitializeSettings();
        base.Start();
    }

    private void InitializeSettings() =>
    Console.WriteLine("Reinitializing printer settings.");
}
```

In this example:

- **AdvancedPrinter Class**: Overrides the Restart method inherited from IDevice to add specific initialization steps.
- **Custom Restart Sequence**: AdvancedPrinter's Restart implementation customizes the process while reusing the core Stop and Start functionality from the base class.

Constraints of Default Interface Methods

While default interface methods offer flexibility, there are some important constraints to keep in mind:

1. **No Instance Fields or State**: Default interface methods cannot access instance fields, as interfaces do not hold state. They can only operate on parameters or static members.
2. **Limited Access to this**: Default methods can access this but cannot call other instance methods directly, making them less flexible for methods that require full object context.
3. **Compatibility Limitations**: Default interface methods are not fully compatible with all versions of .NET or all runtime environments. When targeting frameworks that don't support them, alternative solutions are necessary.

Best Practices for Using Default Interface Methods

1. **Use Sparingly for Optional Behaviors**: Default methods are best suited for optional behaviors rather than critical functionality. Avoid overusing default methods to keep interfaces focused and cohesive.
2. **Keep Implementations Simple**: Since default methods have limited access to object state, keep implementations simple and focused on functionality that doesn't depend on specific object instances.
3. **Leverage for Backward Compatibility**: Use default methods to add new functionality to interfaces without breaking existing code, particularly in shared libraries or frameworks.
4. **Document Default Methods Clearly**: Make it clear when a method is intended as a default so developers understand its role and whether they should override it.

Real-World Use Cases for Default Interface Methods

Default interface methods shine in scenarios where backward compatibility and extensibility are key concerns. Here are a few real-world examples:

1. Extending a Logging Interface

In a logging system, you may want to add a LogDebug method to the existing ILogger interface without requiring all implementations to change immediately. By providing a default implementation, you can offer debug logging functionality without breaking existing loggers.

```csharp
public interface ILogger
{
    void Log(string message);

    // New method with default implementation
    void LogDebug(string message)
    {
        Log($"DEBUG: {message}");
    }
}
```

Existing classes implementing ILogger gain LogDebug functionality without additional code, while new or updated classes can override it if needed.

2. Adding Optional Features to a Payment Processor Interface

In a payment processing system, you might want to add a Refund method to an existing IPaymentProcessor interface. By making it a default interface method, you avoid requiring every payment provider to implement refunds immediately.

```csharp
public interface IPaymentProcessor
{
    void ProcessPayment(decimal amount);

    // Adding a default method for refunds
    void Refund(decimal amount)
    {
```

```
    Console.WriteLine("Refunds are not supported by this
    processor.");
  }
}
```

New processors can override Refund to implement refund logic, while existing implementations inherit the default message.

Default interface methods in C# 8 enhance flexibility in interface design, allowing developers to provide default implementations without modifying existing code. By reducing boilerplate code and enabling backward-compatible interface evolution, default interface methods are invaluable for large or evolving codebases. However, they should be used judiciously, with a focus on optional or secondary behaviors, to avoid diluting the core responsibilities of an interface. When used strategically, default interface methods provide a powerful tool for creating adaptable, maintainable, and user-friendly libraries and applications.

Hands-On Project: Refactoring Legacy Code to Use C# 8 Features

Refactoring legacy code to leverage C# 8 features can enhance readability, performance, and maintainability. By integrating advanced features like nullable reference types, default interface methods, async streams, and pattern matching, you can modernize your codebase and streamline complex logic. In this project, we'll walk through the refactoring of a simple legacy application to take advantage of C# 8 features, improving both code quality and functionality.

Project Overview: Refactoring a Simple Data Processing Application

We'll start with a legacy application that processes customer orders. This application performs tasks like filtering, data transformations, and error handling. Our goal is to refactor the code to use C# 8 features, such as:

1. **Nullable Reference Types**: Improving null safety and reducing potential errors.
2. **Default Interface Methods**: Providing backward-compatible enhancements to interfaces.
3. **Async Streams**: Enabling non-blocking data retrieval and processing.
4. **Pattern Matching Enhancements**: Simplifying complex conditions with advanced pattern matching.

Step 1: Reviewing and Understanding the Legacy Code

Here's a simplified version of the legacy code, which includes a class OrderProcessor that filters and processes orders.

```csharp
public interface IOrderService
{
    IEnumerable<Order> GetOrders();
    Order GetOrderById(int id);
}


public class Order
{
    public int Id { get; set; }
    public string? CustomerName { get; set; }
    public decimal Amount { get; set; }
    public DateTime OrderDate { get; set; }
    public bool IsProcessed { get; set; }
}


public class OrderProcessor
{
    private readonly IOrderService _orderService;

    public OrderProcessor(IOrderService orderService)
    {
        _orderService = orderService;
    }
```

```
    public void ProcessPendingOrders()
    {
        foreach (var order in _orderService.GetOrders())
        {
            if (!order.IsProcessed && order.Amount > 100)
            {
                Console.WriteLine($"Processing order {order.Id}
                for customer {order.CustomerName}");
                order.IsProcessed = true;
            }
        }
    }
}
```

In this code:

- **Order Filtering**: Orders are filtered based on whether they are processed and have an amount greater than 100.
- **Basic Interface and Classes:** The interface IOrderService provides methods for retrieving orders.

Step 2: Enabling and Using Nullable Reference Types

C# 8 introduced nullable reference types to improve null safety. By enabling nullable reference types, we'll annotate reference types to clarify whether they should allow null values.

Enable Nullable Reference Types: In the project file (.csproj), add <Nullable>enable</Nullable> to enable nullable reference types.

Refactor Code with Nullable Annotations: Adjust the Order class and interface methods to use nullable reference types appropriately.

```csharp
public class Order
{
```

```csharp
    public int Id { get; set; }
    public string CustomerName { get; set; } = string.Empty; // No
    null allowed
    public decimal Amount { get; set; }
    public DateTime OrderDate { get; set; }
    public bool IsProcessed { get; set; }
}

public interface IOrderService
{
    IEnumerable<Order> GetOrders();
    Order? GetOrderById(int id); // Indicates that the return
    value may be null
}
```

In this refactored code:

- **Nullable Annotations**: Order properties like CustomerName are marked as non-nullable, while GetOrderById can return null.

Step 3: Introducing Default Interface Methods

Suppose we want to add a new method, GetPendingOrders, to IOrderService without requiring all implementations to change. We can use a default interface method to provide a default implementation.

Refactor IOrderService with a Default Method

csharp

```csharp
public interface IOrderService
{
    IEnumerable<Order> GetOrders();
    Order? GetOrderById(int id);

    // Default interface method
    IEnumerable<Order> GetPendingOrders()
    {
```

```
        return GetOrders().Where(order => !order.IsProcessed);
    }
}
```

With this change:

- **Backward Compatibility**: GetPendingOrders is implemented in IOrderService, providing default functionality to return pending orders without requiring modifications to existing classes.

Step 4: Using Async Streams for Non-Blocking Data Retrieval

Let's assume we want to process large numbers of orders asynchronously, fetching them in batches. Async streams allow us to process these batches one at a time, improving responsiveness.

Update the Interface to Use Async Streams

csharp

```
public interface IOrderService
{
    IAsyncEnumerable<Order> GetOrdersAsync();
    Order? GetOrderById(int id);
}
```

Refactor the OrderProcessor to Use Async Streams

Update OrderProcessor to handle GetOrdersAsync using await foreach to process orders as they become available.

csharp

```
public class OrderProcessor
{
    private readonly IOrderService _orderService;
```

```csharp
    public OrderProcessor(IOrderService orderService)
    {
        _orderService = orderService;
    }

    public async Task ProcessPendingOrdersAsync()
    {
        await foreach (var order in _orderService.GetOrdersAsync())
        {
            if (!order.IsProcessed && order.Amount > 100)
            {
                Console.WriteLine($"Processing order {order.Id}
                for customer {order.CustomerName}");
                order.IsProcessed = true;
            }
        }
    }
}
```

In this refactored code:

- **Async Stream Processing**: By using await foreach, ProcessPendingOrd ersAsync processes each order asynchronously as it becomes available.

Step 5: Simplifying Conditions with Pattern Matching

Let's use pattern matching to simplify the filtering conditions in ProcessPe ndingOrdersAsync.

Refactor with Pattern Matching

csharp

```csharp
public async Task ProcessPendingOrdersAsync()
{
    await foreach (var order in _orderService.GetOrdersAsync())
    {
        if (order is { IsProcessed: false, Amount: > 100 })
```

```
    {
        Console.WriteLine($"Processing order {order.Id} for
        customer {order.CustomerName}");
        order.IsProcessed = true;
    }
  }
}
```

In this example:

- **Property Pattern Matching**: The condition order is { IsProcessed: false, Amount: > 100 } directly matches unprocessed orders with an amount greater than 100, simplifying the condition.

Step 6: Testing and Validating the Refactored Code

Run tests to validate the refactored code, checking for:

- **Null Safety**: Ensure nullable annotations are correctly handled and null values are appropriately managed.
- **Async Behavior**: Confirm that async streams work as expected, processing orders asynchronously.
- **Pattern Matching Accuracy**: Validate that pattern matching filters orders correctly.

By refactoring the legacy code with C# 8 features, we achieved:

1. **Improved Null Safety**: Enabled nullable reference types to clarify null handling.
2. **Backward-Compatible Extensions**: Used default interface methods to add functionality without modifying existing implementations.
3. **Asynchronous Processing**: Leveraged async streams for efficient, non-blocking data processing.
4. **Simplified Logic**: Applied pattern matching to streamline conditional checks.

This refactoring process demonstrates how modern C# features can make legacy code more efficient, maintainable, and easier to read. By using these techniques, you can enhance your codebase with minimal disruption, making it more adaptable to future requirements.

Introduction to Cross-Platform Development with .NET Core

Introduction to Cross-Platform Development with .NET Core .NET Core has transformed the landscape of .NET development by enabling the creation of cross-platform applications that run on Windows, macOS, and Linux. This open-source, modular framework allows developers to build high-performance, scalable applications while maintaining compatibility across different operating systems. With .NET Core, Microsoft provided a streamlined, versatile environment that supports a wide range of application types, from web and cloud services to desktop applications, mobile applications, and microservices.

In this introduction, we'll explore the core aspects of cross-platform development with .NET Core, including its benefits, architecture, ecosystem, and how it supports a unified development experience. By the end, you'll have a foundational understanding of why .NET Core is a powerful choice for developers aiming to create applications that are platform-agnostic, scalable, and high-performing.

Why Choose .NET Core for Cross-Platform Development?

.NET Core was designed with cross-platform capabilities at its core, allowing applications to run seamlessly on multiple operating systems. This adaptability makes .NET Core ideal for modern software development needs, where flexibility and scalability are crucial. Key benefits of using .NET Core for cross-platform development include:

1. **Broad Platform Support**: .NET Core runs on major operating systems, including Windows, macOS, and Linux, enabling applications to reach a wider user base.

2. **High Performance and Scalability**: Optimized for high-performance workloads, .NET Core is particularly effective for cloud-based and microservices architectures where performance and scalability are critical.

3. **Unified Development Framework**: .NET Core provides a consistent environment for developing various application types, from web and desktop to cloud and IoT applications, supporting multiple project types under a single framework.

4. **Open Source and Community-Driven**: As an open-source project under the .NET Foundation, .NET Core benefits from contributions by a broad developer community, ensuring constant improvement and innovation.

5. **Modularity and Flexibility**: .NET Core's modular design allows developers to choose only the necessary libraries for their projects, leading to leaner applications with fewer dependencies and a smaller footprint.

The Architecture of .NET Core

Understanding the architecture of .NET Core is essential to leveraging its cross-platform capabilities effectively. The framework's architecture is designed to be modular, flexible, and optimized for modern development needs.

Key Components of .NET Core Architecture

1. **CoreCLR:** The Core Common Language Runtime (CoreCLR) is the runtime environment for .NET Core applications. It provides features such as memory management, garbage collection, and just-in-time (JIT) compilation, enabling code to run efficiently across different platforms.

2. **CoreFX:** CoreFX is the set of foundational libraries that provide common functionalities, such as file handling, networking, collections,

and data access. CoreFX libraries are platform-agnostic, enabling code reuse across different operating systems.

3. **ASP.NET Core**: ASP.NET Core is a cross-platform web framework built on top of .NET Core for developing high-performance web applications and APIs. It offers improved performance, modular components, and the flexibility to deploy on any operating system.

4. **CLI (Command-Line Interface)**: The .NET Core CLI provides a consistent command-line interface for managing, building, and deploying .NET Core applications. It simplifies development workflows across platforms, especially in environments without an IDE.

5. **Language Support (C#, F#, and Visual Basic)**: .NET Core supports multiple languages, primarily C#, but also includes F# and Visual Basic, allowing developers to choose a language that best suits their project's requirements.

This modular architecture allows developers to build applications that perform optimally across different platforms, with each component contributing to the flexibility and adaptability of .NET Core.

.NET Core Ecosystem and Tooling

The .NET Core ecosystem includes a comprehensive set of tools and libraries designed to simplify cross-platform development. Some essential tools and platforms in the .NET Core ecosystem include:

1. **Visual Studio and Visual Studio Code**: Visual Studio is a fully-featured IDE for .NET development, while Visual Studio Code is a lightweight, cross-platform editor that supports .NET Core. Both offer rich debugging, testing, and code completion features.

2. **NuGet Package Manager**: NuGet is a package manager for .NET, allowing developers to install, update, and manage third-party libraries and tools easily. It integrates seamlessly with .NET Core, providing access to thousands of packages.

3. **Docker and Containerization**: .NET Core's support for Docker

enables containerized applications, making it easier to build, deploy, and scale applications consistently across environments. Containers simplify cross-platform development by encapsulating dependencies within the application.

4. **Azure Integration**: Microsoft Azure offers native support for .NET Core applications, providing a suite of cloud services to host, manage, and scale applications. Azure's integration with .NET Core streamlines deployment and scalability in cloud environments.

5. **Testing Frameworks (e.g., xUnit, NUnit, MSTest)**: .NET Core supports popular testing frameworks, allowing developers to write and execute unit tests across platforms. This support is essential for maintaining code quality in cross-platform projects.

These tools and libraries collectively enhance the .NET Core development experience, enabling developers to build robust, scalable, and platform-independent applications.

Developing Cross-Platform Applications with .NET Core

.NET Core allows developers to create a wide range of applications, from web services to desktop and mobile apps. Its cross-platform support ensures that developers can target any platform without having to rewrite code or make significant adjustments.

1. Web Applications and APIs

ASP.NET Core, a web framework built on top of .NET Core, provides a powerful foundation for developing web applications and RESTful APIs. It includes features such as MVC (Model-View-Controller) architecture, Razor Pages, dependency injection, and middleware, which simplify web development.

- **Unified Web Application Framework**: ASP.NET Core combines MVC and Web API, providing a unified framework for building dynamic web applications and services.

- **Cross-Platform Hosting**: ASP.NET Core applications can be hosted on Linux, Windows, or macOS, offering flexibility in deployment options.
- **Enhanced Performance**: Optimized for speed, ASP.NET Core is suitable for handling high-traffic web applications and APIs.

2. Desktop Applications

.NET Core supports desktop application development through frameworks like Windows Presentation Foundation (WPF) and Windows Forms, which are available on .NET Core (for Windows-only applications). Additionally, the cross-platform .NET MAUI (Multi-platform App UI) allows for building native applications across multiple platforms from a single codebase.

- **Platform Flexibility**: With .NET MAUI, developers can create applications that run natively on Windows, macOS, Android, and iOS, reducing the need to maintain separate codebases.
- **Shared Codebase**: MAUI enables code sharing across platforms, making it easier to manage updates and reduce maintenance overhead.
- **Enhanced UI Development**: .NET MAUI provides cross-platform UI components, helping developers create visually consistent applications across operating systems.

3. Cloud and Microservices Applications

.NET Core's support for cloud-native development, including microservices architectures, makes it a strong choice for building distributed, scalable applications. The framework's performance and containerization support make it ideal for deploying microservices on cloud platforms like Azure, AWS, or Google Cloud.

- **Containerization with Docker**: .NET Core is optimized for Docker, allowing applications to be containerized for consistent deployment across environments.
- **High Scalability**: Microservices can be independently deployed, scaled, and maintained, making .NET Core an ideal framework for building

scalable cloud applications.

- **Azure Integration**: Azure's close integration with .NET Core simplifies deployment, scaling, and management of cloud applications.

4. Mobile Applications

With .NET MAUI, .NET Core supports cross-platform mobile development. This framework enables developers to build native mobile applications that work on Android and iOS from a single codebase, improving efficiency and reducing development time.

- **Single Codebase for Multiple Platforms**: .NET MAUI allows developers to build applications that run natively on multiple platforms, reducing code duplication and simplifying maintenance.
- **Cross-Platform UI Design**: Developers can create consistent, platform-optimized user interfaces that work seamlessly across different devices.

Key Considerations for Cross-Platform Development

When developing cross-platform applications with .NET Core, there are a few essential considerations to ensure a smooth development process and consistent user experience:

1. **Consistent Testing Across Platforms**: Since behavior may vary slightly between platforms, it's important to test applications thoroughly on all targeted platforms to ensure consistent functionality and user experience.
2. **Platform-Specific Libraries**: Be aware of platform-specific libraries or APIs that may limit compatibility across systems. .NET Core's modular design allows for conditional compilation, enabling you to target specific platforms where necessary.
3. **Deployment Environment**: Choose the appropriate deployment strategy based on your target platform. For example, containerization with Docker can simplify deployments across platforms, while cloud services like Azure provide a flexible, scalable environment for .NET

Core applications.

.NET Core provides a powerful, versatile environment for cross-platform development, offering high performance, a unified ecosystem, and compatibility across major operating systems. With tools like ASP.NET Core, .NET MAUI, and support for containerization, .NET Core enables developers to build applications that scale from desktops to the cloud. Whether developing web applications, desktop applications, cloud-native microservices, or mobile apps, .NET Core's cross-platform capabilities make it a compelling choice for modern software development.

Setting Up a Multi-Platform Project

Setting up a multi-platform project in .NET Core requires careful consideration of the tools, project structure, and configurations needed to ensure compatibility across different operating systems. The .NET Core framework offers powerful tools to streamline this process, including Visual Studio, Visual Studio Code, and the .NET Core CLI. By establishing a clear project structure and following best practices for cross-platform compatibility, you can create a flexible foundation for building applications that run seamlessly on Windows, macOS, and Linux.

This section covers the key steps in setting up a multi-platform project, from configuring your development environment to creating and organizing project files and handling platform-specific dependencies.

Step 1: Configuring the Development Environment

The first step in creating a multi-platform project is setting up a development environment that supports all targeted operating systems.

Choosing an IDE

Several IDE options support .NET Core development, each with its strengths:

- **Visual Studio** (Windows and macOS): A full-featured IDE with comprehensive .NET Core support, offering rich debugging, profiling, and testing tools.
- **Visual Studio Code** (Windows, macOS, and Linux): A lightweight, cross-platform editor with support for .NET Core development through extensions, particularly well-suited for cross-platform projects due to its compatibility with all major OS platforms.
- **Rider by JetBrains** (Windows, macOS, and Linux): A powerful cross-platform IDE with extensive support for .NET Core, offering advanced code analysis and navigation.

Installing .NET Core SDK

The .NET Core SDK is necessary to develop, build, and run .NET Core applications across platforms. To install:

Download the SDK from dotnet.microsoft.com.

Verify the Installation by running the following command in your terminal or command prompt:

```bash
dotnet --version
```

This command displays the installed SDK version, confirming that .NET Core is ready for development.

Using the .NET CLI for Cross-Platform Development

The .NET Core CLI is a powerful tool for managing .NET projects, particularly useful in cross-platform environments. With the CLI, you can create, build, test, and deploy applications directly from the terminal, offering flexibility across Windows, macOS, and Linux.

Common commands include:

- **Creating a New Project**:

```bash
dotnet new console -o MultiPlatformApp
```

- **Building the Project**:

```bash
dotnet build
```

- **Running the Application**:

```bash
dotnet run
```

- **Adding a Package**:

```bash
dotnet add package <PackageName>
```

Step 2: Creating a Multi-Platform Project

To begin, you'll create a solution and organize it with separate projects for different layers, such as UI, business logic, and data access, ensuring a clean, modular structure.

2.1 Creating a Solution and Adding Projects

Create a Solution: A solution can group multiple projects, simplifying dependency management and organization.

```bash
dotnet new sln -o MultiPlatformSolution
```

Add Core Project(s): Create the main application project(s), such as a console or web project, that will serve as the entry point for the application.

```bash
dotnet new console -o MultiPlatformApp
dotnet sln add MultiPlat
formApp/MultiPlatformApp.csproj
```

Add Class Library Projects: Separate reusable components, such as data models or business logic, into class library projects.

```bash
dotnet new classlib -o MultiPlatformApp.Core
dotnet sln add
 MultiPlatformApp.
Core/Multi
PlatformApp.Core.csproj
```

By organizing your solution with separate projects for different concerns, you establish a foundation that supports scalability and easier maintenance.

Configuring Project Files for Cross-Platform Compatibility

Edit the .csproj files to ensure they are set up for cross-platform compatibility. Common configurations include:

- **Target Framework**: Set the target framework to netcoreappX.Y, where X.Y is the version of .NET Core you are using. For example:

```xml
<TargetFramework>netcoreapp3.1</TargetFramework>
```

- **Platform-Neutral Packages**: Avoid packages with platform-specific dependencies unless they support multiple operating systems or have conditionally compiled code for cross-platform use.
- **Runtime Identifiers (RIDs)**: Define runtime identifiers to specify which operating systems the project should support. For example, win-x64, osx-x64, and linux-x64.

Step 3: Managing Platform-Specific Code

Even in cross-platform projects, some functionality may require platform-specific implementations. .NET Core provides ways to manage platform-specific code gracefully.

Conditional Compilation

Use conditional compilation to handle platform-specific code, allowing different implementations depending on the target OS.

```csharp
public string GetPlatformSpecificPath()
{
    #if WINDOWS
        return "C:\\Program Files";
    #elif LINUX
        return "/usr/local/bin";
    #elif OSX
```

```
        return "/Applications";
    #else
        return string.Empty;
    #endif
}
```

In this example:

- **Conditional Directives**: #if, #elif, and #endif directives specify code for each platform, ensuring that only relevant code is compiled and executed.

Platform-Specific Assemblies and Dependencies

Some libraries may offer platform-specific assemblies that need conditional references. Define them in the project file to ensure correct dependencies are loaded on each platform.

```xml
xml

<ItemGroup Condition="
'$(RuntimeIdentifier)' == 'win-x64' ">
    <PackageReference Include="WindowsSpecificLibrary"
    Version="1.0.0" />
</ItemGroup>
<ItemGroup Condition="
'$(RuntimeIdentifier)' == 'linux-x64' ">
    <PackageReference Include="
LinuxSpecificLibrary" Version="1.0.0" />
</ItemGroup>
```

Step 4: Testing for Cross-Platform Compatibility

Testing is critical to ensure the application behaves consistently across platforms. Key areas to focus on include:

Unit Testing: Use cross-platform testing frameworks like xUnit, NUnit, or MSTest to write tests that validate core functionality.

Platform-Specific Testing: Run platform-specific tests if your application uses platform-dependent code, ensuring each OS handles code as expected.

Automated CI/CD Pipelines: Set up CI/CD pipelines to automatically test, build, and deploy the application across platforms. Use services like GitHub Actions, Azure Pipelines, or GitLab CI, which support multi-platform builds.

Example of Platform-Specific Tests

```csharp
[Fact]
public void ShouldReturnCorrectPathForWindows()
{
    if (RuntimeInformation.
IsOSPlatform(OSPlatform.Windows))
    {
        Assert.Equal("C:\\Program Files",
 GetPlatformSpecificPath());
    }
}
```

In this example:

- **Runtime Information**: The RuntimeInformation class determines the OS at runtime, enabling platform-specific test conditions.

Step 5: Deploying a Multi-Platform Application

Deployment strategies for .NET Core applications vary depending on the type of application and target platforms. Some common deployment options include:

Self-Contained Deployment: Packages the application with all necessary .NET Core dependencies, making it platform-specific but not requiring .NET Core to be installed on the host system. Use this for distributing applications to multiple platforms without assuming .NET Core availability.

```bash
dotnet publish -c Release -r
win-x64 --self-contained true
```

Framework-Dependent Deployment: Assumes the .NET Core runtime is installed on the target system, making the deployment smaller and more portable. Suitable for controlled environments where .NET Core runtime versions are consistent.

Containerization: Containerizing .NET Core applications with Docker offers a highly portable deployment method, ensuring the application runs consistently across different environments.

```dockerfile
FROM mcr.microsoft.com/dotnet/core/runtime:3.1 AS base
WORKDIR /app
COPY . .
ENTRYPOINT ["dotnet", "MultiPlatformApp.dll"]
```

Setting up a multi-platform project in .NET Core involves configuring a flexible, scalable project structure that supports multiple operating systems. By selecting the right tools, using conditional compilation, managing platform-specific dependencies, and testing rigorously across environments, you can create applications that perform consistently on Windows, macOS, and Linux.

With a well-organized, cross-platform setup in .NET Core, you're equipped to build applications that are robust, adaptable, and ready for deployment in a variety of environments. Next, we'll delve into handling platform-specific requirements and dependencies in more detail, ensuring compatibility and optimal performance across all supported platforms.

Working with Platform-Specific Code

Cross-platform development often requires handling platform-specific code, as certain features and APIs may behave differently or only be available on particular operating systems. In .NET Core, developers can manage platform-specific requirements through techniques like conditional compilation, runtime detection, and platform-specific dependencies. This allows applications to provide a consistent experience across platforms while accounting for OS-specific behaviors.

This section covers techniques for working with platform-specific code in .NET Core, including best practices for detecting platforms, using conditional compilation, and integrating platform-specific libraries.

Understanding Platform-Specific Code Requirements

Platform-specific code is often necessary when an application needs to:

1. **Access OS-Specific Features**: Some features, such as file system paths, native libraries, or certain APIs, behave differently on each platform.
2. **Optimize Performance**: Certain platforms may have performance considerations that can be optimized by using platform-specific code paths.
3. **Handle UI Differences**: In cross-platform desktop or mobile applications, UI components and rendering may require platform-specific customization.

By implementing platform-specific code, .NET Core applications can adapt to the nuances of each operating system, delivering a more seamless and optimized experience.

Step 1: Detecting the Target Platform at Runtime

.NET Core provides classes and methods to detect the platform at runtime, allowing you to tailor functionality based on the operating system. The System.Runtime.InteropServices.RuntimeInformation and OperatingSystem classes are commonly used for this purpose.

Example of Runtime Platform Detection

The RuntimeInformation.IsOSPlatform method enables you to check the current platform and execute platform-specific code as needed.

```csharp
using System;
using System.Runtime.InteropServices;

public void DisplayPlatformInfo()
{
    if (RuntimeInformation.IsOSPlatform(OSPlatform.Windows))
    {
        Console.WriteLine("Running on Windows");
    }
    else if (RuntimeInformation.IsOSPlatform(OSPlatform.Linux))
    {
        Console.WriteLine("Running on Linux");
    }
    else if (RuntimeInformation.IsOSPlatform(OSPlatform.OSX))
    {
        Console.WriteLine("Running on macOS");
    }
    else
    {
        Console.WriteLine("Unknown platform");
    }
}
```

In this example:

- **Platform Checks**: RuntimeInformation.IsOSPlatform checks if the application is running on Windows, Linux, or macOS, allowing platform-specific logic to be executed.
- **Fallback**: An optional fallback (Unknown platform) ensures that unrecognized platforms are handled gracefully.

Step 2: Using Conditional Compilation
Conditional compilation allows developers to define platform-specific

187

code at compile time, preventing unnecessary code from being included on unsupported platforms. This approach is particularly effective for features that rely on platform-specific libraries or configurations.

Example of Conditional Compilation for Platform-Specific Code

Conditional compilation can be implemented using preprocessor directives like #if, #elif, and #endif.

```csharp
public string GetDefaultFilePath()
{
    #if WINDOWS
        return "C:\\ProgramData\\MyApp\\data.txt";
    #elif LINUX
        return "/var/lib/myapp/data.txt";
    #elif OSX
        return "/Library/Application Support/MyApp/data.txt";
    #else
        return string.Empty;
    #endif
}
```

In this example:

- **Platform-Specific Paths**: Each OS receives its path format, ensuring compatibility with each file system.
- **Preprocessor Directives**: #if, #elif, and #endif are used to compile code specific to each platform, reducing runtime checks and ensuring only relevant code is included in each build.

Setting Platform Symbols: Ensure platform symbols (e.g., WINDOWS, LINUX, OSX) are defined in your project's build configuration, so the compiler recognizes these conditional blocks.

Step 3: Managing Platform-Specific Dependencies

In some cases, platform-specific functionality depends on external libraries that are only available for certain operating systems. .NET Core's project file (.csproj) allows you to include conditional dependencies, ensuring that platform-specific packages are only loaded when needed.

Example of Platform-Specific Package References in .csproj

Define platform-specific packages by using conditions in the .csproj file. This approach allows you to specify dependencies based on the runtime identifier (RID).

```xml

<Project Sdk="Microsoft.NET.Sdk">

  <PropertyGroup>
    <TargetFramework>net5.0</TargetFramework>
  </PropertyGroup>

  <ItemGroup Condition=" '$(RuntimeIdentifier)' == 'win-x64' ">
    <PackageReference Include="WindowsSpecificLibrary"
    Version="1.0.0" />
  </ItemGroup>

  <ItemGroup Condition="
'$(RuntimeIdentifier)' == 'linux-x64' ">
    <PackageReference Include=
"LinuxSpecificLibrary" Version="1.0.0" />
  </ItemGroup>

  <ItemGroup Condition="
'$(RuntimeIdentifier)' == 'osx-x64' ">
    <PackageReference Include=
"MacOSSpecificLibrary" Version="1.0.0" />
  </ItemGroup>

</Project>
```

In this example:

- **Conditional Package References**: Each <ItemGroup> conditionally references platform-specific libraries based on the runtime identifier, ensuring only relevant libraries are included in each build.

Step 4: Creating Platform-Specific Services with Dependency Injection

For platform-specific functionality, such as file management or network access, dependency injection can help separate platform-agnostic logic from platform-specific implementations. This method provides flexibility and makes it easier to unit test platform-specific code.

Example of Platform-Specific Services

Define an Interface for platform-specific functionality.

```csharp
public interface IFileService
{
    string GetDefaultFilePath();
}
```

Implement Platform-Specific Services for each target platform.

```csharp
public class WindowsFileService : IFileService
{
    public string GetDefaultFilePath() =>
    "C:\\ProgramData\\MyApp\\data.txt";
}

public class LinuxFileService : IFileService
{
    public string GetDefaultFilePath() =>
"/var/lib/myapp/data.txt";
}
```

Register Services Conditionally based on the platform.

csharp

```csharp
public void ConfigureServices
(IServiceCollection services)
{
    if (RuntimeInformation.IsOSPlatform
(OSPlatform.Windows))
    {
        services.AddSingleton<IFileService,
WindowsFileService>();
    }
    else if (RuntimeInformation.
IsOSPlatform(OSPlatform.Linux))
    {
        services.AddSingleton<IFileService,
 LinuxFileService>();
    }
    else if (RuntimeInformation.
IsOSPlatform(OSPlatform.OSX))
    {
        services.AddSingleton<IFileService,
 MacOSFileService>();
    }
}
```

In this example:

- **Interface and Implementation Separation**: By defining an interface (IFileService) and providing platform-specific implementations, the code becomes modular and easier to maintain.
- **Conditional Registration**: Services are conditionally registered at runtime based on the detected OS, allowing each platform to use its specific implementation.

Step 5: Testing and Validating Platform-Specific Code

Testing platform-specific code requires ensuring that each platform behaves as expected. This may involve creating tests that run on multiple operating systems or setting up conditional test cases.

Cross-Platform Testing with xUnit and Conditional Fact

Using xUnit's [Fact] attribute with conditional checks, you can create tests that only run on certain platforms.

```csharp
[Fact]
public void TestWindowsFilePath()
{
    if (RuntimeInformation.IsOSPlatform(OSPlatform.Windows))
    {
        var fileService =
new WindowsFileService();
        Assert.Equal
("C:\\ProgramData\\
MyApp\\data.txt",
fileService.GetDefaultFilePath());
    }
}
```

In this example:

- **Platform-Specific Assertions**: By checking the platform before executing the test, this approach ensures that the test is only run on Windows, avoiding platform-related failures.

Working with platform-specific code in .NET Core involves a combination of runtime detection, conditional compilation, platform-specific dependencies, and dependency injection to ensure consistent functionality across operating systems. By using these techniques effectively, you can develop .NET Core applications that seamlessly adapt to each platform's requirements, delivering optimized and consistent performance. Additionally, implementing robust testing strategies ensures that platform-specific code works reliably across environments, providing a seamless experience for end users.

Hands-On Project: Building a Simple Cross-Platform Application for Windows, macOS, and Linux

In this hands-on project, we'll create a simple cross-platform .NET Core console application that reads and writes to a configuration file and displays platform-specific messages for Windows, macOS, and Linux. The project will demonstrate techniques for handling platform-specific code, setting up the application to run seamlessly across multiple operating systems, and managing dependencies and configurations for a consistent user experience.

Project Overview

Our **Cross-Platform Config Reader** application will:

1. Read and write configuration data from a platform-specific file path.
2. Display customized messages based on the operating system.
3. Use dependency injection to separate platform-specific functionality from the core logic.
4. Provide testing to validate behavior across platforms.

This project will reinforce skills in managing platform-specific code, working with runtime identifiers, and structuring cross-platform applications effectively.

Step 1: Setting Up the Project

Create the Project and Solution: Start by creating a new solution and console project using the .NET CLI.

```bash
dotnet new sln -o CrossPlatformConfigApp
dotnet new console -o CrossPlatformConfigApp
dotnet sln add
CrossPlatformConfigApp/
CrossPlatformConfigApp.csproj
```

Add a Class Library for shared logic and services. This library will separate the core application logic from platform-specific details.

```bash
dotnet new classlib -o CrossPlatformConfigApp.Core
dotnet sln add
 CrossPlatformConfigApp.Core/
CrossPlatform
ConfigApp.Core.csproj
```

Step 2: Designing Platform-Specific File Services

We'll create an interface for a configuration service and provide platform-specific implementations. Each implementation will define a default file path based on the operating system.

Define the Configuration Interface in CrossPlatformConfigApp.Core

In CrossPlatformConfigApp.Core, create an IConfigService interface.

```csharp
namespace CrossPlatformConfigApp.Core
{
    public interface IConfigService
    {
        string GetConfigPath();
        void WriteConfig(string content);
        string ReadConfig();
    }
}
```

This interface:

- **Defines a Configuration Path**: GetConfigPath retrieves the default configuration path for each platform.
- **Read and Write Methods**: WriteConfig and ReadConfig handle config-

uration file interactions.

Create Platform-Specific Implementations

In CrossPlatformConfigApp, add classes for each platform-specific configuration service.

Windows Implementation:

csharp

```csharp
using CrossPlatformConfigApp.Core;
using System;
using System.IO;

namespace CrossPlatformConfigApp
{
    public class WindowsConfigService : IConfigService
    {
        private readonly string _configPath =
        "C:\\ProgramData\\CrossPlatformConfigApp\\config.txt";

        public string GetConfigPath() => _configPath;

        public void WriteConfig(string content)
        {
            Directory.CreateDirectory(Path.
GetDirectoryName(_configPath) ?? string.Empty);
            File.WriteAllText(_configPath, content);
        }

        public string ReadConfig()
        {
            return File.Exists(_configPath) ?
            File.ReadAllText(_configPath) : "No config file
            found.";
        }
    }
}
```

Linux Implementation:

```csharp
csharp

using CrossPlatformConfigApp.Core;
using System;
using System.IO;

namespace CrossPlatformConfigApp
{
    public class LinuxConfigService : IConfigService
    {
        private readonly string _configPath =
        "/var/lib/crossplatformconfigapp/config.txt";

        public string GetConfigPath() => _configPath;

        public void WriteConfig(string content)
        {
            Directory.CreateDirectory(Path.
GetDirectoryName(_configPath) ?? string.Empty);
            File.WriteAllText(_configPath, content);
        }

        public string ReadConfig()
        {
            return File.Exists(_configPath) ?
            File.ReadAllText(_configPath) : "No config file
            found.";
        }
    }
}
```

macOS Implementation:

```csharp
csharp

using CrossPlatformConfigApp.Core;
using System;
using System.IO;
```

```
namespace CrossPlatformConfigApp
{
    public class MacOSConfigService : IConfigService
    {
        private readonly string
 _configPath = "/Library/Application
 Support/CrossPlatformConfigApp/config.txt";

        public string GetConfigPath() => _configPath;

        public void WriteConfig(string content)
        {
            Directory.CreateDirectory
(Path.GetDirectoryName
(_configPath) ?? string.Empty);
            File.WriteAllText(_configPath, content);
        }

        public string ReadConfig()
        {
            return File.Exists(_configPath) ?
            File.ReadAllText(_configPath) : "No config file
            found.";
        }
    }
}
```

Step 3: Registering Platform-Specific Services Using Dependency Injection

Use conditional logic to register the appropriate platform-specific service at runtime.

Add Dependency Injection to the project by adding the Microsoft.Exten sions.DependencyInjection package.

bash

```
dotnet add package Microsoft.
Extensions.DependencyInjection
```

Configure Dependency Injection in the Program.cs file.

```
csharp
```

```csharp
using CrossPlatformConfigApp.Core;
using Microsoft.Extensions.DependencyInjection;
using System;
using System.Runtime.InteropServices;

namespace CrossPlatformConfigApp
{
    class Program
    {
        static void Main(string[] args)
        {
            var services = new ServiceCollection();
            ConfigureServices(services);

            var serviceProvider =
   services.BuildServiceProvider();
            var configService =
            serviceProvider.GetService<IConfigService>();

            Console.WriteLine
   ("Cross-Platform Config Reader");
            Console.WriteLine($"Config path:
            {configService?.GetConfigPath()}");

            // Write to config
            configService?.WriteConfig
   ("Sample configuration data.");

            // Read from config
            Console.WriteLine("Config contents:");
            Console.WriteLine(configService?.ReadConfig());
        }
```

```
        private static void
ConfigureServices(IServiceCollection services)
        {
            if (RuntimeInformation.
IsOSPlatform(OSPlatform.Windows))
            {
                services.AddSingleton<IConfigService,
                WindowsConfigService>();
            }
            else if
            (RuntimeInformation.IsOSPlatform(OSPlatform.Linux))
            {
                services.AddSingleton<IConfigService,
                LinuxConfigService>();
            }
            else if (RuntimeInformation.
IsOSPlatform(OSPlatform.OSX))
            {
                services.AddSingleton<IConfigService,
                MacOSConfigService>();
            }
        }
    }
}
```

In this code:

- **Dependency Injection**: The appropriate IConfigService implementation is injected based on the OS.
- **Platform Detection**: RuntimeInformation.IsOSPlatform checks the OS at runtime, ensuring that each platform loads its specific configuration service.

Step 4: Testing the Cross-Platform Application

To validate the application's behavior across different platforms, we'll conduct tests for the following:

Configuration Path: Ensuring the correct path is retrieved for each OS.

File Writing and Reading: Verifying that configuration data is written and read accurately.

Run the application on each target OS to confirm the expected behavior.

bash

```
dotnet run
```

Expected output:

Displays the configuration file path based on the platform.

Writes "Sample configuration data." to the file.

Reads and displays the file contents.

Step 5: Packaging and Deploying the Application

To distribute the application, use self-contained deployment or Docker for platform-specific builds.

Self-Contained Deployment:

bash

```
dotnet publish -c Release -r win-x64 --self-contained true
dotnet publish -c Release -r linux-x64 --self-contained true
dotnet publish -c Release -r osx-x64 --self-contained true
```

These commands produce binaries for Windows, Linux, and macOS that include the necessary .NET runtime, allowing the application to run without requiring .NET Core to be installed on the host system.

Docker Containerization (Optional): Docker allows you to containerize the application, making it easy to deploy and run on any OS that supports Docker.

Example Dockerfile:

```dockerfile
FROM mcr.microsoft.com/dotnet/runtime:6.0 AS base
WORKDIR /app
COPY . .
ENTRYPOINT ["dotnet", "CrossPlatformConfigApp.dll"]
```

Build and run the Docker container:

```bash
docker build -t cross-platform-config-app .
docker run cross-platform-config-app
```

Summary of the Cross-Platform Config Reader Project

In this hands-on project, we created a simple .NET Core console application capable of running on Windows, macOS, and Linux. We demonstrated how to:

1. **Implement Platform-Specific Services** using dependency injection to provide OS-optimized functionality.
2. **Manage File Paths and I/O** for each operating system through platform-specific implementations.
3. **Leverage Runtime Detection and Conditional Service Registration** to load the appropriate services based on the platform.

This project provides a solid foundation for building cross-platform .NET Core applications that adapt seamlessly to different operating systems, ensuring flexibility, compatibility, and a consistent user experience.

Building Interactive User Interfaces with WPF and XAML

Getting Started with WPF and XAML for Desktop Apps
Windows Presentation Foundation (WPF) and XAML (Extensible Application Markup Language) are central to creating interactive, visually rich desktop applications for the Windows operating system. WPF is a UI framework for building Windows applications, and XAML is the declarative markup language used to define the layout, styling, and functionality of WPF elements. Together, they enable developers to create scalable and maintainable applications with advanced graphics, animations, and data-binding capabilities.

This section introduces WPF and XAML, covering their fundamental principles, the benefits of using WPF for desktop applications, and the core concepts that form the foundation of WPF applications.

Why Choose WPF and XAML for Desktop Applications?

WPF and XAML provide significant advantages over traditional Windows Forms applications, allowing developers to create applications that are both visually appealing and functionally robust. Here are some key reasons to choose WPF and XAML for desktop application development:

1. **Declarative UI with XAML**: XAML enables developers to define user interfaces declaratively, making UI layouts easier to read, understand, and maintain.

2. **Separation of Concerns**: WPF applications separate UI design from application logic, enabling designers and developers to work more independently.

3. **Rich Graphics and Animation Support**: WPF includes powerful graphics capabilities, such as vector-based rendering, animations, and hardware acceleration, allowing for high-quality visuals and smooth animations.

4. **Data Binding and MVVM Pattern**: WPF's data-binding capabilities support the Model-View-ViewModel (MVVM) pattern, which facilitates cleaner code organization and improved testing.

5. **Scalability and Resolution Independence**: WPF automatically scales UI elements based on screen resolution and DPI, ensuring that applications look sharp across a range of screen sizes and resolutions.

Understanding XAML Basics

XAML is an XML-based language used to define UI elements, layouts, and styles in a hierarchical structure. Each element in XAML represents a UI component, layout, or style, and properties are set using XML attributes or nested elements. WPF interprets XAML and translates it into the visual and interactive components of a WPF application.

Example of XAML Structure

```
xaml

<Window x:Class="MyApp.MainWindow"
       xmlns="http://
schemas.microsoft.
com/winfx/2006/
xaml/presentation"
       xmlns:x="http:
//schemas.microsoft.
com/winfx/2006/xaml"
       Title="My WPF Application" Height="400" Width="600">
    <Grid>
        <TextBlock Text="Hello, WPF!"
```

```
HorizontalAlignment="Center" VerticalAlignment="Center"
FontSize="24"/>
        <Button Content="Click Me" Width="100" Height="50"
        HorizontalAlignment="Center" VerticalAlignment="Bottom"
        Margin="0,0,0,30"/>
    </Grid>
</Window>
```

In this example:

- **Root Element (Window)**: Defines the main window of the application, setting properties like title, height, and width.
- **Grid Layout**: A flexible container that organizes child elements in rows and columns.
- **UI Elements (TextBlock and Button)**: Display text and provide interactivity, with properties like alignment, font size, and margins specified directly in XAML.

Core WPF Concepts

To build WPF applications effectively, it's essential to understand several key concepts: layouts, controls, data binding, and the application lifecycle.

1. Layouts in WPF

WPF offers a variety of layout controls that help organize and position UI elements. Each layout control arranges elements differently, providing flexibility in creating responsive UIs.

- **Grid**: Divides the window into rows and columns, allowing precise control over element positioning. It's commonly used for complex, grid-based layouts.
- **StackPanel**: Arranges elements in a single line, either horizontally or vertically. Useful for simple, stacked layouts.
- **DockPanel**: Positions elements along the edges of the container, allowing elements to dock to the top, bottom, left, or right.

- **Canvas**: Provides absolute positioning, giving full control over where elements appear, ideal for custom graphics and animations.

2. Common Controls in WPF

WPF includes a rich set of controls, ranging from simple buttons and labels to complex data grids and sliders. Some commonly used controls include:

- **TextBlock and Label**: Display text within the application.
- **Button**: Represents a clickable button that can trigger actions.
- **TextBox**: Allows users to input text.
- **CheckBox and RadioButton**: Enable selection and choice options within forms.
- **ListBox and ComboBox**: Display lists of selectable items.

Each control can be customized extensively with properties, styles, and templates, making it easy to create visually consistent and functional UIs.

3. Data Binding and MVVM

Data binding in WPF connects the UI to data sources, such as objects, collections, or databases, making it easier to manage data flows and synchronize UI elements with underlying data models. WPF data binding works seamlessly with the Model-View-ViewModel (MVVM) pattern, which separates application logic (model), UI structure (view), and data-binding logic (view model).

- **Data Binding Syntax**: Bindings are established using the {Binding} syntax in XAML.

```xaml
<TextBox Text="{Binding UserName}" Width="200" />
```

In this example:

- **Binding Path**: UserName is a property on the data context (often set in the view model) bound to the TextBox's Text property.

4. Styles, Templates, and Resources

WPF allows developers to customize the look and feel of applications using styles, templates, and resources:

- **Styles**: Define common visual characteristics, such as font size, color, and control dimensions, and apply them consistently across the application.
- **Control Templates**: Customize the appearance of WPF controls, allowing for unique, custom-designed buttons, text boxes, and other controls.
- **Resources**: Define reusable styles, templates, and other values in a resource dictionary, making them accessible throughout the application.

Creating a Simple WPF Application

Let's create a basic WPF application using Visual Studio that demonstrates how to use XAML to define UI elements, apply styles, and set up basic data binding.

Step 1: Setting Up the Project

Open Visual Studio and create a new WPF App (.NET Core) project. Name the project SimpleWPFApp and click **Create**.

Step 2: Designing the User Interface in XAML

In MainWindow.xaml, define the UI structure using XAML.

```xaml
<Window x:Class="SimpleWPFApp.MainWindow"
        xmlns="http://schemas.microsoft
```

```
.com/winfx/2006/xaml/presentation"
        xmlns:x="http:
//schemas.microsoft.com/winfx/2006/xaml"
        Title="Simple WPF App" Height="400" Width="600">
    <Grid>
        <StackPanel HorizontalAlignment="Center"
        VerticalAlignment="Center">
            <TextBlock Text="Enter your name:" FontSize="16"
            Margin="0,0,0,10"/>
            <TextBox Name="NameTextBox" Width="200" Height="30"
            Margin="0,0,0,20"/>
            <Button Content="Submit" Width="100" Height="30"
            Click="SubmitButton_Click"/>
            <TextBlock Name="GreetingTextBlock" FontSize="16"
            Margin="0,20,0,0"/>
        </StackPanel>
    </Grid>
</Window>
```

In this example:

- **StackPanel Layout**: Positions elements vertically in the center.
- **TextBox and Button**: Provide an input field and a clickable button.
- **TextBlock (GreetingTextBlock)**: Displays the greeting message.

Step 3: Adding Interactivity with Event Handlers

In MainWindow.xaml.cs, add an event handler for the button's Click event to display a greeting message.

```csharp
using System.Windows;

namespace SimpleWPFApp
{
    public partial class MainWindow : Window
```

```
    {
        public MainWindow()
        {
            InitializeComponent();
        }

        private void SubmitButton_Click(object sender,
        RoutedEventArgs e)
        {
            string name = NameTextBox.Text;
            GreetingTextBlock.Text = $"Hello, {name}!";
        }
    }
}
```

In this code:

- **Event Handling**: The SubmitButton_Click method retrieves the text from NameTextBox and updates GreetingTextBlock with a personalized greeting.

Running the Application

Press F5 to build and run the application. In the running application:

Enter a name in the text box.

Click the **Submit** button to display the greeting message below.

This example demonstrates the core concepts of WPF and XAML, including layout management, event handling, and basic interactivity.

WPF and XAML provide a powerful framework for building interactive, visually appealing desktop applications. By combining XAML's declarative syntax with WPF's rich layout controls, data binding, and customizable styles, developers can create applications that are both functional and user-friendly. The separation of concerns inherent in WPF applications, combined with XAML's readability, makes it easier to develop, maintain, and scale applications over time.

Exploring Data Binding and MVVM Architecture

Data binding and the Model-View-ViewModel (MVVM) architecture are core components of WPF, enabling clean separation of concerns and facilitating the development of maintainable, testable applications. Data binding in WPF connects UI elements directly to data sources, while the MVVM pattern organizes code into three distinct layers, each responsible for specific aspects of the application. Together, they empower developers to build responsive, scalable applications with minimal code-behind and maximum flexibility.

This section covers the principles of data binding in WPF, introduces the MVVM architecture, and demonstrates how these components work together to streamline UI development and improve code organization.

Understanding Data Binding in WPF

Data binding in WPF allows UI elements to automatically update when data changes, creating a dynamic link between the UI and the underlying data model. WPF's data binding capabilities are highly flexible, supporting complex data structures, collections, and real-time updates, making it an ideal choice for applications that display or manipulate data.

Key Concepts of Data Binding

1. **Binding Sources and Targets**: Data binding connects a source (data) to a target (UI element). Common binding sources include properties, objects, and collections, while binding targets are UI elements like TextBox, TextBlock, and ListBox.
2. **Binding Modes**: WPF supports different binding modes, each determining the direction in which data flows:

- **One-Way**: Data flows from the source to the target only.
- **Two-Way**: Data flows both ways, allowing changes in the UI to update the source and vice versa.
- **One-Way to Source**: Data flows from the target to the source only, useful

for capturing user input.

- **One-Time**: Data flows from source to target only once, ideal for static data.

Data Context: The DataContext property of a WPF element sets the source for all bindings within that element's scope, simplifying binding syntax by eliminating the need to specify the full binding path.

Example of Data Binding in XAML

Let's explore a simple example of one-way data binding in XAML, binding a TextBlock to a property in the code-behind.

```xaml
<Window x:Class="DataBindingExample.MainWindow"
        xmlns="http:
//schemas.microsoft
.com/winfx/2006/
xaml/presentation"
        xmlns:x="http://schemas.
microsoft.com/winfx/2006/xaml"
        Title="Data Binding Example"
Height="200" Width="400">
    <StackPanel>
        <TextBlock Text="
{Binding GreetingMessage}" FontSize="24"
HorizontalAlignment="Center"/>
    </StackPanel>
</Window>
```

In this example:

- **Binding Syntax**: The Text property of TextBlock is bound to a property named GreetingMessage. WPF automatically updates the TextBlock whenever GreetingMessage changes.

Code-Behind for Binding Source

In MainWindow.xaml.cs, define the GreetingMessage property and set the DataContext of the window to itself.

```csharp
using System.ComponentModel;
using System.Runtime.CompilerServices;
using System.Windows;

namespace DataBindingExample
{
    public partial class MainWindow : Window,
    INotifyPropertyChanged
    {
        private string _greetingMessage;

        public string GreetingMessage
        {
            get => _greetingMessage;
            set
            {
                _greetingMessage = value;
                OnPropertyChanged();
            }
        }

        public MainWindow()
        {
            InitializeComponent();
            DataContext = this;
            GreetingMessage = "Welcome to WPF Data Binding!";
        }

        public event PropertyChangedEventHandler PropertyChanged;

        protected void OnPropertyChanged([CallerMemberName] string
        propertyName = null)
        {
            PropertyChanged?.Invoke(this, new
            PropertyChangedEventArgs(propertyName));
```

```
        }
    }
}
```

In this code:

- **INotifyPropertyChanged Interface**: Implements property change notification, which is necessary for WPF to detect when a property changes and update the UI.
- **OnPropertyChanged Method**: Notifies WPF of changes to properties, ensuring that bound UI elements update automatically.

Introducing the MVVM Architecture

The MVVM (Model-View-ViewModel) pattern is a widely used architecture in WPF that separates application logic into three components:

1. **Model**: Represents the data and business logic of the application. The model is responsible for managing and manipulating data and is often independent of the UI.
2. **View**: Defines the user interface, created with XAML. The view is responsible for displaying data and responding to user interactions but contains no business logic.
3. **ViewModel**: Serves as the intermediary between the view and model. The view model holds the data displayed by the view and implements commands and property change notifications, allowing for clean data binding.

The MVVM pattern enhances the modularity and testability of WPF applications, making it easier to manage complex projects.

Setting Up MVVM Components

To demonstrate the MVVM pattern, we'll build a simple WPF application with a view model that exposes a data-bound property and command.

Step 1: Create the Model
In this example, the model represents a simple Person object.

```csharp
namespace MVVMExample.Models
{
    public class Person
    {
        public string Name { get; set; }
        public int Age { get; set; }
    }
}
```

Step 2: Create the ViewModel

The view model contains properties that the view will bind to and commands to handle user actions.

```csharp
using System.ComponentModel;
using System.Runtime.CompilerServices;
using System.Windows.Input;

namespace MVVMExample.ViewModels
{
    public class PersonViewModel : INotifyPropertyChanged
    {
        private Person _person;

        public Person Person
        {
            get => _person;
            set
            {
                _person = value;
                OnPropertyChanged();
            }
```

```
        }

        public string DisplayMessage =>
$"Hello, {Person?.Name}! You are {Person?.Age} years old.";

        public ICommand UpdateCommand { get; }

        public PersonViewModel()
        {
            Person = new Person { Name = "John Doe", Age = 30 };
            UpdateCommand = new RelayCommand(UpdatePerson);
        }

        private void UpdatePerson(object parameter)
        {
            Person = new Person { Name = "Jane Doe", Age = 25 };
            OnPropertyChanged(nameof(DisplayMessage));
        }

        public event PropertyChangedEventHandler PropertyChanged;

        protected void OnPropertyChanged([CallerMemberName] string
        propertyName = null)
        {
            PropertyChanged?.Invoke(this, new
            PropertyChangedEventArgs(propertyName));
        }
    }
}
```

In this code:

- **Properties and Commands**: DisplayMessage is a calculated property
  that updates when Person changes. UpdateCommand allows the view to
  trigger changes to the data.
- **RelayCommand**: A custom implementation of ICommand that allows
  binding commands in the view.

Step 3: Create the View

The view binds to the properties and commands of the view model, displaying DisplayMessage and providing a button to trigger UpdateCommand.

```xaml
<Window x:Class="MVVMExample.MainWindow"
        xmlns="http:
//schemas.microsoft.
com/winfx/2006/xaml/presentation"
        xmlns:x="http:
//schemas
.microsoft.com/winfx/2006/xaml"
        Title="MVVM Example"
 Height="200" Width="400">
    <Window.DataContext>
        <local:PersonViewModel />
    </Window.DataContext>
    <StackPanel HorizontalAlignment="Center"
    VerticalAlignment="Center">
        <TextBlock Text="{Binding
 DisplayMessage}" FontSize="16"
Margin="0,10,0,20"/>
        <Button Content="Update
 Person" Command="{Binding
 UpdateCommand}" Width="100"/>
    </StackPanel>
</Window>
```

In this example:

- **DataContext**: Sets the data context to PersonViewModel, enabling binding for all elements in the window.
- **Bindings and Commands**: DisplayMessage and UpdateCommand are bound to the TextBlock and Button, respectively, allowing UI elements to interact directly with the view model.

Testing the MVVM Application

Run the application to observe the following behavior:

Initial Data Display: The TextBlock displays the initial DisplayMessage from PersonViewModel.

Update Command: When the button is clicked, UpdateCommand changes the Person properties, and the DisplayMessage updates automatically.

Data binding and the MVVM pattern are fundamental to building organized, scalable WPF applications. Data binding connects UI elements to the underlying data model, while the MVVM pattern separates UI, logic, and data for improved maintainability and testability. By using data binding and MVVM, developers can create responsive, testable, and easily maintainable applications with minimal code-behind, allowing for a more modular and flexible architecture.

Designing Responsive UIs: Tips and Tricks

Responsive design is critical for desktop applications, ensuring that UIs adapt smoothly to different screen sizes, resolutions, and user preferences. In WPF, creating responsive layouts requires an understanding of layout controls, grid structures, alignment, and dynamic resizing. By leveraging WPF's powerful layout and styling capabilities, developers can build UIs that adjust gracefully to various screen dimensions, enhancing usability and visual appeal.

This section explores key tips and techniques for designing responsive UIs in WPF, covering effective use of layout controls, adaptive grids, alignment strategies, dynamic resizing, and visual states.

1. Using Flexible Layout Controls for Responsiveness

WPF provides several layout controls, each with unique features suited to different responsive design needs. The most commonly used layout controls are Grid, StackPanel, DockPanel, and WrapPanel.

Grid Layout

The Grid layout is highly flexible and allows for complex, grid-based layouts that adapt well to different screen sizes. Grids support defining rows and columns with fixed, star-sized, or auto-sized values.

- **Star Sizing (*)**: This approach dynamically allocates space based on available room. For example, setting Width="*", Width="2*", etc., proportionally allocates space based on screen size.

```xaml
<Grid>
    <Grid.ColumnDefinitions>
        <ColumnDefinition Width="*" /> <!--
Adapts to available space -->
        <ColumnDefinition Width="2*" /> <!--
Occupies twice the space of the first column -->
    </Grid.ColumnDefinitions>
    <TextBlock Text="Responsive Column 1" Grid.Column="0"/>
    <TextBlock Text="Responsive Column 2" Grid.Column="1"/>
</Grid>
```

- **Auto Sizing (Auto)**: Adapts column or row size to the content's natural size, ensuring a flexible yet responsive layout.

StackPanel Layout

StackPanel arranges elements in a single line, either vertically or horizontally. While simple, it is less adaptive than Grid but useful for basic stacked layouts.

```xaml
<StackPanel Orientation="Vertical"
 HorizontalAlignment="Center">
```

```
    <TextBlock Text="Item 1" />
    <TextBlock Text="Item 2" />
    <TextBlock Text="Item 3" />
</StackPanel>
```

DockPanel and WrapPanel

- **DockPanel**: Allows elements to dock to specific edges (top, bottom, left, right), useful for layouts where elements should anchor to screen borders.

xaml

```
<DockPanel>
    <Button Content="Top" DockPanel.Dock="Top"/>
    <Button Content="Bottom" DockPanel.Dock="Bottom"/>
</DockPanel>
```

- **WrapPanel**: Arranges elements in a row, wrapping them to a new line when the edge is reached, making it ideal for responsive, flow-based layouts.

2. Implementing Adaptive Grids for Dynamic Resizing

To create adaptive layouts, use grids with rows and columns that respond to window resizing and screen orientation changes. Dynamic grids automatically redistribute space as the window resizes, ensuring that content remains accessible and visually organized.

Example of an Adaptive Grid Layout

xaml

```
<Grid>
    <Grid.RowDefinitions>
```

```
        <RowDefinition Height="Auto" />
        <RowDefinition Height="*" />
    </Grid.RowDefinitions>
    <Grid.ColumnDefinitions>
        <ColumnDefinition Width="3*" />
        <ColumnDefinition Width="2*" />
        <ColumnDefinition Width="1*" />
    </Grid.ColumnDefinitions>

    <TextBlock Text="Main Content" Grid.Row="1" Grid.Column="0"/>
    <TextBlock Text="Side Panel" Grid.Row="1" Grid.Column="1"/>
    <TextBlock Text="Ads" Grid.Row="1" Grid.Column="2"/>
</Grid>
```

In this example:

- **Auto and Star Sizing**: The header row adjusts to its content's height, while the main content row (*) adapts to available space.
- **Column Width Ratios**: Proportionally distributed columns ensure that the layout maintains balance across various screen sizes.

3. Using Alignment and Margin for Flexibility

Proper alignment and margin settings prevent controls from becoming misaligned or overlapping. Key considerations include:

- **Horizontal and Vertical Alignment**: Control positioning within the parent container. Center alignment is effective for creating centered, adaptive layouts.
- **Margins and Padding**: Consistent use of margins and padding creates breathing space around elements, ensuring readability and preventing UI crowding.

```xaml
```

```xaml
<Button Content="Responsive Button" Width="200"
HorizontalAlignment="Center" Margin="10"/>
```

In this example, the button centers itself horizontally and maintains a uniform margin, making it adaptable to resizing without crowding nearby elements.

4. Enabling Dynamic Resizing with Viewbox and ScrollViewer

Viewbox and ScrollViewer are invaluable for managing dynamic resizing and content overflow:

- **Viewbox**: Scales child elements to fit the available space. Useful for applications with complex visuals or when scaling entire layouts.

```xaml
```

```xaml
<Viewbox>
    <Grid Width="600" Height="400">
        <!-- Content goes here -->
    </Grid>
</Viewbox>
```

- **ScrollViewer**: Adds scrollbars when content exceeds available space, ensuring access to overflowed content.

```xaml
```

```xaml
<ScrollViewer VerticalScrollBarVisibility="Auto">
    <StackPanel>
        <!-- Scrollable content goes here -->
```

```
    </StackPanel>
  </ScrollViewer>
```

5. Utilizing Data Triggers and Visual State Manager for Responsive States

Data triggers and the Visual State Manager (VSM) allow you to define responsive behaviors that adjust to user interactions or window resizing, adding flexibility and interactivity to the UI.

Data Triggers

Data triggers in XAML enable property changes in response to data conditions, such as resizing or state changes. For example, change a TextBlock color when window width exceeds a certain threshold.

xaml

```
<TextBlock Text="Responsive Text">
    <TextBlock.Style>
        <Style TargetType="TextBlock">
            <Setter Property="Foreground" Value="Black"/>
            <Style.Triggers>
                <DataTrigger Binding=
"{Binding ActualWidth,
RelativeSource={RelativeSource
AncestorType=Window}}" Value="800">
                    <Setter Property=
"Foreground" Value="Green"/>
                </DataTrigger>
            </Style.Triggers>
        </Style>
    </TextBlock.Style>
</TextBlock>
```

In this example:

- **Data Trigger**: When the window width exceeds 800 pixels, the text color changes, providing a simple, adaptive UI behavior.

Visual State Manager

The Visual State Manager allows defining UI states based on application triggers or conditions, making it easier to handle complex visual changes. Commonly used for adapting to layout changes or screen orientation.

```xaml
<Grid>
    <VisualStateManager.VisualStateGroups>
        <VisualStateGroup x:Name="WindowStates">
            <VisualState x:Name="Narrow">
                <Storyboard>
                    <!-- Adjust properties for narrow view -->
                </Storyboard>
            </VisualState>
            <VisualState x:Name="Wide">
                <Storyboard>
                    <!-- Adjust properties for wide view -->
                </Storyboard>
            </VisualState>
        </VisualStateGroup>
    </VisualStateManager.VisualStateGroups>
</Grid>
```

6. Best Practices for Responsive UI Design in WPF

1. **Use Relative Sizing**: Prefer Auto and * sizing over fixed pixel sizes, enabling components to adapt naturally to screen size.
2. **Test on Multiple Resolutions**: Ensure the layout looks and behaves correctly on various resolutions and screen sizes, accounting for high DPI settings.
3. **Minimize Code-Behind for Layout Changes**: Use XAML-based triggers, bindings, and state managers for layout adaptations instead of code-behind logic.
4. **Optimize for Readability and Accessibility**: Ensure that text, buttons, and interactive elements are accessible on different screen sizes without crowding or reducing readability.

Responsive UI design in WPF is essential for creating flexible, user-friendly applications that adapt to different screen sizes and resolutions. By using layout controls effectively, implementing adaptive grids, leveraging dynamic resizing, and applying visual states, developers can create applications that provide a seamless user experience. These techniques ensure that WPF applications remain accessible, visually consistent, and functional across a wide range of screen dimensions, enhancing both usability and aesthetic appeal.

Integrating C# 8 Features into WPF Applications

Integrating C# 8 features into WPF applications brings modern programming techniques, improves code readability, and enhances performance. Features like nullable reference types, async streams, pattern matching, and default interface methods can streamline the development process, reduce runtime errors, and make your WPF applications more responsive and robust.

This section covers practical applications of C# 8 features in WPF, including examples and best practices for integrating these features into your UI and application logic.

1. Nullable Reference Types for Improved Null Safety

Nullable reference types allow developers to designate whether a reference type can hold null values, enhancing safety and reducing NullReferenceExcep tion errors at runtime. This is particularly useful in WPF applications, where null values can arise frequently, such as in data bindings and user inputs.

Enabling Nullable Reference Types

Enable nullable reference types in your project file:

```xml
<Project Sdk="Microsoft.NET.Sdk.WindowsDesktop">
  <PropertyGroup>
```

```xml
    <TargetFramework>netcoreapp3.1</TargetFramework>
    <UseWPF>true</UseWPF>
    <Nullable>enable</Nullable>
  </PropertyGroup>
</Project>
```

Applying Nullable Reference Types in a WPF ViewModel

Using nullable reference types helps prevent null-related issues in data-bound properties. In a view model, you can explicitly define which properties can be null, allowing WPF's data-binding engine to respond appropriately.

csharp

```csharp
using System.ComponentModel;
using System.Runtime.CompilerServices;

namespace WpfApp.ViewModels
{
    public class CustomerViewModel : INotifyPropertyChanged
    {
        private string? _firstName;
        private string? _lastName;

        public string? FirstName
        {
            get => _firstName;
            set
            {
                _firstName = value;
                OnPropertyChanged();
            }
        }

        public string? LastName
        {
            get => _lastName;
            set
```

```
        {
            _lastName = value;
            OnPropertyChanged();
        }
    }

    public event PropertyChangedEventHandler?
PropertyChanged;

    protected void OnPropertyChanged
([CallerMemberName] string propertyName = null!)
        {
            PropertyChanged?.Invoke(this, new
            PropertyChangedEventArgs(propertyName));
        }
    }
}
```

In this example:

- **Nullable Annotations**: Properties like FirstName and LastName are explicitly marked as nullable (string?), signaling that these fields can accept null values, which is common in form-based WPF applications where fields may be empty.

2. Async Streams for Asynchronous Data Loading

Async streams provide a way to handle asynchronous sequences of data, ideal for scenarios where data arrives over time, such as when fetching data from a network or streaming data from an API.

Using Async Streams with Data Binding

Suppose we're fetching data in a WPF application, such as loading records in chunks. You can use IAsyncEnumerable<T> to load data incrementally, improving responsiveness and allowing partial data display as it arrives.

Example: Loading Data with Async Streams

csharp

```csharp
public async IAsyncEnumerable<string> FetchRecordsAsync()
{
    for (int i = 1; i <= 10; i++)
    {
        await Task.Delay(500); // Simulate network delay
        yield return $"Record {i}";
    }
}
```

Consuming Async Streams in ViewModel

csharp

```csharp
public class RecordsViewModel : INotifyPropertyChanged
{
    private ObservableCollection<string> _records = new
    ObservableCollection<string>();

    public ObservableCollection<string> Records
    {
        get => _records;
        set
        {
            _records = value;
            OnPropertyChanged();
        }
    }

    public async Task LoadRecordsAsync()
    {
        await foreach (var record in FetchRecordsAsync())
        {
            Records.Add(record);
        }
    }
}
```

```
public event PropertyChangedEventHandler? PropertyChanged;

protected void OnPropertyChanged([CallerMemberName] string
propertyName = null!)
{
    PropertyChanged?.Invoke(this, new
    PropertyChangedEventArgs(propertyName));
}
}
```

In this example:

- **Async Data Loading**: FetchRecordsAsync asynchronously retrieves records, yielding each one individually. The view model updates Records incrementally, which the UI reflects immediately.
- **Improved Responsiveness**: The UI remains responsive, as records are added gradually without blocking the main thread.

3. Pattern Matching Enhancements for Cleaner Control Logic

C# 8's pattern matching enhancements simplify conditional logic by allowing more expressive conditions. In WPF, pattern matching can enhance code readability in commands or event handlers that need to respond based on specific control states or types.

Example of Pattern Matching in a Command

Suppose we have a command that needs to handle different types of items in a ListBox selection. Using pattern matching, we can handle each type directly within the switch expression.

```csharp
public void HandleItemSelected(object selectedItem)
{
    switch (selectedItem)
    {
```

```csharp
        case Customer customer when customer.IsActive:
            MessageBox.Show($"Active customer: {customer.Name}");
            break;
        case Customer customer:
            MessageBox.Show($"Inactive customer: {customer.Name}");
            break;
        case Order order:
            MessageBox.Show($"Order ID: {order.OrderId}");
            break;
        default:
            MessageBox.Show("Unknown item selected");
            break;
    }
}
```

In this example:

- **Type Pattern Matching**: Pattern matching simplifies the logic by directly handling each type, such as Customer and Order, reducing the need for if statements or type checks.

4. Default Interface Methods for Extensible Services

Default interface methods allow interfaces to contain implementation logic, making it easier to evolve services without affecting existing implementations. In WPF, default interface methods are particularly useful for extending service classes in a modular way.

Example of Default Interface Methods in a Data Service

Imagine a data service for fetching records. By adding a default method to the interface, you can extend its functionality without modifying each implementation.

```csharp
csharp


public interface IDataService
{
```

```
Task<IEnumerable<string>> GetRecordsAsync();

// Default method for getting a count of records
async Task<int> GetRecordCountAsync()
{
    var records = await GetRecordsAsync();
    return records.Count();
}
}
```

In this code:

- **Backward Compatibility**: Adding GetRecordCountAsync as a default method extends the interface without breaking existing implementations.
- **Consistent Behavior**: All implementations of IDataService gain a record-counting method without requiring additional changes, enhancing code modularity.

5. Indexes and Ranges for Simplified Data Manipulation

C# 8's indexes and ranges can streamline data access and manipulation in collections, enhancing readability and efficiency in WPF applications where lists or arrays are common.

Example of Using Indexes and Ranges

Indexes and ranges are particularly useful when displaying a subset of data in WPF controls, such as paginating a list.

```csharp
public ObservableCollection<string> GetRecentRecords()
{
    var allRecords = new ObservableCollection<string>
    {
        "Record 1", "Record 2", "Record 3", "Record 4", "Record 5"
    };
```

```
// Return the last three records
return new ObservableCollection<string>(allRecords[^3..]);
}
```

In this example:

- **Range Syntax (^3..)**: The range syntax selects the last three records from allRecords, making the code more concise and readable.

Integrating C# 8 features into WPF applications can significantly improve code clarity, reduce potential errors, and enhance application responsiveness. Nullable reference types improve null safety, async streams support responsive data loading, pattern matching simplifies control logic, and default interface methods make services extensible. By incorporating these features, WPF applications become more maintainable, flexible, and aligned with modern development practices, enabling developers to create sophisticated and robust desktop applications.

Hands-On Project: Building a Cross-Platform WPF App with MVVM

This hands-on project guides you through building a cross-platform WPF application that leverages the Model-View-ViewModel (MVVM) architecture, integrating C# 8 features to create a clean, maintainable, and responsive application. Our application, **Task Manager**, will manage a list of tasks, allowing users to add, edit, and delete tasks. The MVVM pattern will ensure that the code is modular and testable, while WPF and C# 8 features provide responsiveness and maintainability.

Project Overview: Task Manager Application

The **Task Manager** application will:

1. Display a list of tasks with descriptions and completion status.

2. Allow users to add new tasks, update existing tasks, and mark tasks as completed.
3. Showcase MVVM architecture with data binding, commands, and property notifications.
4. Implement C# 8 features like nullable reference types, async streams, and pattern matching for enhanced safety and usability.

Step 1: Setting Up the Project Structure

Create a New Solution and WPF Project: Open Visual Studio, create a new WPF App (.NET Core) project, and name it TaskManagerApp. Set the project as part of a new solution.

bash

```
dotnet new wpf -n TaskManagerApp
```

Add Folders for MVVM Layers: Inside TaskManagerApp, create folders for each MVVM component:

- Models: Contains the data models for tasks.
- ViewModels: Contains view models with properties, commands, and business logic.
- Views: Contains the XAML views defining the UI layout and binding elements.

Add Required NuGet Packages (Optional for Dependency Injection and Commands): You may use Microsoft.Extensions.DependencyInjection for DI and Microsoft.Toolkit.Mvvm for MVVM support, including RelayCommand for commands.

Step 2: Creating the Model

The Task model represents a single task, including properties for its description and completion status.

```
csharp

namespace TaskManagerApp.Models
{
    public class TaskModel
    {
        public int Id { get; set; }
        public string Description { get; set; } = string.Empty;
        public bool IsCompleted { get; set; }
    }
}
```

Step 3: Designing the ViewModel

The TaskViewModel will manage a collection of TaskModel objects and define commands for adding, updating, and deleting tasks.

Implement TaskViewModel:

```
csharp

using System.Collections.ObjectModel;
using System.ComponentModel;
using System.Runtime.CompilerServices;
using System.Windows.Input;

namespace TaskManagerApp.ViewModels
{
    public class TaskViewModel : INotifyPropertyChanged
    {
        public ObservableCollection<TaskModel> Tasks { get; set; }
        private TaskModel _selectedTask;
        public TaskModel SelectedTask
        {
            get => _selectedTask;
            set { _selectedTask = value; OnPropertyChanged(); }
        }

        public ICommand AddTaskCommand { get; }
```

```csharp
public ICommand RemoveTaskCommand { get; }
public ICommand UpdateTaskCommand { get; }

public TaskViewModel()
{
    Tasks = new ObservableCollection<TaskModel>();
    AddTaskCommand = new RelayCommand(AddTask);
    RemoveTaskCommand = new RelayCommand(RemoveTask,
    CanRemoveTask);
    UpdateTaskCommand = new RelayCommand(UpdateTask,
    CanUpdateTask);
}

private void AddTask()
{
    Tasks.Add(new TaskModel { Description = "New Task",
    IsCompleted = false });
}

private void RemoveTask()
{
    if (SelectedTask != null)
    {
        Tasks.Remove(SelectedTask);
    }
}

private bool CanRemoveTask() => SelectedTask != null;

private void UpdateTask()
{
    // Update task logic can be implemented here
}

private bool CanUpdateTask() => SelectedTask != null;

public event PropertyChangedEventHandler PropertyChanged;
protected void OnPropertyChanged([CallerMemberName] string
propertyName = null)
{
```

```
        PropertyChanged?.Invoke(this, new
        PropertyChangedEventArgs(propertyName));
    }
  }
}
```

- **ObservableCollection**: Holds the list of tasks, enabling the UI to update automatically when tasks are added or removed.
- **Commands**: AddTaskCommand, RemoveTaskCommand, and Update-TaskCommand are bound to UI actions for managing tasks.
- **Property Change Notification**: Implements INotifyPropertyChanged to notify the UI of property changes.

Step 4: Designing the View (MainWindow.xaml)

Define the main UI layout in MainWindow.xaml, binding elements to TaskViewModel properties and commands.

```xaml
xaml

<Window x:Class="TaskManagerApp.MainWindow"
        xmlns="http:
//schemas.microsoft.
com/winfx
/2006/xaml/presentation"
        xmlns:x="http://schemas.
microsoft.com/winfx/2006/xaml"
        xmlns:local="clr-namespace:TaskManagerApp.ViewModels"
        Title="Task Manager"
Height="400" Width="600">
    <Window.DataContext>
        <local:TaskViewModel />
    </Window.DataContext>

    <Grid Margin="10">
        <Grid.RowDefinitions>
```

```xml
            <RowDefinition Height="Auto"/>
            <RowDefinition Height="*"/>
            <RowDefinition Height="Auto"/>
        </Grid.RowDefinitions>

        <TextBlock Text="Task List"
FontSize="24" HorizontalAlignment=
"Center" Margin="0,10"/>

        <ListBox ItemsSource="{Binding Tasks}"
        SelectedItem="{Binding SelectedTask}"
        DisplayMemberPath="Description"
                Grid.Row="1" Margin="0,10">
        </ListBox>

        <StackPanel Orientation="Horizontal" Grid.Row="2"
        HorizontalAlignment="Center" Margin="0,20">
            <Button Content=
"Add Task" Command="{Binding AddTaskCommand}"
 Width="100" Margin="5"/>
            <Button Content=
"Remove Task" Command=
"{Binding RemoveTaskCommand}"
 Width="100" Margin="5"/>
            <Button Content=
"Update Task" Command="
{Binding UpdateTaskCommand}"
Width="100" Margin="5"/>
        </StackPanel>
    </Grid>
</Window>
```

- **Data Binding**: The ListBox is bound to the Tasks collection, displaying task descriptions, and SelectedTask binds to the selected item.
- **Command Binding**: The buttons for adding, removing, and updating tasks are bound to respective commands in TaskViewModel.

Step 5: Adding Async Data Loading with C# 8 Async Streams

235

We'll simulate async data loading for tasks using async streams.

Define an Async Method in the ViewModel:

csharp

```
public async IAsyncEnumerable<TaskModel> LoadTasksAsync()
{
    for (int i = 1; i <= 5; i++)
    {
        await Task.Delay(300); // Simulate delay
        yield return new TaskModel { Description = $"Task {i}",
        IsCompleted = false };
    }
}

public async Task InitializeTasksAsync()
{
    await foreach (var task in LoadTasksAsync())
    {
        Tasks.Add(task);
    }
}
```

Call InitializeTasksAsync in the MainWindow Code-Behind:

csharp

```
public partial class MainWindow : Window
{
    public MainWindow()
    {
        InitializeComponent();
        Loaded += MainWindow_Loaded;
    }

    private async void MainWindow_Loaded(object sender,
    RoutedEventArgs e)
    {
        if (DataContext is TaskViewModel viewModel)
```

236

```
            {
                await viewModel.InitializeTasksAsync();
            }
        }
    }
```

In this example:

- **Async Stream**: LoadTasksAsync asynchronously loads tasks, yielding each item with a delay.
- **Async Data Initialization**: InitializeTasksAsync loads tasks into the Tasks collection upon application start.

Step 6: Testing and Running the Application
Run the application to ensure it behaves as expected:

1. **Task Display and Selection**: The initial tasks are displayed in the ListBox.
2. **Command Execution**: The Add, Remove, and Update buttons respond to commands, adding, removing, and updating tasks.
3. **Async Data Loading**: Tasks load asynchronously at startup, demonstrating async streams and responsive data handling.

In this project, we built a simple Task Manager application using WPF with the MVVM pattern, demonstrating:

1. **MVVM Architecture**: Organized code into models, views, and view models, ensuring a modular and testable application.
2. **Data Binding and Commands**: Leveraged WPF's data binding and commands to create a responsive, interactive UI.
3. **Async Streams**: Utilized async streams for responsive, incremental data loading, enhancing performance.

This foundation can be expanded with additional features and complexity, using WPF and C# 8's capabilities to build a scalable, modern desktop application.

Cloud Integration and Microservices Architecture

O

verview of Cloud Integration: Why It Matters for Modern Apps

Cloud integration has become essential for building scalable, resilient, and efficient applications. By leveraging cloud infrastructure and services, modern applications can dynamically adjust to changing workloads, integrate seamlessly with external services, and deliver a consistent user experience across various devices and geographies. Cloud integration enables applications to move beyond traditional on-premises limitations, offering a suite of tools and resources that streamline deployment, enhance performance, and improve operational efficiency.

In this overview, we'll examine the key benefits and capabilities of cloud integration, explore why it's critical for modern application development, and look at foundational aspects of building cloud-integrated applications.

Why Cloud Integration Is Essential for Modern Applications

The need for applications that are accessible, flexible, and scalable has transformed cloud integration from a competitive advantage to a necessity. The cloud provides an environment where applications can leverage a host of services, from data storage and compute power to security and analytics, enhancing capabilities without requiring additional on-premises infrastructure.

Key Advantages of Cloud Integration

1. **Scalability and Elasticity**: Cloud platforms provide on-demand scalability, allowing applications to handle fluctuations in traffic and data load effortlessly. Horizontal and vertical scaling options let applications add or remove resources dynamically, ensuring efficient resource utilization.

2. **Cost Efficiency**: With cloud integration, businesses only pay for the resources they use, making it cost-effective, especially for applications with variable or unpredictable traffic. Traditional on-premises solutions often require significant upfront investment, while cloud services reduce capital expenditure and lower operational costs.

3. **Global Reach and Availability**: Cloud providers operate data centers around the world, enabling applications to deploy closer to end-users and reduce latency. This geographic flexibility enhances the user experience by ensuring faster response times and higher availability across regions.

4. **Improved Security and Compliance**: Leading cloud providers invest heavily in security measures, such as encryption, identity management, and network monitoring. They also adhere to industry standards and regulations (e.g., GDPR, HIPAA), ensuring that applications meet compliance requirements without the added overhead of managing on-premises security infrastructure.

5. **Streamlined Development and Deployment**: Cloud integration supports a streamlined development process with tools like continuous integration/continuous deployment (CI/CD), automated testing, and version control. These tools enable faster, more reliable deployments, minimizing downtime and allowing teams to roll out updates or new features more frequently.

Key Components of Cloud Integration

A successful cloud-integrated application is built upon several key components, each supporting different aspects of the application lifecycle, from development and deployment to data management and security.

1. Infrastructure as a Service (IaaS)

IaaS provides virtualized computing resources over the internet, including storage, networking, and computing power. It enables developers to provision and scale resources as needed without physical infrastructure, supporting applications that require substantial computing power or large-scale data storage.

Example: Amazon Web Services (AWS) Elastic Compute Cloud (EC2) allows applications to run virtual servers in the cloud, scaling up or down based on demand.

2. Platform as a Service (PaaS)

PaaS offers a development and deployment platform with managed infrastructure, allowing developers to focus on writing code rather than managing hardware and software layers. PaaS provides a controlled environment for building, testing, and deploying applications, often including tools for application hosting, database management, and scaling.

Example: Microsoft Azure App Service provides a managed environment for deploying web applications, enabling automatic scaling and integration with other Azure services.

3. Software as a Service (SaaS)

SaaS delivers software applications over the internet as a service, accessible via web or mobile applications. SaaS applications are fully managed by the provider, offering end-users a convenient, subscription-based model that includes updates, security, and support.

Example: Google Workspace provides productivity tools like Google Docs and Google Sheets as a SaaS offering, accessible from any internet-connected device.

4. Serverless Architecture

Serverless architecture enables developers to write and deploy code without provisioning or managing servers, allowing applications to scale automatically based on demand. This architecture suits applications with unpredictable or fluctuating workloads, as it charges based on execution time rather than fixed resource allocation.

Example: AWS Lambda lets developers run functions in response to events, such as API requests, without managing the underlying infrastructure.

5. Containerization and Orchestration

Containers encapsulate application code and dependencies, enabling consistent performance across different environments. Container orchestration platforms like Kubernetes automate the deployment, scaling, and management of containerized applications, supporting microservices architectures that require isolated, flexible components.

Example: Docker enables application components to run in isolated containers, while Kubernetes orchestrates these containers, managing their lifecycle and scaling.

Cloud Integration Strategies for Modern Applications

Choosing the right cloud integration strategy depends on the application's architecture, performance requirements, and business goals. Key strategies include:

1. **Hybrid Cloud**: A hybrid approach combines on-premises infrastructure with cloud services, offering the flexibility to run applications in the most suitable environment. This approach is ideal for businesses needing to meet specific data residency requirements or gradually transition to the cloud.

2. **Multi-Cloud**: A multi-cloud strategy uses multiple cloud providers (e.g., AWS, Azure, Google Cloud) to diversify resources and minimize dependency on a single vendor. This approach enhances resilience, reduces latency by distributing services across different locations, and enables access to best-in-class services from each provider.

3. **Cloud-Native**: Cloud-native applications are designed specifically for cloud environments, often using microservices, containers, and serverless architecture to take full advantage of cloud scalability and

resilience.

4. **Lift and Shift**: This strategy involves migrating existing applications to the cloud without significant changes to the architecture. It provides a straightforward path to cloud integration, though it may limit the application's ability to leverage cloud-native features.

Cloud Integration Challenges and Best Practices

While cloud integration offers substantial benefits, it also presents challenges, particularly in areas such as data management, security, and cost control. Addressing these challenges with best practices ensures a smooth transition and reliable cloud operations.

Key Challenges

1. **Data Security and Privacy**: Protecting data in transit and at rest, managing access control, and ensuring compliance with data regulations are critical. Misconfigurations, lack of encryption, or inadequate access policies can expose applications to risks.

2. **Latency and Performance**: Geographic distance between users and data centers can introduce latency, impacting user experience. Ensuring that applications are hosted close to end-users or leveraging content delivery networks (CDNs) can mitigate this issue.

3. **Cost Management**: While cloud services reduce capital expenditure, unchecked usage can lead to high operational costs. Effective monitoring and management tools help control spending, while resource optimization (e.g., scaling down unused resources) prevents unnecessary expenses.

4. **Complexity of Integration**: Integrating cloud services with existing on-premises systems or third-party applications can be complex, requiring careful planning and a clear understanding of data flow, security requirements, and interoperability.

Best Practices for Cloud Integration

1. **Implement Security Best Practices**: Use identity and access management (IAM), encryption, and regular security audits. Cloud providers offer native security tools, such as AWS Identity and Access Management (IAM) or Azure Active Directory (AAD), which control user permissions and protect sensitive data.

2. **Adopt a Microservices Architecture**: For new applications, consider breaking down functionality into microservices. Each microservice can be independently deployed, scaled, and managed, allowing for greater flexibility and resilience.

3. **Automate with Infrastructure as Code (IaC)**: Tools like Terraform and AWS CloudFormation automate the provisioning and management of cloud resources, reducing human error and ensuring consistent environments.

4. **Use Monitoring and Analytics**: Cloud providers offer built-in monitoring tools (e.g., Azure Monitor, AWS CloudWatch) to track resource utilization, detect anomalies, and optimize performance. Monitoring is crucial for maintaining application health and avoiding costly downtime.

5. **Optimize Cost with Autoscaling and Reserved Instances**: Autoscaling automatically adjusts resource allocation based on demand, while reserved instances lock in lower prices for long-term usage. This combination optimizes cost without compromising performance.

The Importance of Cloud Integration in Modern Application Development

Cloud integration offers a host of advantages for modern applications, from flexibility and cost savings to improved performance and security. With the ability to deploy and scale applications globally, leverage microservices and serverless architectures, and automate development and deployment processes, cloud integration represents a paradigm shift in software development. By understanding and implementing best practices, developers and organizations can maximize the value of cloud integration, ensuring their applications remain competitive, resilient, and capable of meeting the demands of a digital-first world.

Setting Up and Managing Microservices

Microservices architecture has become a standard approach for building large-scale, modular applications, breaking down complex systems into independently deployable services that interact over a network. Microservices enable greater flexibility, scalability, and resilience, especially in cloud-native applications, where each service can be independently managed, scaled, and updated. However, managing microservices effectively requires strategic planning, robust infrastructure, and a comprehensive approach to deployment, communication, and monitoring.

This section covers the key steps for setting up and managing microservices, focusing on best practices and tools for deploying, monitoring, and maintaining a microservices-based architecture.

1. Defining the Microservices Architecture

Microservices architecture organizes an application as a collection of loosely coupled, independently deployable services. Each microservice typically represents a specific business capability, such as user authentication, payment processing, or inventory management. These services communicate over APIs or messaging protocols, which allow them to function together as a unified application.

Key Characteristics of Microservices

Single Responsibility: Each microservice focuses on a single functionality or business process.

Independent Deployment: Services are loosely coupled, allowing independent deployment without affecting other services.

Decentralized Data Management: Each service manages its own data and database, avoiding a monolithic database structure.

Polyglot Development: Services can be developed using different programming languages and technologies, depending on the specific requirements.

2. Setting Up the Microservices Infrastructure

Setting up a microservices infrastructure requires a combination of containers, orchestration tools, and networking solutions. Key components include containerization (e.g., Docker), orchestration (e.g., Kubernetes), and a managed service platform like AWS or Azure.

Step 1: Containerizing Services

Containers encapsulate the application code, runtime, libraries, and dependencies, making services portable and consistent across environments. Docker is the most widely used containerization tool.

Example Dockerfile for a Microservice:

```
dockerfile


# Use a base image
FROM mcr.microsoft.com/dotnet/aspnet:5.0 AS base
WORKDIR /app
COPY . .


# Expose port for communication
EXPOSE 80


# Start the microservice
ENTRYPOINT ["dotnet", "MyMicroservice.dll"]
```

Step 2: Setting Up Kubernetes for Orchestration

Kubernetes automates the deployment, scaling, and management of containerized applications, ensuring that microservices run reliably and are easily scalable.

Create Kubernetes Manifests: Define Kubernetes manifests for each microservice to configure pods, deployments, and services.

Example Deployment Manifest:

```
yaml


apiVersion: apps/v1
kind: Deployment
metadata:
```

```
  name: my-microservice
spec:
  replicas: 3
  selector:
    matchLabels:
      app: my-microservice
  template:
    metadata:
      labels:
        app: my-microservice
    spec:
      containers:
      - name: my-microservice-container
        image: my-microservice-image
        ports:
        - containerPort: 80
```

Define Services for Communication: Kubernetes services expose microservices within the cluster or to the external network. ClusterIP services provide internal access, while LoadBalancer or NodePort exposes services externally.

Set Up Auto-Scaling: Kubernetes enables horizontal scaling by adding or removing replicas based on metrics like CPU and memory usage, making it ideal for handling varying loads.

Step 3: Implementing API Gateway for Routing

An API gateway acts as a single entry point for all client requests, routing them to the appropriate microservices, managing cross-cutting concerns like authentication, rate limiting, and load balancing.

Choose an API Gateway Tool: Options include Amazon API Gateway, Kong, and NGINX. These tools handle request routing, authentication, and rate limiting.

Define Routing Rules: Set up routes for each microservice, specifying endpoints and path rules. The gateway directs incoming requests based on these routes, ensuring efficient load distribution and secure access.

Centralize Cross-Cutting Concerns: Implement cross-cutting concerns such as logging, request throttling, and API authentication through the gateway to simplify microservice logic.

3. Managing Communication Between Microservices

Microservices need to communicate with each other, either synchronously or asynchronously. Each approach has specific use cases and requires different tools.

Synchronous Communication

In synchronous communication, services interact in real-time using protocols like HTTP or gRPC. This approach is suitable for low-latency and tightly coupled services.

- **RESTful APIs**: Representational State Transfer (REST) APIs are a common approach for synchronous communication. They are simple, stateless, and compatible with HTTP-based services.
- **gRPC**: Google Remote Procedure Call (gRPC) is a high-performance, binary protocol that uses HTTP/2, supporting faster communication and data serialization than REST. Ideal for high-performance scenarios.

Asynchronous Communication

Asynchronous communication decouples services, allowing them to communicate without blocking each other. This approach is ideal for event-driven architectures and scenarios where response times are not critical.

- **Message Queues**: Message queues like RabbitMQ and Apache Kafka enable asynchronous messaging between microservices, ensuring that services continue functioning even if one service is down.
- **Event Streaming**: Tools like Kafka and AWS Kinesis support event-driven communication, where services react to events asynchronously, ideal for distributed systems.

4. Implementing Service Discovery and Load Balancing

In a microservices environment, instances of services may come and go due to scaling and deployment. Service discovery and load balancing ensure that requests are routed to the appropriate instances.

Service Discovery: Tools like Consul and Eureka register each microservice instance, enabling dynamic discovery. This ensures that services can locate and communicate with each other without hardcoded endpoints.

Load Balancing: Load balancing distributes incoming requests across service instances, optimizing resource utilization and ensuring that no single instance is overloaded. Kubernetes has built-in load balancing for internal services, while API gateways manage load balancing for external requests.

5. Monitoring and Logging Microservices

Effective monitoring and logging are essential for troubleshooting, ensuring reliability, and identifying performance bottlenecks.

Implementing Centralized Logging

Microservices generate logs in different instances and locations. Centralized logging aggregates these logs, making it easier to search, filter, and analyze logs.

- **ELK Stack (Elasticsearch, Logstash, and Kibana)**: The ELK stack is a popular solution for centralized logging in microservices. Elasticsearch stores log data, Logstash collects and processes logs, and Kibana provides visualization.
- **Cloud Logging Services**: Cloud providers offer managed logging solutions, such as AWS CloudWatch and Azure Monitor, which simplify logging and monitoring.

Monitoring with Distributed Tracing

Distributed tracing tracks requests across multiple services, providing insights into performance and dependencies.

- **OpenTelemetry**: OpenTelemetry is an open-source solution for distributed tracing, providing standardized APIs and libraries for monitoring applications.

- **Jaeger**: Jaeger is a tool for distributed tracing, allowing visualization of service dependencies, latency, and request flow across services.

6. Securing Microservices

Security is critical in a microservices architecture due to the large number of components and potential attack vectors. Key security practices include:

Authentication and Authorization: Use OAuth or JWT (JSON Web Tokens) for secure authentication and authorization, allowing each microservice to verify the identity and permissions of requests.

Service-to-Service Encryption: Implement TLS (Transport Layer Security) for secure communication between services, preventing data interception.

Network Segmentation and Firewalls: Limit network access using virtual private clouds (VPCs), firewalls, and network policies to prevent unauthorized access to microservices.

Secrets Management: Store sensitive information, such as API keys and database credentials, securely using tools like HashiCorp Vault or AWS Secrets Manager.

7. Deploying Microservices in Production

Deploying microservices requires a robust CI/CD pipeline to automate building, testing, and deploying services. A continuous deployment strategy enables rapid updates and reduces downtime.

1. **Set Up a CI/CD Pipeline**: Use tools like Jenkins, GitHub Actions, or GitLab CI/CD to automate build, test, and deployment processes. These pipelines ensure that code changes are verified before being deployed to production.

2. **Blue-Green and Canary Deployments**: Use advanced deployment strategies, such as blue-green and canary deployments, to minimize risk during updates. Blue-green deployment maintains two environments, while canary deployment releases updates to a subset of users before a full rollout.

3. **Rolling Updates and Rollbacks**: Use rolling updates to deploy new versions gradually, reducing impact on users. Rollbacks revert to the previous version if an update fails, ensuring stability.

Setting up and managing microservices architecture requires a coordinated approach to deployment, communication, scaling, monitoring, and security. By leveraging tools like Docker, Kubernetes, API gateways, service discovery, and centralized logging, developers can build resilient, scalable, and secure applications that harness the full potential of cloud-native microservices. With effective management practices, microservices architecture enables modular, flexible, and high-performing applications that can scale seamlessly to meet the demands of modern digital experiences.

Deploying C# Applications on Azure

Deploying C# applications on Microsoft Azure allows developers to take advantage of cloud scalability, high availability, and seamless integration with the .NET ecosystem. Azure provides several deployment models and services tailored to various application types, from simple web apps to complex microservices architectures. This section delves into the primary Azure services suited for deploying C# applications, offering practical steps and best practices to ensure a reliable and scalable deployment.

Key Deployment Options for C# Applications on Azure

Azure offers a range of services designed to host different types of C# applications:

Azure App Service: A fully managed platform ideal for web applications, RESTful APIs, and mobile backends.

Azure Functions: A serverless compute service suited for event-driven applications or background tasks.

Azure Kubernetes Service (AKS): Provides managed Kubernetes clusters for orchestrating containerized microservices.

Azure Virtual Machines (VMs): Virtualized servers that allow complete control over the operating system and runtime environment.

1. Deploying a C# Application to Azure App Service

Azure App Service is a highly popular option for deploying C# web applications and APIs. It provides automatic scaling, load balancing, and integration with Visual Studio, making it easy to deploy and manage applications.

Steps to Deploy a C# Application Using Azure App Service

Create an App Service Instance:

- Log into the Azure Portal.
- Navigate to **App Services** and click **Create**.
- Choose the **Web App** template, then select your subscription, resource group, runtime stack (.NET Core or ASP.NET), and region.

Deploy from Visual Studio:

- Open your C# project in Visual Studio.
- Right-click on the project in Solution Explorer, select **Publish**, and choose **Azure** as the target.
- Select your App Service instance from the available options or create a new one within the dialog box.
- Click **Publish** to deploy directly from Visual Studio to Azure App Service.

Set Up Continuous Deployment:

- To automate deployments, configure a CI/CD pipeline by linking your App Service to GitHub, Azure Repos, or another source control provider.
- Go to the **Deployment Center** in Azure Portal under your App Service instance, select **GitHub** as the source, and complete the setup.

Monitor and Scale:

- Enable **Application Insights** from the Azure Portal for real-time monitoring of your application.
- Set up autoscaling based on CPU, memory, or other metrics to handle traffic surges automatically.

2. Deploying Event-Driven C# Applications with Azure Functions

Azure Functions is a serverless option for running C# code in response to events, such as HTTP requests, database changes, or timer triggers. It is ideal for background tasks, microservices, or workloads that don't require continuous operation.

Steps to Deploy C# Azure Functions
Create a Function App:

- In the Azure Portal, go to **Function App** and click **Create**.
- Select a unique name, runtime stack (e.g., .NET Core), region, and storage account.

Develop and Deploy from Visual Studio:

- Open Visual Studio and create a new **Azure Functions Project**.
- Define functions with specific triggers, such as HTTP, Timer, or Cosmos DB triggers.
- Right-click the project, select **Publish**, choose **Azure** as the target, and deploy directly to your Function App in Azure.

Monitor and Scale:

- Azure Functions automatically scales based on demand, so there's no need to configure scaling manually.
- Use **Application Insights** to track function performance and usage metrics.

3. Deploying Microservices to Azure Kubernetes Service (AKS)

For C# applications built with microservices architecture, AKS provides a managed Kubernetes environment to orchestrate and manage containerized services. This approach supports complex, distributed systems where each microservice is isolated and independently deployable.

Steps to Deploy C# Microservices Using AKS

Create an AKS Cluster:

- In the Azure Portal, go to **Kubernetes Service** and click **Create**.
- Configure the cluster's basic settings, including region, node size, and node count.

Containerize Each Microservice:

- Use Docker to create containers for each C# microservice by defining Dockerfiles and building images.
- Push the Docker images to a container registry, such as Azure Container Registry (ACR).

```bash
docker build -t myservice .
docker tag myservice <AzureContainerRegistry>/myservice
docker push <AzureContainerRegistry>/myservice
```

Deploy to AKS:

- Create Kubernetes manifests (.yaml files) for each microservice, defining Deployments, Services, and Ingress configurations.
- Use kubectl commands to deploy to the AKS cluster:

```bash
bash
```

```
kubectl apply -f deployment.yaml
```

Configure Monitoring and Scaling:

- Integrate AKS with **Azure Monitor** and **Prometheus** for centralized monitoring.
- Set up horizontal pod autoscaling (HPA) to scale services based on CPU or memory usage.

4. Deploying C# Applications on Azure Virtual Machines

Azure VMs offer a flexible option for applications that need custom configurations, such as legacy systems or applications with specialized requirements.

Steps to Deploy C# Applications Using Azure VMs

Create and Configure a VM:

- In the Azure Portal, navigate to **Virtual Machines** and click **Create**.
- Choose the desired OS (Windows or Linux) and configure the VM's size, region, and network settings.
- Connect to the VM via RDP (Windows) or SSH (Linux).

Install .NET Runtime and Application Dependencies:

- On Windows, use PowerShell or the Azure CLI to install the .NET runtime.
- Deploy the application files to the VM, either by copying them manually or setting up a CI/CD pipeline.

Configure Load Balancing and Scaling:

- Use Azure Load Balancer to distribute traffic across multiple VM instances.

- Configure **Autoscale** to adjust the number of VMs based on demand.

Monitoring and Optimization Tools on Azure

Monitoring, logging, and optimization are essential for ensuring that deployed applications run efficiently. Azure provides several tools to support these needs:

- **Application Insights**: Integrated monitoring for tracking application performance, logging errors, and gathering user metrics. Especially useful for web applications and Azure Functions.
- **Azure Monitor**: Provides a comprehensive view of resource health, performance, and system metrics. It includes alerts, diagnostics, and insights for VMs, AKS, and more.
- **Azure Cost Management**: Helps monitor and manage spending, providing insights into resource usage and cost-optimization opportunities.
- **Azure Security Center**: Provides security recommendations, including vulnerability assessment, access control, and encryption options to secure applications and data.

Best Practices for Deploying C# Applications on Azure

1. **Automate Deployments with CI/CD Pipelines**: Use Azure DevOps or GitHub Actions to create automated pipelines that streamline deployment, testing, and updates.
2. **Optimize Resource Allocation**: Scale resources according to demand, use reserved instances or savings plans, and monitor resource usage to minimize costs.
3. **Secure Application and Data**: Implement Azure's identity management, network security, and encryption services to protect applications and data.
4. **Leverage Autoscaling and Load Balancing**: Use Azure's autoscaling and load balancing options to handle traffic spikes and ensure high

availability.

5. **Centralize Logging and Monitoring**: Use tools like Application Insights and Azure Monitor to gain visibility into application performance and identify areas for optimization.

Azure offers a versatile, scalable platform for deploying C# applications, whether it's a straightforward web app on Azure App Service, an event-driven function with Azure Functions, a microservices architecture on AKS, or a custom VM-based deployment. By leveraging Azure's cloud infrastructure, developers can focus on building high-quality applications while ensuring they are secure, performant, and ready to scale. Through effective use of deployment models and cloud services, C# applications on Azure can achieve high availability, resilience, and the flexibility needed for modern, cloud-based solutions.

RESTful API Design with C# 8

Designing a robust, scalable, and easy-to-maintain RESTful API in C# 8 involves careful planning, adherence to best practices, and leveraging modern C# language features to streamline development. RESTful APIs serve as the backbone for many applications, allowing communication between client applications and back-end services through standardized HTTP methods. With C# 8, developers have access to new features, such as nullable reference types, async streams, and pattern matching, which enhance API design, improve performance, and reduce common errors.

In this section, we'll explore the fundamentals of RESTful API design and how C# 8 features can be utilized to build more efficient and maintainable APIs.

Key Principles of RESTful API Design

A well-designed RESTful API should adhere to REST principles, ensuring it is easy to use, reliable, and efficient. RESTful APIs are built around resources, identified by unique URIs, and manipulated using HTTP methods (e.g., GET, POST, PUT, DELETE).

RESTful API Principles

1. **Statelessness**: Each request from the client to the server must contain all the necessary information for the server to understand and process it. The server does not store any client context between requests.
2. **Uniform Interface**: Use standard HTTP methods, resource URIs, and status codes to ensure consistency and predictability.
3. **Client-Server Separation**: The client and server should operate independently, allowing each to evolve separately.
4. **Layered System**: Design the API to support layers, such as authentication or caching, that can be added or removed without affecting the core functionality.
5. **Cacheability**: Implement caching where applicable to improve response times and reduce server load.

Building a RESTful API with ASP.NET Core and C# 8

ASP.NET Core provides an ideal framework for building RESTful APIs in C#. With its modular architecture, built-in dependency injection, and middleware support, ASP.NET Core simplifies the process of setting up an API. We'll also incorporate C# 8 features to enhance functionality, error handling, and performance.

1. Setting Up the API Project

Create a New ASP.NET Core Web API Project: Open a terminal or command prompt and create a new Web API project:

```bash
dotnet new webapi -n MyRestfulApi
```

Define the API Structure: Organize the project into folders for Controllers,

Models, and Services to maintain separation of concerns and simplify navigation.

2. Designing RESTful Endpoints

Each resource in a RESTful API should have its own set of endpoints, with each endpoint following HTTP conventions:

- **GET**: Retrieve a resource or collection.
- **POST**: Create a new resource.
- **PUT**: Update an existing resource.
- **DELETE**: Delete a resource.

Let's create a sample ProductController with basic CRUD operations for a product resource.

```csharp
using Microsoft.AspNetCore.Mvc;
using MyRestfulApi.Models;
using MyRestfulApi.Services;

namespace MyRestfulApi.Controllers
{
    [Route("api/[controller]")]
    [ApiController]
    public class ProductController : ControllerBase
    {
        private readonly IProductService _productService;

        public ProductController(IProductService productService)
        {
            _productService = productService;
        }

        [HttpGet]
        public ActionResult<IEnumerable<Product>> GetProducts() =>
```

```
    _productService.GetAllProducts();

    [HttpGet("{id}")]
    public ActionResult<Product> GetProduct(int id)
    {
        var product = _productService.GetProductById(id);
        if (product == null) return NotFound();
        return Ok(product);
    }

    [HttpPost]
    public ActionResult<Product> CreateProduct(Product product)
    {
        var createdProduct =
        _productService.AddProduct(product);
        return CreatedAtAction(nameof(GetProduct), new { id =
        createdProduct.Id }, createdProduct);
    }

    [HttpPut("{id}")]
    public IActionResult UpdateProduct(int id, Product product)
    {
        if (!_productService.UpdateProduct(id, product))
        return NotFound();
        return NoContent();
    }

    [HttpDelete("{id}")]
    public IActionResult DeleteProduct(int id)
    {
        if (!_productService.DeleteProduct(id)) return
        NotFound();
        return NoContent();
    }
    }
}
```

In this example:

- **Routing**: The [Route("api/[controller]")] attribute sets the route to api/product.

- **Status Codes**: Each method returns HTTP status codes according to the operation's result (e.g., NotFound, Ok, CreatedAtAction).

Leveraging C# 8 Features in RESTful APIs

C# 8 introduces language features that improve code readability, reduce runtime errors, and streamline data handling in RESTful APIs.

1. Nullable Reference Types

Nullable reference types help identify potential null reference issues, reducing runtime errors. In an API context, nullable annotations can make it clear when a property or parameter is optional.

Example:

```csharp
public class Product
{
    public int Id { get; set; }
    public string Name { get; set; } = string.Empty;
    public string? Description { get; set; }  // Nullable field
    public decimal Price { get; set; }
}
```

- **string? Description**: By marking Description as nullable, we signal to consumers that this field is optional, enabling clearer API contracts.

2. Async Streams for Data Fetching

Async streams (IAsyncEnumerable<T>) enable efficient streaming of data from a data source, such as a database or external service, without blocking the request thread.

Example of Async Stream in a Data Service:

csharp

```csharp
public interface IProductService
{
    IAsyncEnumerable<Product> GetProductsAsync();
}

public class ProductService : IProductService
{
    public async IAsyncEnumerable<Product> GetProductsAsync()
    {
        // Simulate data fetching
        for (int i = 1; i <= 10; i++)
        {
            await Task.Delay(100); // Simulate delay
            yield return new Product { Id = i, Name = $"Product
            {i}", Price = i * 10 };
        }
    }
}
```

Consuming Async Stream in Controller:

csharp

```csharp
[HttpGet("stream")]
public async IAsyncEnumerable<Product> GetProductsStream()
{
    await foreach (var product in
    _productService.GetProductsAsync())
    {
        yield return product;
    }
}
```

- **Async Streaming**: This enables clients to consume data as it's available rather than waiting for all data to load, improving responsiveness for large datasets.

3. Pattern Matching for Error Handling

Pattern matching can simplify error handling by allowing you to handle specific cases directly in your controller logic.

Example of Pattern Matching in ActionResult:

csharp

```
[HttpGet("{id}")]
public ActionResult<Product> GetProduct(int id) =>
    _productService.GetProductById(id) switch
    {
        null => NotFound(),
        var product => Ok(product)
    };
```

In this example:

- **Pattern Matching with switch**: Directly matches the result of GetProductById. If the result is null, it returns NotFound(), otherwise, it returns Ok() with the product.

Implementing Best Practices in RESTful API Design

1. **Versioning**: Use versioning in URLs or headers to manage breaking changes, such as api/v1/products.
2. **Error Handling**: Provide consistent error responses by using custom middleware or filters to capture exceptions and return standardized error messages.
3. **Pagination and Filtering**: Implement pagination and filtering for large data sets to improve response times and reduce payload sizes.
4. **Caching**: Use HTTP cache headers (e.g., Cache-Control, ETag) to reduce server load and improve response times for frequently accessed resources.
5. **Validation**: Validate request data with data annotations or FluentValidation to ensure inputs meet the required format before processing.

Securing RESTful APIs

1. **Authentication**: Use OAuth2 or JWTs for secure, token-based authentication, ensuring that only authorized users can access protected resources.
2. **Authorization**: Apply role-based or claims-based authorization policies to control access to specific resources or operations.
3. **HTTPS**: Enforce HTTPS to protect data in transit and prevent interception by encrypting requests and responses.
4. **Rate Limiting**: Implement rate limiting to control the number of requests a client can make in a given timeframe, protecting against abuse and DoS attacks.

Testing and Monitoring RESTful APIs

Testing and monitoring are essential for maintaining API reliability and performance:

1. **Unit and Integration Testing**: Write unit tests for business logic and integration tests to ensure endpoint functionality using tools like xUnit or NUnit.
2. **Load Testing**: Use tools like Apache JMeter or Azure Load Testing to simulate high traffic and measure the API's ability to handle concurrent requests.
3. **API Monitoring**: Use tools like Application Insights or New Relic to monitor API performance, identify bottlenecks, and track usage.

Building a RESTful API with C# 8 and ASP.NET Core provides a flexible, scalable platform for modern web applications. By following REST principles, leveraging C# 8 features, and implementing best practices for error handling, security, and performance, developers can create APIs that are reliable, maintainable, and responsive. Integrating tools for testing and monitoring ensures the API remains performant and resilient, capable of supporting a range of client applications and services.

Hands-On Project: Building a Cloud-Connected Microservices App

In this project, we'll create a cloud-connected microservices application using Azure Kubernetes Service (AKS) and ASP.NET Core. This **E-Commerce Microservices App** will consist of independent services for managing products, orders, and user accounts. By leveraging Azure's cloud resources, the application will be designed for scalability, flexibility, and maintainability.

Project Architecture and Overview

The application will consist of three main microservices:

Product Service: Handles product catalog information such as names, prices, and inventory.

Order Service: Manages order creation, updating, and status tracking.

User Service: Handles user registration, authentication, and profile management.

Each microservice will:

- **Use RESTful APIs**: Expose APIs for inter-service and client communication.
- **Be Containerized with Docker**: Each microservice will be packaged in a Docker container.
- **Deployed on Azure Kubernetes Service (AKS)**: AKS will provide scalability, load balancing, and automated orchestration.
- **Use Azure Resources**: Azure SQL, Cosmos DB, and Azure Key Vault for database and secrets management.

Step 1: Setting Up the Project Structure
Create a New Solution:

- Open a terminal and create a new solution called ECommerceMicroserv icesApp.

```bash
bash
```

```bash
dotnet new sln -n ECommerceMicroservicesApp
```

Add ASP.NET Core Web API Projects:

- For each microservice (ProductService, OrderService, and UserService), create a new ASP.NET Core Web API project.

```bash
bash
```

```bash
dotnet new webapi -n ProductService
dotnet new webapi -n OrderService
dotnet new webapi -n UserService
```

Organize the Solution:

- Add each project to the solution and create folders for Controllers, Models, and Services to maintain separation of concerns.

Step 2: Designing Each Microservice API

Each service will handle distinct functionality with standard RESTful endpoints.

Product Service

The ProductService will manage products, allowing CRUD operations.

```csharp
csharp
```

```csharp
[ApiController]
[Route("api/[controller]")]
public class ProductController : ControllerBase
{
    private readonly IProductService _productService;
```

```csharp
    public ProductController(IProductService productService)
    {
        _productService = productService;
    }

    [HttpGet("{id}")]
    public ActionResult<Product> GetProduct(int id)
    {
        var product = _productService.GetProductById(id);
        return product != null ? Ok(product) : NotFound();
    }

    [HttpPost]
    public ActionResult<Product> CreateProduct(Product product)
    {
        var createdProduct = _productService.AddProduct(product);
        return CreatedAtAction(nameof(GetProduct), new { id =
        createdProduct.Id }, createdProduct);
    }
}
```

Order Service

The OrderService will handle order management, including placing,
updating, and retrieving orders.

csharp

```csharp
[ApiController]
[Route("api/[controller]")]
public class OrderController : ControllerBase
{
    private readonly IOrderService _orderService;

    public OrderController(IOrderService orderService)
    {
        _orderService = orderService;
    }
```

```
[HttpPost]
public ActionResult<Order> PlaceOrder(Order order)
{
    var createdOrder = _orderService.PlaceOrder(order);
    return CreatedAtAction(nameof(GetOrder), new { id =
    createdOrder.Id }, createdOrder);
}
}
```

User Service

The UserService will handle user account management and authentication.

csharp

```
[ApiController]
[Route("api/[controller]")]
public class UserController : ControllerBase
{
    private readonly IUserService _userService;

    public UserController(IUserService userService)
    {
        _userService = userService;
    }

    [HttpPost("register")]
    public ActionResult Register(UserRegistrationDto
    registrationDto)
    {
        var result = _userService.RegisterUser(registrationDto);
        return result.IsSuccess ? Ok() :
        BadRequest(result.ErrorMessage);
    }
}
```

Step 3: Containerizing Each Microservice

Each service will be containerized with Docker for deployment on AKS.

Create Dockerfiles:

- Add Dockerfiles to each project directory. Here's an example Dockerfile for ProductService.

```dockerfile
FROM mcr.microsoft.com/dotnet/aspnet:6.0 AS base
WORKDIR /app
COPY . .
EXPOSE 80
ENTRYPOINT ["dotnet", "ProductService.dll"]
```

Build and Push Docker Images:

- Build Docker images for each service and push them to a container registry (e.g., Azure Container Registry).

```bash
docker build -t myacr.azurecr.io/productservice .
docker push myacr.azurecr.io/productservice
```

Step 4: Deploying Microservices on AKS
Create an AKS Cluster:

- In the Azure Portal, navigate to **Kubernetes Service** and create a new AKS cluster.
- Configure the cluster with the appropriate node size and networking options.

Define Kubernetes Manifests:

- Create deployment YAML files for each service, specifying replicas, container images, and ports.

```yaml
yaml

apiVersion: apps/v1
kind: Deployment
metadata:
  name: productservice
spec:
  replicas: 3
  selector:
    matchLabels:
      app: productservice
  template:
    metadata:
      labels:
        app: productservice
    spec:
      containers:
      - name: productservice
        image: myacr.azurecr.io/productservice:latest
        ports:
        - containerPort: 80
```

Apply the Manifests:

- Use kubectl to deploy the services to AKS.

```bash
bash

kubectl apply -f productservice-deployment.yaml
```

Set Up API Gateway:

- Configure an API gateway (e.g., Azure API Management) to route external requests to the microservices. This provides security, load balancing, and simplified access.

Step 5: Integrating Azure Resources
Use Azure SQL for Relational Data:

- Create an Azure SQL Database to store order and user data.
- Configure connection strings in AKS as secrets for secure database access.

Cosmos DB for NoSQL Storage:

- Set up Cosmos DB for product catalog data to support flexibility in product data modeling.
- Connect using managed identities to ensure secure access.

Secure Secrets with Azure Key Vault:

- Store sensitive data, such as API keys and database credentials, in Azure Key Vault.
- Use managed identity to grant the AKS cluster access to Key Vault.

Step 6: Implementing Monitoring and Autoscaling
Monitoring:

- Enable **Application Insights** for each service for real-time monitoring of performance and errors.
- Configure **Azure Monitor** to track metrics and set up alerts.

Auto-Scaling:

- Configure horizontal pod autoscaling in AKS to dynamically adjust replicas based on load.

```yaml
yaml

apiVersion: autoscaling/v2beta2
kind: HorizontalPodAutoscaler
metadata:
  name: productservice-hpa
spec:
  scaleTargetRef:
    apiVersion: apps/v1
    kind: Deployment
    name: productservice
  minReplicas: 2
  maxReplicas: 10
  metrics:
  - type: Resource
    resource:
      name: cpu
      target:
        type: Utilization
        averageUtilization: 70
```

In this project, we built a cloud-connected e-commerce application using AKS and ASP.NET Core. The application leverages containerization, Kubernetes orchestration, and Azure's managed services for security, data management, and scalability. By utilizing these tools and services, we ensured that our microservices app is scalable, resilient, and capable of handling high volumes with ease.

Data Management and Access

Working with Databases in C#: Introduction to Entity Framework Core

Entity Framework Core (EF Core) is a modern, open-source object-relational mapper (ORM) for .NET applications. It allows developers to interact with databases using C# code rather than SQL, enabling a streamlined approach to data access and management. EF Core simplifies CRUD (Create, Read, Update, Delete) operations and provides a set of tools for managing relational data within .NET applications, while remaining database-agnostic.

This section introduces EF Core and its key features, focusing on its configuration, the basics of setting up models and relationships, querying, and some best practices for working efficiently with databases in C#.

Why Choose Entity Framework Core?

EF Core is a popular ORM choice because of its flexibility, efficiency, and developer-friendly design. Here's why it stands out:

1. **Productivity**: EF Core eliminates boilerplate code by managing data access patterns and allowing developers to focus on business logic rather than SQL.
2. **Database-Agnostic**: EF Core supports multiple databases (e.g., SQL Server, SQLite, PostgreSQL), making it easier to switch database providers if needed.
3. **LINQ Integration**: EF Core supports LINQ (Language Integrated

Query), allowing developers to write complex, type-safe queries directly in C#.

4. **Change Tracking**: EF Core keeps track of changes made to entities and only updates modified data in the database.

5. **Schema Migrations**: EF Core's migrations tool simplifies schema management, enabling seamless database schema changes as the application evolves.

Setting Up EF Core in a C# Application

To start using EF Core, you'll need to install the necessary packages, define your data model, and set up a database context.

Step 1: Installing EF Core Packages

The EF Core NuGet packages provide the libraries and tools needed to interact with the database. For this example, we'll use SQL Server as the database provider.

bash

```
dotnet add package Microsoft.EntityFrameworkCore
dotnet add package Microsoft.EntityFrameworkCore.SqlServer
dotnet add package Microsoft.EntityFrameworkCore.Tools
```

- **Microsoft.EntityFrameworkCore**: The main EF Core library.
- **Microsoft.EntityFrameworkCore.SqlServer**: The SQL Server provider for EF Core.
- **Microsoft.EntityFrameworkCore.Tools**: Tools for EF Core commands, like migrations.

Step 2: Defining the Data Model

In EF Core, you define entities as C# classes representing tables in the database. Each entity's properties map to database columns, and relationships are defined through navigation properties.

Example: Creating a Product Entity

```csharp
public class Product
{
    public int ProductId { get; set; }  // Primary Key
    public string Name { get; set; } = string.Empty;
    public decimal Price { get; set; }
    public int StockQuantity { get; set; }
    public int CategoryId { get; set; }  // Foreign Key

    public Category? Category { get; set; }  // Navigation Property
}
```

Example: Creating a Category Entity

```csharp
public class Category
{
    public int CategoryId { get; set; }  // Primary Key
    public string Name { get; set; } = string.Empty;

    public List<Product> Products { get; set; } = new();  // Navigation Property
}
```

- **Primary Key**: EF Core identifies primary keys by convention using the property name Id or <EntityName>Id.
- **Navigation Properties**: Define relationships between tables, allowing EF Core to load related data automatically when needed.

Step 3: Configuring the Database Context

The DbContext class in EF Core manages database access and tracks changes to entities. In EF Core, each context corresponds to a session with the database.

Example: Creating an AppDbContext

csharp

```
using Microsoft.EntityFrameworkCore;

public class AppDbContext : DbContext
{
    public DbSet<Product> Products { get; set; }
    public DbSet<Category> Categories { get; set; }

    protected override void OnConfiguring(DbContextOptionsBuilder
    optionsBuilder)
    {
        optionsBuilder.UseSqlServer("YourConnectionStringHere");
    }

    protected override void OnModelCreating(ModelBuilder
    modelBuilder)
    {
        // Configure relationships or additional constraints if
        necessary
    }
}
```

- **DbSet Properties**: Represent tables in the database. DbSet<Product> will map to the Products table.
- **OnConfiguring**: Sets up the database connection string for the SQL Server provider.
- **OnModelCreating**: Provides an optional configuration space for customizing relationships and table mappings.

CRUD Operations with EF Core

EF Core provides a simple, powerful API for performing CRUD operations, all while handling SQL generation and execution internally.

Inserting Data

To insert data, create a new entity instance, add it to the context, and save the changes.

```csharp
using (var context = new AppDbContext())
{
    var category = new Category { Name = "Electronics" };
    context.Categories.Add(category);

    var product = new Product
    {
        Name = "Laptop",
        Price = 1000,
        StockQuantity = 50,
        Category = category
    };
    context.Products.Add(product);

    context.SaveChanges();
}
```

- **SaveChanges()**: Commits all changes to the database in a single transaction.

Querying Data with LINQ

EF Core fully supports LINQ for querying, enabling developers to write concise, type-safe database queries.

Example: Fetching Products by Category

```csharp
using (var context = new AppDbContext())
{
    var electronics = context.Products
        .Where(p => p.Category.Name == "Electronics")
```

```
        .ToList();
}
```

- **ToList()**: Executes the query, retrieving all products in the "Electronics" category.

Updating Data

To update data, retrieve the entity, modify its properties, and call SaveChanges().

```csharp
csharp

using (var context = new AppDbContext())
{
    var product = context.Products.FirstOrDefault(p => p.ProductId
    == 1);
    if (product != null)
    {
        product.Price = 899.99m;
        context.SaveChanges();
    }
}
```

Deleting Data

To delete data, retrieve the entity, remove it from the context, and call SaveChanges().

```csharp
csharp

using (var context = new AppDbContext())
{
    var product = context.Products.FirstOrDefault(p => p.ProductId
    == 1);
    if (product != null)
```

```
    {
        context.Products.Remove(product);
        context.SaveChanges();
    }
}
```

Advanced Configuration and Relationships in EF Core

Configuring Relationships

EF Core uses conventions to infer relationships between entities, but you can also configure relationships explicitly using the OnModelCreating method.

Example: Configuring One-to-Many Relationship

csharp

```
protected override void OnModelCreating(ModelBuilder modelBuilder)
{
    modelBuilder.Entity<Product>()
        .HasOne(p => p.Category)
        .WithMany(c => c.Products)
        .HasForeignKey(p => p.CategoryId);
}
```

Using Migrations for Schema Management

EF Core migrations track and apply database schema changes, making it easier to evolve the database schema as your application grows.

Create Initial Migration: Generates migration files based on the current data model.

bash

```
dotnet ef migrations add InitialCreate
```

Apply Migration: Updates the database schema to reflect changes.

bash

dotnet ef database update

Managing Migrations: You can add, remove, or revert migrations as needed, allowing precise control over schema changes.

Seeding Data

Data seeding populates the database with initial values during the migration process, which is helpful for default data or testing.

csharp

```
protected override void OnModelCreating(ModelBuilder modelBuilder)
{
    modelBuilder.Entity<Category>().HasData(
        new Category { CategoryId = 1, Name = "Electronics" },
        new Category { CategoryId = 2, Name = "Home Appliances" }
    );
}
```

Best Practices for Using EF Core

1. **Use Asynchronous Methods**: Prefer async methods like ToListAsync() and SaveChangesAsync() for non-blocking database access.
2. **Limit Data Loading**: Use Include for eager loading of related data and restrict the amount of data retrieved to only what's needed.
3. **Manage Connection Strings Securely**: Store connection strings in secure configurations, such as environment variables or Azure Key Vault.
4. **Avoid Raw SQL Queries**: Use LINQ and EF Core's API to benefit from strong typing and SQL injection prevention.
5. **Optimize Performance**: Avoid loading unnecessary data or over-querying the database. Index frequently queried fields and consider caching frequently accessed data.

Entity Framework Core provides a powerful ORM for .NET applications, simplifying data access and reducing the need for raw SQL queries. With features like change tracking, LINQ integration, and schema migrations, EF Core enables efficient database management while maintaining a clean and readable codebase. Following best practices and leveraging EF Core's advanced capabilities can help developers build scalable, maintainable applications that handle data efficiently and securely.

Handling Complex Data with LINQ and C# 8 Enhancements

LINQ (Language Integrated Query) is a powerful feature in C# that enables developers to perform complex data manipulation and querying directly within C# code. LINQ provides a unified syntax for querying data sources, including databases, collections, XML, and more. With C# 8, LINQ has become even more versatile, thanks to language enhancements like nullable reference types, async streams, and pattern matching, which make it easier to handle complex data structures and write efficient, concise code.

In this section, we'll explore the fundamentals of using LINQ for complex data operations and examine how C# 8 enhancements improve LINQ's capabilities for handling diverse and sophisticated data sets.

Overview of LINQ: Core Concepts and Query Patterns

LINQ integrates querying capabilities into C#, allowing developers to work with data in a declarative, SQL-like syntax. There are two primary syntax styles in LINQ: query syntax and method syntax.

- **Query Syntax**: Uses SQL-like keywords (e.g., from, where, select) for filtering, projecting, and ordering data.
- **Method Syntax**: Uses extension methods (e.g., .Where(), .Select(), .OrderBy()) for chaining complex operations, often preferred for its readability and flexibility.

LINQ Operations and Query Composition

LINQ supports several operations, each suited for different types of data manipulation. These core operations enable developers to filter, sort, transform, and aggregate data.

1. **Filtering**: Using .Where() to specify conditions on data, akin to the SQL WHERE clause.
2. **Projection**: Using .Select() to shape or transform data, similar to the SQL SELECT clause.
3. **Sorting**: Using .OrderBy() and .OrderByDescending() to order results.
4. **Grouping**: Using .GroupBy() to group data by specific criteria.
5. **Aggregation**: Using .Count(), .Sum(), .Average(), and .Min()/.Max() for data summarization.

Example: Basic LINQ Query for Filtering and Sorting

```csharp
var expensiveProducts = products
    .Where(p => p.Price > 1000)
    .OrderByDescending(p => p.Price)
    .Select(p => new { p.Name, p.Price })
    .ToList();
```

In this example:

- .Where() filters for products priced above 1000.
- .OrderByDescending() sorts products by price in descending order.
- .Select() projects each product into an anonymous type containing only the Name and Price.

C# 8 Enhancements for LINQ: Streamlining Complex Queries

C# 8 introduced several features that enhance LINQ's expressiveness, enabling developers to handle complex data scenarios more efficiently.

1. Nullable Reference Types: Safeguarding Data Integrity

Nullable reference types in C# 8 provide compile-time checks to help avoid NullReferenceException errors. In LINQ, this feature ensures that queries handle nullable data safely, especially when dealing with optional fields or related data that might be missing.

Example: Querying Nullable Properties with Null Checks

```csharp
var productsWithDescriptions = products
    .Where(p => p.Description != null)
    .Select(p => new { p.Name, Description = p.Description! }) //
    Use '!' to indicate non-null
    .ToList();
```

- **Nullable Annotations**: By annotating Description as nullable (string?), the compiler warns if Description might be null. Using ! (null-forgiving operator) indicates the developer is certain the value is non-null.

2. Async Streams: Asynchronous Data Streaming with IAsyncEnumerable<T>

Async streams in C# 8 allow LINQ to work with asynchronous data sequences using IAsyncEnumerable<T>. This is particularly useful for handling large data sets or remote data sources that require incremental loading, such as reading data from a database or API.

Example: Using Async Streams to Fetch Data Incrementally

```csharp
public async IAsyncEnumerable<Product>
GetExpensiveProductsAsync(decimal minPrice)
{
    foreach (var product in products.Where(p => p.Price >
```

```
        minPrice))
        {
            await Task.Delay(100); // Simulate async data fetch
            yield return product;
        }
    }
}

public async Task DisplayProductsAsync()
{
    await foreach (var product in GetExpensiveProductsAsync(1000))
    {
        Console.WriteLine($"{product.Name}: ${product.Price}");
    }
}
```

- **IAsyncEnumerable<T>**: Enables asynchronous iteration, useful for data sources where results arrive over time.
- **await foreach**: Allows iteration over asynchronous streams, providing data as it becomes available without blocking the main thread.

3. Pattern Matching: Simplifying Conditional Logic in Queries

Pattern matching in C# 8 improves LINQ's ability to handle complex filtering based on multiple conditions. Patterns like switch expressions and property patterns help streamline query logic for data transformations or type-checking scenarios.

Example: Using Pattern Matching in LINQ with Property Patterns

csharp

```
var filteredProducts = products
    .Where(p => p is { Category: "Electronics", StockQuantity: > 0
    })
    .Select(p => new { p.Name, p.Price })
    .ToList();
```

In this example:

- **Property Patterns**: Filters products with Category of "Electronics" and a StockQuantity greater than zero.
- **Readable Conditions**: Pattern matching provides a concise way to apply multiple conditions, especially in complex queries.

4. Indexes and Ranges: Working with Subsets of Data

C# 8's index (^) and range (..) operators simplify working with data subsets. Although primarily used with arrays and lists, these operators can also be beneficial in LINQ queries when selecting specific data ranges.

Example: Using Indexes and Ranges with LINQ

```csharp
var topProducts = products
    .OrderByDescending(p => p.Price)
    .Take(10)
    .ToList();
```

- **Range Operator**: Using .Take(10) retrieves the first 10 elements. Alternatively, .Skip(10).Take(10) retrieves a specific range of items, supporting pagination scenarios.

Advanced LINQ Techniques for Complex Data Management
1. Joining Data from Multiple Sources

Joining data from multiple sources is essential when working with complex data structures. LINQ supports joins, similar to SQL joins, allowing you to correlate data across collections or tables.

Example: Inner Join with LINQ

```csharp
var productOrders = from product in products
                    join order in orders on product.ProductId
                    equals order.ProductId
                    select new { product.Name, order.Quantity,
                    order.OrderDate };
```

- **Inner Join**: Joins products with orders based on a common key (ProductId).

2. Grouping and Aggregating Data

LINQ's .GroupBy() method enables data grouping, which is often followed by aggregation operations such as Sum(), Average(), Count(), or Max().

Example: Grouping Data and Calculating Totals

```csharp
var categoryTotals = products
    .GroupBy(p => p.Category)
    .Select(g => new { Category = g.Key, TotalStock = g.Sum(p =>
    p.StockQuantity) })
    .ToList();
```

- **Grouping**: Groups products by category.
- **Aggregating**: Calculates the total stock quantity for each category.

3. Handling Complex Transformations with SelectMany

The SelectMany operator is useful for flattening nested collections or transforming collections of collections into a single sequence.

Example: Flattening Nested Collections with SelectMany

```
csharp

var allOrderProducts = customers
    .SelectMany(c => c.Orders)
    .Select(o => new { o.ProductId, o.Quantity })
    .ToList();
```

In this example:

- **SelectMany**: Flattens each customer's orders, producing a single sequence of orders across all customers.

Best Practices for Handling Complex Data with LINQ and C# 8

1. **Use Asynchronous LINQ for High-Latency Data**: For database or network-bound data, prefer asynchronous LINQ with async streams to avoid blocking operations.
2. **Minimize Data Fetching**: Use projection (Select) to retrieve only necessary fields rather than entire objects, reducing memory consumption and improving performance.
3. **Combine Filters and Projections**: Apply .Where() and .Select() together to narrow down and shape data, improving readability and efficiency.
4. **Optimize with Method Syntax**: Use method syntax for complex chaining, which can be more readable than query syntax for intricate data transformations.
5. **Handle Nulls with Care**: Use nullable reference types and null-coalescing operators (??) to handle optional data fields and prevent runtime exceptions.

Handling complex data with LINQ in C# is further enhanced by C# 8's new features, including nullable reference types, async streams, pattern matching, and range operators. These enhancements allow developers to work more effectively with sophisticated data scenarios, supporting better error handling, improved performance with asynchronous data, and concise code for conditional filtering. By leveraging these techniques and following best practices, developers can build efficient, maintainable, and expressive data manipulation logic within C# applications.

CRUD Operations: Best Practices for Efficiency

Efficient CRUD (Create, Read, Update, Delete) operations are essential for application performance and scalability, especially in data-intensive applications. By following best practices for handling CRUD operations in C#, particularly with Entity Framework Core (EF Core), developers can ensure that data access is optimized and that the application performs reliably, even with large datasets or high transaction volumes. This section covers best practices for writing efficient CRUD operations in C# and EF Core, including optimization tips for queries, data fetching, and transaction management.

1. Optimizing Create Operations: Efficient Data Insertion

Efficiently managing data insertion is crucial, especially when dealing with bulk data. In C# and EF Core, there are several ways to optimize data insertion.

Best Practices for Create Operations

Use AddRange for Bulk Inserts: When inserting multiple records, use AddRange() instead of Add() to minimize the number of database calls. This approach reduces round trips to the database and speeds up bulk insert operations.

```csharp
var products = new List<Product>
{
    new Product { Name = "Product1", Price = 100 },
    new Product { Name = "Product2", Price = 150 },
```

```
};
```

```
context.Products.AddRange(products);
context.SaveChanges();
```

Consider Batch Operations: When handling very large datasets, batch inserts (processing data in smaller chunks) can improve performance and reduce memory usage.

Use SaveChanges Carefully: Minimize the use of SaveChanges() within loops. Instead, accumulate changes and call SaveChanges() once outside the loop, reducing the number of database transactions.

Disable Change Tracking for Bulk Inserts: Disabling change tracking for bulk inserts can increase performance since EF Core won't monitor the state of each entity.

csharp

```
context.ChangeTracker.AutoDetectChangesEnabled = false;
```

2. Optimizing Read Operations: Efficient Data Retrieval

Read operations are often the most frequent data access pattern in applications. Inefficient reads can significantly affect application performance, especially in high-traffic scenarios.

Best Practices for Read Operations

Use Projection to Minimize Data Transfer: Only retrieve the necessary columns by using Select(). This minimizes data transfer, reduces memory usage, and improves performance, particularly for large tables.

csharp

```
var productSummaries = context.Products
    .Select(p => new { p.ProductId, p.Name, p.Price })
    .ToList();
```

Leverage Asynchronous Queries: Use asynchronous methods like ToLis-tAsync() for high-latency data sources (e.g., databases). This approach keeps the application responsive by avoiding blocking operations.

```csharp
var products = await context.Products.ToListAsync();
```

Use Eager Loading for Related Data: When fetching related data, use Include() to eagerly load related entities. This prevents the "N+1" query problem, where multiple round trips are required to fetch related data.

```csharp
var productsWithCategories = context.Products
    .Include(p => p.Category)
    .ToList();
```

Use AsNoTracking for Read-Only Data: When querying data that doesn't require updates, use AsNoTracking() to disable change tracking. This reduces memory usage and improves query performance.

```csharp
var products = context.Products.AsNoTracking().ToList();
```

Filter Early and Often: Apply filters (Where()) as early as possible in the query to reduce the amount of data being processed and transferred.

```csharp
var affordableProducts = context.Products
    .Where(p => p.Price < 500)
    .ToList();
```

3. Optimizing Update Operations: Handling Data Modifications Efficiently

Update operations can become costly if not handled properly, especially with large datasets or frequent updates.

Best Practices for Update Operations

Retrieve Only What's Necessary for Updates: When updating records, retrieve only the fields you intend to modify, reducing data transfer and memory usage.

```csharp
var product = context.Products
    .Where(p => p.ProductId == 1)
    .Select(p => new Product { ProductId = p.ProductId, Price =
    p.Price })
    .FirstOrDefault();

if (product != null)
{
    product.Price = 120;
    context.SaveChanges();
}
```

Use UpdateRange for Bulk Updates: Similar to AddRange(), using UpdateRange() can reduce the number of database calls when updating multiple entities.

```csharp
var productsToUpdate = context.Products.Where(p => p.Price <
50).ToList();
foreach (var product in productsToUpdate)
{
    product.Price += 10;
}
context.UpdateRange(productsToUpdate);
context.SaveChanges();
```

Consider Optimistic Concurrency Control: Enable optimistic concurrency control by using concurrency tokens (e.g., a Timestamp column) to detect conflicting updates. This is useful in multi-user environments.

Minimize SaveChanges Calls in Loops: Like inserts, avoid calling SaveChanges() within loops for bulk updates. Accumulate changes and call SaveChanges() once outside the loop.

4. Optimizing Delete Operations: Efficiently Removing Data

Efficient deletion is essential for maintaining performance, particularly when removing large datasets or dealing with cascading deletions.

Best Practices for Delete Operations

Use RemoveRange for Bulk Deletes: When deleting multiple records, use RemoveRange() to perform the deletion in a single transaction.

```csharp
var oldProducts = context.Products.Where(p =>
p.IsDiscontinued).ToList();
context.Products.RemoveRange(oldProducts);
context.SaveChanges();
```

Handle Cascade Deletes Carefully: When deleting entities with relationships, configure cascade delete policies wisely to avoid accidentally removing related data.

```csharp
modelBuilder.Entity<Product>()
    .HasOne(p => p.Category)
    .WithMany(c => c.Products)
    .OnDelete(DeleteBehavior.Cascade);
```

Use SQL Commands for Massive Deletes: For very large deletions, consider using raw SQL commands to bypass EF Core's change tracking, which can improve performance.

```csharp
context.Database.ExecuteSqlRaw("DELETE FROM Products WHERE
IsDiscontinued = 1");
```

5. Transaction Management: Ensuring Data Integrity and Consistency

EF Core automatically wraps SaveChanges() in a transaction, but for complex operations that span multiple calls, explicit transactions provide control and help maintain data consistency.

Best Practices for Transactions

Use Explicit Transactions for Multi-Step Operations: For complex operations that modify multiple tables or involve multiple SaveChanges() calls, use explicit transactions.

```csharp
using (var transaction = context.Database.BeginTransaction())
{
    try
    {
        // First operation
        context.SaveChanges();

        // Second operation
        context.SaveChanges();

        transaction.Commit();
    }
    catch
    {
        transaction.Rollback();
    }
}
```

Minimize Locks with Optimistic Concurrency: In multi-user scenarios, use optimistic concurrency rather than locking database rows to avoid

293

blocking other operations.

Use Savepoints in Long Transactions: For complex workflows, using savepoints within a transaction allows partial rollbacks, maintaining data integrity without rolling back the entire transaction.

6. Caching Strategies to Minimize Database Hits

Caching can significantly improve performance by reducing the number of database queries, especially for frequently accessed data.

Caching Techniques

Use In-Memory Caching for Frequently Accessed Data: In-memory caching, such as the .NET MemoryCache or distributed caching options like Redis, stores frequently accessed data, reducing repeated database hits.

```csharp
// Configure and use caching as needed
```

Leverage Query Caching for Static Data: For data that doesn't change often (e.g., lookup tables), implement caching to avoid unnecessary database queries.

Use a Distributed Cache for Web Applications: In multi-server environments, distributed caching (e.g., Redis) ensures data consistency across instances.

Efficient CRUD operations in C# require a combination of EF Core best practices, caching, and transaction management. Optimizing data fetching, minimizing calls to SaveChanges(), using asynchronous methods, and applying caching strategies are fundamental to building responsive and scalable applications. By following these best practices, developers can ensure that CRUD operations are performant, reducing the load on the database and improving the overall user experience.

Unit of Work and Repository Patterns for Data-Driven Applications

The Unit of Work and Repository patterns are widely used in data-driven applications to create a clean separation between data access logic and business logic. These patterns abstract data access code, making it easier to manage data changes, maintain code consistency, and implement testable, maintainable codebases. Together, the Unit of Work and Repository patterns support efficient data management, enabling developers to work with data more effectively and reducing the direct dependency on specific database technologies.

This section provides an in-depth guide to implementing the Unit of Work and Repository patterns in C# with Entity Framework Core (EF Core), focusing on best practices for creating flexible, testable, and maintainable data access layers.

Understanding the Repository Pattern

The Repository pattern provides a consistent interface to perform CRUD operations on data sources. It abstracts database interactions, so the application doesn't directly interact with EF Core or other data access frameworks, enabling flexible data management and enhancing testability.

Key Benefits of the Repository Pattern

Encapsulation of Data Access Logic: All database operations are centralized, simplifying code maintenance and reducing duplication.

Abstraction for Flexibility: The application remains agnostic of specific data access technologies, making it easier to switch databases if needed.

Improved Testability: By abstracting EF Core, repositories can be mocked in unit tests, enabling isolated testing of business logic.

Implementing the Repository Pattern

In a typical implementation, each entity has a corresponding repository that provides basic CRUD operations. Here's how to create a generic repository interface and a concrete implementation for Entity Framework Core.

Step 1: Define a Generic Repository Interface

The generic repository interface defines the standard CRUD operations.

csharp

```
public interface IRepository<T> where T : class
{
    Task<IEnumerable<T>> GetAllAsync();
    Task<T?> GetByIdAsync(int id);
    Task AddAsync(T entity);
    void Update(T entity);
    void Delete(T entity);
    Task SaveChangesAsync();
}
```

- **GetAllAsync** and **GetByIdAsync**: Fetch data from the database.
- **AddAsync**, **Update**, and **Delete**: Handle data creation, modification, and deletion.
- **SaveChangesAsync**: Commits changes to the database, commonly handled in the Unit of Work pattern.

Step 2: Implement the Generic Repository with EF Core

Create a concrete repository implementation that uses EF Core for data access.

csharp

```
using Microsoft.EntityFrameworkCore;

public class Repository<T> : IRepository<T> where T : class
{
    protected readonly DbContext _context;
    private readonly DbSet<T> _dbSet;

    public Repository(DbContext context)
    {
```

```
        _context = context;
        _dbSet = _context.Set<T>();
    }

    public async Task<IEnumerable<T>> GetAllAsync()
    {
        return await _dbSet.ToListAsync();
    }

    public async Task<T?> GetByIdAsync(int id)
    {
        return await _dbSet.FindAsync(id);
    }

    public async Task AddAsync(T entity)
    {
        await _dbSet.AddAsync(entity);
    }

    public void Update(T entity)
    {
        _dbSet.Update(entity);
    }

    public void Delete(T entity)
    {
        _dbSet.Remove(entity);
    }

    public async Task SaveChangesAsync()
    {
        await _context.SaveChangesAsync();
    }
}
```

- **DbContext and DbSet**: The DbContext and DbSet are used to interact with the database.
- **Async Operations**: All operations are asynchronous to avoid blocking

the main thread during database access.

Step 3: Create Specific Repositories for Complex Scenarios

For more complex entities, you can create specific repository interfaces and implementations to handle specialized data access requirements.

```csharp
public interface IProductRepository : IRepository<Product>
{
    Task<IEnumerable<Product>> GetProductsByCategoryAsync(int
    categoryId);
}

public class ProductRepository : Repository<Product>,
IProductRepository
{
    public ProductRepository(DbContext context) : base(context) { }

    public async Task<IEnumerable<Product>>
    GetProductsByCategoryAsync(int categoryId)
    {
        return await _dbSet.Where(p => p.CategoryId ==
        categoryId).ToListAsync();
    }
}
```

Understanding the Unit of Work Pattern

The Unit of Work pattern groups multiple database operations within a single transaction, ensuring that changes are atomic and consistent. It manages repository instances and provides a centralized point for saving changes to the database, allowing you to commit all operations or roll them back if an error occurs.

Key Benefits of the Unit of Work Pattern

Transactional Consistency: Ensures that multiple database operations within a transaction either all succeed or fail together.

Centralized Save Operation: Consolidates all changes, reducing redundant calls to SaveChanges.

Dependency Management: Manages multiple repository instances in a single transaction, ensuring all repositories share the same context.

Implementing the Unit of Work Pattern

The Unit of Work pattern implementation involves creating a Unit of Work interface and a class that manages repository instances and transaction handling.

Step 1: Define the Unit of Work Interface

The Unit of Work interface manages repositories and provides a method to save changes.

```csharp
public interface IUnitOfWork : IDisposable
{
    IProductRepository Products { get; }
    ICategoryRepository Categories { get; }
    Task<int> SaveChangesAsync();
}
```

- **Repositories**: The Unit of Work holds instances of repositories, ensuring they operate within a single context.
- **SaveChangesAsync**: Commits all changes to the database.

Step 2: Implement the Unit of Work Class

The Unit of Work class initializes and manages repository instances, allowing them to share the same DbContext.

```csharp
public class UnitOfWork : IUnitOfWork
{
```

```
private readonly AppDbContext _context;
private IProductRepository? _productRepository;
private ICategoryRepository? _categoryRepository;

public UnitOfWork(AppDbContext context)
{
    _context = context;
}

public IProductRepository Products => _productRepository ??=
new ProductRepository(_context);
public ICategoryRepository Categories => _categoryRepository
??= new CategoryRepository(_context);

public async Task<int> SaveChangesAsync()
{
    return await _context.SaveChangesAsync();
}

public void Dispose()
{
    _context.Dispose();
}
}
```

- **Lazy Initialization**: Repositories are instantiated only when accessed, reducing overhead.
- **Shared DbContext**: All repositories within the Unit of Work share the same DbContext, supporting consistent transactions.
- **Dispose**: Ensures that the DbContext is disposed of properly, freeing resources.

Using the Unit of Work and Repository Patterns in the Application

With the patterns implemented, you can now leverage them in your application's services or controllers.

Example Usage in a Service Layer

```csharp
public class ProductService
{
    private readonly IUnitOfWork _unitOfWork;

    public ProductService(IUnitOfWork unitOfWork)
    {
        _unitOfWork = unitOfWork;
    }

    public async Task<IEnumerable<Product>> GetAllProductsAsync()
    {
        return await _unitOfWork.Products.GetAllAsync();
    }

    public async Task AddProductAsync(Product product)
    {
        await _unitOfWork.Products.AddAsync(product);
        await _unitOfWork.SaveChangesAsync();
    }
}
```

- **Single Unit of Work Instance**: All repository actions within the ProductService use a single IUnitOfWork instance, ensuring consistency.
- **SaveChangesAsync**: Only one call to SaveChangesAsync is needed, committing all changes at once.

Benefits of Using the Unit of Work and Repository Patterns Together

Combining the Unit of Work and Repository patterns creates a structured approach to data access. Key benefits include:

1. **Centralized Data Access Logic**: All data access operations are handled through repositories, simplifying code maintenance.
2. **Transaction Consistency**: Ensures that all operations within a service

method are consistent and wrapped in a single transaction.

3. **Loose Coupling**: Abstracts database dependencies from business logic, making it easier to change database providers or refactor code.

Testing with the Unit of Work and Repository Patterns

The Unit of Work and Repository patterns make it easier to mock data access logic for testing, as they provide well-defined interfaces that can be substituted with mock implementations.

Example: Mocking Repositories in Unit Tests

Using a mocking framework like Moq, you can create mock repositories and Unit of Work instances to test business logic in isolation.

```csharp
var mockProductRepo = new Mock<IProductRepository>();
var mockUnitOfWork = new Mock<IUnitOfWork>();

mockUnitOfWork.Setup(u =>
u.Products).Returns(mockProductRepo.Object);
mockUnitOfWork.Setup(u => u.SaveChangesAsync()).ReturnsAsync(1);

// Inject mockUnitOfWork into service and test
```

- **Mocked Repositories**: Allows you to test the service without actual database interactions.
- **Mocked Unit of Work**: Verifies that SaveChangesAsync() is called, ensuring transactional behavior.

Best Practices for Using the Unit of Work and Repository Patterns

1. **Limit Repository Scope**: Repositories should focus on data access. Avoid placing business logic within repositories.
2. **Use Specific Repositories for Complex Data**: Implement specific repositories for entities requiring complex or custom queries.

3. **Avoid Overusing Repositories**: If EF Core's DbContext already meets your needs, avoid unnecessary abstraction that could complicate your code.

4. **Inject Unit of Work into Services**: Use dependency injection to provide services with Unit of Work instances, ensuring a consistent approach to data access and transactions.

The Unit of Work and Repository patterns offer a structured, maintainable approach to data access in data-driven applications. By abstracting data access through repositories and managing transactions with a Unit of Work, these patterns simplify data operations, improve testability, and maintain consistency across the application. Used together, they provide a flexible foundation for building scalable, data-centric applications in C#.

Hands-On Project: Developing a Data-Driven App with EF Core

This project will guide you through building a **Library Management System** using Entity Framework Core (EF Core) as the ORM. The system will allow CRUD (Create, Read, Update, Delete) operations for managing books and authors in a library. We'll implement the Repository and Unit of Work patterns to ensure a scalable and maintainable code structure, enabling clean data access and efficient transaction management.

Project Overview: Library Management System

Our Library Management System will consist of two main components:

Book Management: Manage book details, including title, publication year, genre, and associated author.

Author Management: Manage author details and their associated books. The project will cover:

- Data modeling and relationships in EF Core
- CRUD operations through repositories

- Unit of Work pattern for managing transactions
- Basic API endpoints to interact with the application

Step 1: Setting Up the Project and Installing Dependencies

Create a New ASP.NET Core Web API Project: Open a terminal and create a new Web API project for the Library Management System.

```bash
dotnet new webapi -n LibraryManagementSystem
```

Add EF Core and SQL Server Packages: Install EF Core and the SQL Server provider to enable database interactions.

```bash
dotnet add package Microsoft.EntityFrameworkCore
dotnet add package Microsoft.EntityFrameworkCore.SqlServer
dotnet add package Microsoft.EntityFrameworkCore.Tools
```

Define Folder Structure: Organize the project into folders for Models, Data, Repositories, and Services to maintain a clean and modular architecture.

Step 2: Designing the Data Model

Define **Book** and **Author** models with relationships and validation using data annotations.

Book Model

```csharp
using System.ComponentModel.DataAnnotations;

public class Book
{
```

```
    public int BookId { get; set; }

    [Required]
    [MaxLength(200)]
    public string Title { get; set; } = string.Empty;

    public int PublicationYear { get; set; }

    public int AuthorId { get; set; } // Foreign Key

    public Author? Author { get; set; } // Navigation Property
}
```

Author Model

```csharp
using System.ComponentModel.DataAnnotations;

public class Author
{
    public int AuthorId { get; set; }

    [Required]
    [MaxLength(100)]
    public string Name { get; set; } = string.Empty;

    public List<Book> Books { get; set; } = new(); // Navigation
    Property
}
```

Step 3: Setting Up the Database Context

Create LibraryDbContext to manage database access for the Book and Author entities.

```csharp
```

```
using Microsoft.EntityFrameworkCore;

public class LibraryDbContext : DbContext
{
    public DbSet<Book> Books { get; set; }
    public DbSet<Author> Authors { get; set; }

    public LibraryDbContext(DbContextOptions<LibraryDbContext>
    options) : base(options) { }

    protected override void OnModelCreating(ModelBuilder
    modelBuilder)
    {
        modelBuilder.Entity<Author>()
            .HasMany(a => a.Books)
            .WithOne(b => b.Author)
            .HasForeignKey(b => b.AuthorId)
            .OnDelete(DeleteBehavior.Cascade);
    }
}
```

Step 4: Implementing the Repository and Unit of Work Patterns

Step 4.1: Create a Generic Repository Interface

Define a generic repository interface to handle common data operations.

```csharp
public interface IRepository<T> where T : class
{
    Task<IEnumerable<T>> GetAllAsync();
    Task<T?> GetByIdAsync(int id);
    Task AddAsync(T entity);
    void Update(T entity);
    void Delete(T entity);
    Task SaveChangesAsync();
}
```

Step 4.2: Implement the Generic Repository

Create a concrete repository implementation that uses EF Core for data

306

access.

```csharp
using Microsoft.EntityFrameworkCore;

public class Repository<T> : IRepository<T> where T : class
{
    private readonly LibraryDbContext _context;
    private readonly DbSet<T> _dbSet;

    public Repository(LibraryDbContext context)
    {
        _context = context;
        _dbSet = _context.Set<T>();
    }

    public async Task<IEnumerable<T>> GetAllAsync() => await
    _dbSet.ToListAsync();

    public async Task<T?> GetByIdAsync(int id) => await
    _dbSet.FindAsync(id);

    public async Task AddAsync(T entity) => await
    _dbSet.AddAsync(entity);

    public void Update(T entity) => _dbSet.Update(entity);

    public void Delete(T entity) => _dbSet.Remove(entity);

    public async Task SaveChangesAsync() => await
    _context.SaveChangesAsync();
}
```

Step 4.3: Implement the Unit of Work Pattern

The Unit of Work class will manage repositories and transactions, providing a single access point to save changes.

csharp

```csharp
public interface IUnitOfWork : IDisposable
{
    IRepository<Book> Books { get; }
    IRepository<Author> Authors { get; }
    Task<int> SaveChangesAsync();
}

public class UnitOfWork : IUnitOfWork
{
    private readonly LibraryDbContext _context;
    private IRepository<Book>? _bookRepository;
    private IRepository<Author>? _authorRepository;

    public UnitOfWork(LibraryDbContext context)
    {
        _context = context;
    }

    public IRepository<Book> Books => _bookRepository ??= new
    Repository<Book>(_context);
    public IRepository<Author> Authors => _authorRepository ??=
    new Repository<Author>(_context);

    public async Task<int> SaveChangesAsync() => await
    _context.SaveChangesAsync();

    public void Dispose() => _context.Dispose();
}
```

Step 5: Implementing CRUD Operations in Services

With the Unit of Work and Repository patterns in place, we can implement CRUD functionality in the service layer.

Book Service

csharp

```
public class BookService
{
    private readonly IUnitOfWork _unitOfWork;

    public BookService(IUnitOfWork unitOfWork)
    {
        _unitOfWork = unitOfWork;
    }

    public async Task<IEnumerable<Book>> GetAllBooksAsync() =>
    await _unitOfWork.Books.GetAllAsync();

    public async Task<Book?> GetBookByIdAsync(int id) => await
    _unitOfWork.Books.GetByIdAsync(id);

    public async Task AddBookAsync(Book book)
    {
        await _unitOfWork.Books.AddAsync(book);
        await _unitOfWork.SaveChangesAsync();
    }

    public async Task UpdateBookAsync(Book book)
    {
        _unitOfWork.Books.Update(book);
        await _unitOfWork.SaveChangesAsync();
    }

    public async Task DeleteBookAsync(int id)
    {
        var book = await _unitOfWork.Books.GetByIdAsync(id);
        if (book != null)
        {
            _unitOfWork.Books.Delete(book);
            await _unitOfWork.SaveChangesAsync();
        }
    }
}
```

Step 6: Creating Controllers for Book and Author Management

Create API endpoints for managing books and authors in BookController and AuthorController.

Book Controller

csharp

```csharp
[Route("api/[controller]")]
[ApiController]
public class BookController : ControllerBase
{
    private readonly BookService _bookService;

    public BookController(BookService bookService)
    {
        _bookService = bookService;
    }

    [HttpGet]
    public async Task<IActionResult> GetAll() => Ok(await
    _bookService.GetAllBooksAsync());

    [HttpGet("{id}")]
    public async Task<IActionResult> Get(int id)
    {
        var book = await _bookService.GetBookByIdAsync(id);
        return book != null ? Ok(book) : NotFound();
    }

    [HttpPost]
    public async Task<IActionResult> Create(Book book)
    {
        await _bookService.AddBookAsync(book);
        return CreatedAtAction(nameof(Get),
new { id = book.BookId }, book);
    }

    [HttpPut("{id}")]
    public async Task<IActionResult> Update(int id, Book book)
    {
        if (id != book.BookId) return BadRequest();
```

```
        await _bookService.UpdateBookAsync(book);
        return NoContent();
    }


    [HttpDelete("{id}")]
    public async Task<IActionResult> Delete(int id)
    {
        await _bookService.DeleteBookAsync(id);
        return NoContent();
    }
}
```

Step 7: Configuring Dependency Injection

Register services and dependencies in Program.cs.

csharp

```
builder.Services.AddDbContext<
LibraryDbContext>(options =>
    options.UseSqlServer
(builder.Configuration.
GetConnectionString("DefaultConnection")));

builder.Services.AddScoped<IUnitOfWork, UnitOfWork>();
builder.Services.AddScoped<BookService>();
builder.Services.AddScoped<AuthorService>();


builder.Services.AddControllers();
```

Step 8: Running Migrations and Testing

Add Initial Migration: Run migrations to create the database schema.

bash

```
dotnet ef migrations add InitialCreate
dotnet ef database update
```

Testing CRUD Operations: Use Swagger or Postman to test the API endpoints for adding, retrieving, updating, and deleting books and authors.

This hands-on project demonstrated how to build a data-driven Library Management System using EF Core, following best practices with the Repository and Unit of Work patterns. The approach provided a structured and maintainable data access layer, facilitating efficient CRUD operations and enabling a scalable, modular application architecture suitable for real-world data-centric applications.

Testing and Debugging in C# 8

I **mportance of Testing in Software Development**
Testing is a cornerstone of successful software development, ensuring that applications perform as intended, meet user expectations, and remain reliable under various conditions. By identifying defects early, testing helps developers produce high-quality software, maintain code integrity, and minimize costly bug fixes after deployment. In a rapidly evolving industry where software complexity is increasing, testing has become indispensable for delivering robust, maintainable, and scalable applications.

Key Benefits of Testing in Software Development

1. **Error Detection and Prevention**: Testing reveals defects that may otherwise go unnoticed. By identifying issues early in the development cycle, testing allows for timely fixes, reducing the risk of major bugs in production. Catching errors during development is far more cost-effective than post-release fixes.

2. **Improved Code Quality**: Quality software doesn't just work well in one scenario; it handles a wide range of cases effectively. Testing ensures that each component functions correctly, adheres to standards, and integrates smoothly with other parts of the application. Unit tests, for example, confirm that specific functions produce expected outputs, while integration tests verify that modules interact seamlessly.

3. **Reliability and Performance**: Reliable software handles high traffic, supports heavy workloads, and provides stable performance over time.

Testing uncovers performance bottlenecks and stress points, helping developers optimize code and configure resources for resilience.

4. **Documentation for Code Understanding**: Tests serve as an additional form of documentation, clarifying how specific modules are intended to work. New developers can refer to tests to understand the application's functionality, expected outputs, and use cases, which speeds up onboarding and reduces misinterpretations.

5. **Validation of User Requirements**: Testing validates that software meets business requirements and user expectations. Acceptance tests, in particular, confirm that features work as expected from a user perspective, ensuring that the software aligns with real-world use cases and stakeholder requirements.

6. **Enhanced Security**: Security testing is essential in protecting user data and application integrity. Testing for vulnerabilities like SQL injection, cross-site scripting, and data leaks ensures that the application is robust against security threats, safeguarding both users and organizations.

Types of Software Testing and Their Role in Development

Different types of testing target various aspects of software quality. Each has its role in confirming that the software performs well across functional, performance, and security dimensions.

1. **Unit Testing**: Unit testing focuses on individual components or functions to ensure they work correctly. By isolating each function, unit tests quickly identify issues at a granular level, making them highly effective for verifying business logic and data processing.

2. **Integration Testing**: Integration tests verify the interactions between multiple components or systems. These tests check that modules or services function as a cohesive unit, identifying issues that might arise from data mismatches or communication errors between components.

3. **System Testing**: System testing evaluates the software in its entirety, validating that all integrated parts function correctly as a whole. System tests ensure that the software performs as expected within the given

environment, covering end-to-end scenarios.

4. **Acceptance Testing**: Acceptance testing confirms that the software meets user expectations and business requirements. Conducted from a user's perspective, acceptance tests often involve real-world scenarios to validate functionality, usability, and adherence to requirements.

5. **Performance Testing**: Performance testing measures the responsiveness, speed, and stability of an application under various conditions. This type of testing includes load testing, stress testing, and endurance testing to ensure the software remains efficient and stable even under heavy usage.

6. **Security Testing**: Security testing identifies vulnerabilities within the application to ensure data protection, user privacy, and compliance with security standards. Tests in this category often focus on authentication, authorization, data encryption, and threat mitigation.

Testing in the Software Development Lifecycle (SDLC)

Testing is not a one-time task but an integral part of the Software Development Lifecycle (SDLC). Incorporating testing at each stage improves the overall quality and helps in achieving a stable release.

1. **Requirement Analysis**: Even before coding begins, teams should define the requirements and establish criteria for acceptance tests. This ensures that development aligns with user expectations and business needs.

2. **Design Phase**: During design, developers can identify potential issues and establish testing strategies, determining the most effective testing types and tools for the project.

3. **Development and Coding**: In this phase, developers write unit tests alongside the code to verify individual components. Test-driven development (TDD) can guide this process, ensuring that code is tested continuously as it's written.

4. **Integration and System Testing**: Once components are integrated, teams conduct integration and system testing to validate the software

as a whole. This phase verifies that the software meets functional and non-functional requirements.

5. **Acceptance and Deployment**: Before deployment, acceptance tests ensure that the software fulfills user requirements and business objectives. After deployment, regression tests ensure that updates or new features do not introduce new bugs.

6. **Maintenance**: During maintenance, regression and performance tests verify that updates and patches work seamlessly with existing features. Continuous testing helps ensure that the software remains robust over time.

Automation in Testing: Accelerating Development and Improving Consistency

Automated testing plays a pivotal role in modern software development by accelerating the testing process, improving accuracy, and enabling continuous integration and continuous deployment (CI/CD). Automated tests are ideal for repetitive tasks, large datasets, and complex scenarios that would otherwise be time-consuming to execute manually.

Benefits of Test Automation

- **Efficiency**: Automated tests run faster and can be executed multiple times across different environments, saving time and resources.
- **Consistency**: Automated tests provide consistent results, reducing human error and ensuring that tests are executed precisely every time.
- **Scalability**: Automated tests scale easily, supporting large projects where manual testing would be infeasible.
- **CI/CD Integration**: Automation allows testing to become a seamless part of the CI/CD pipeline, where tests are run automatically on every commit, ensuring immediate feedback on new code changes.

Types of Automated Testing

1. **Unit Test Automation**: Automated unit tests are invaluable for

verifying individual components. Tools like xUnit, NUnit, or MSTest in C# enable developers to automate unit tests.

2. **UI Test Automation**: Automated UI tests simulate user interactions, checking that the application behaves correctly from an end-user perspective. Tools like Selenium and Cypress help automate these tests.

3. **API Test Automation**: Automated API tests validate data exchanges between system components, ensuring reliable communication and data integrity. Postman and RestSharp are popular choices for API testing.

4. **Performance Test Automation**: Tools like JMeter and LoadRunner automate performance tests to evaluate application response and stability under varying loads.

Challenges in Software Testing

While testing is essential, it also comes with challenges, especially as applications grow in complexity.

1. **Test Maintenance**: As software evolves, test cases must be updated to reflect new functionalities and requirements. This requires regular reviews and updates to maintain accurate tests.

2. **Balancing Coverage and Resources**: Achieving complete test coverage is often impractical due to time and budget constraints. Prioritizing critical features and functionalities is essential for efficient testing.

3. **Choosing the Right Tests to Automate**: Not all tests are suited for automation. Deciding which tests provide the highest ROI when automated helps avoid unnecessary complexity.

4. **Handling Interdependent Modules**: Complex applications with interdependent modules require careful management to ensure that changes don't disrupt functionality in other parts of the application.

Testing is a vital part of the software development process, providing the foundation for delivering quality applications that meet user needs and business goals. By identifying defects early, validating requirements, and verifying performance, testing helps reduce risks, improve software reliability, and enhance user satisfaction. As applications continue to evolve in complexity, the importance of testing grows, making it essential for developers to adopt rigorous testing practices and integrate automation for scalable, efficient testing processes.

Unit Testing with xUnit and NUnit

Unit testing is a fundamental part of software quality assurance, focused on validating that individual components of an application work as intended. Unit tests isolate specific sections of code (typically functions or methods) to verify their correctness under various conditions. In the .NET ecosystem, **xUnit** and **NUnit** are two popular frameworks for writing and running unit tests. Both are widely used due to their rich feature sets, ease of integration, and compatibility with .NET Core and .NET Framework.

This section provides an in-depth guide to unit testing with xUnit and NUnit, covering setup, writing and organizing tests, and exploring best practices for creating effective and maintainable tests.

Why Use xUnit and NUnit for Unit Testing?

Both xUnit and NUnit are open-source testing frameworks designed for .NET applications, offering similar core functionalities. They provide:

- **Attributes** for marking test methods and managing test cases.
- **Assertions** to verify expected results.
- **Support for Test Runners** that allow tests to be executed in development environments or CI/CD pipelines.
- **Parameterization** and **data-driven tests** to cover a range of test scenarios with minimal code duplication.

xUnit Overview

xUnit is a lightweight, opinionated testing framework designed to enhance the developer experience by enforcing best practices in test design. It is the default testing framework for .NET Core projects, integrated directly into Visual Studio.

Key Features of xUnit

- **Theory and Inline Data Attributes**: Simplify data-driven testing with [Theory] and [InlineData] attributes.
- **Constructor Injection**: Inject dependencies into test classes using constructor parameters, supporting more flexible test configurations.
- **Flexible Assertions**: Offers a comprehensive suite of assertions, making it easy to validate conditions across a wide range of scenarios.

NUnit Overview

NUnit is a mature, flexible testing framework for .NET, popular for its versatility and comprehensive features. It supports both .NET Framework and .NET Core, making it ideal for legacy and cross-platform testing.

Key Features of NUnit

- **Parameterized Tests**: Supports [TestCase] for data-driven testing, enabling multiple inputs and expected outputs within a single test method.
- **Test Fixtures and Setup Methods**: Use [TestFixture] and [SetUp] to define initialization and teardown operations for test groups.
- **Asserts and Constraints**: Offers fluent assertions and a constraint-based model, making assertions more expressive and readable.

Setting Up xUnit and NUnit in a .NET Project

Installing xUnit or NUnit

For xUnit: Install xUnit through NuGet.

```bash
dotnet add package xunit
dotnet add package xunit.runner.visualstudio  # For Visual Studio
```

support

For NUnit: Install NUnit and the NUnit test runner.

bash

```
dotnet add package NUnit
dotnet add package NUnit3TestAdapter  # For Visual Studio support
```

Once installed, xUnit and NUnit can be used interchangeably, depending on team preference and project requirements.

Writing Unit Tests with xUnit

Let's create a sample class, Calculator, with basic arithmetic methods and write tests using xUnit.

Calculator Class Example

csharp

```
public class Calculator
{
    public int Add(int a, int b) => a + b;
    public int Subtract(int a, int b) => a - b;
    public int Multiply(int a, int b) => a * b;
    public double Divide(int a, int b) => b != 0 ? (double)a / b :
    throw new DivideByZeroException();
}
```

xUnit Tests for Calculator

csharp

```
using Xunit;

public class CalculatorTests
{
```

```
private readonly Calculator _calculator;

public CalculatorTests()
{
    _calculator = new Calculator();
}

[Fact]
public void Add_ShouldReturnCorrectSum()
{
    var result = _calculator.Add(2, 3);
    Assert.Equal(5, result);
}

[Theory]
[InlineData(4, 2, 2)]
[InlineData(10, 5, 5)]
[InlineData(9, 3, 3)]
public void Divide_ShouldReturnCorrectQuotient(int dividend,
int divisor, double expected)
{
    var result = _calculator.Divide(dividend, divisor);
    Assert.Equal(expected, result);
}

[Fact]
public void Divide_ByZero_ShouldThrowDivideByZeroException()
{
    Assert.Throws<DivideByZeroException>(() =>
    _calculator.Divide(10, 0));
}
}
```

- **[Fact]**: Marks a standard test method.
- **[Theory]** and **[InlineData]**: Used for data-driven testing, allowing multiple sets of input values.

Writing Unit Tests with NUnit

The same Calculator class can be tested using NUnit with similar syntax but slightly different attributes.

NUnit Tests for Calculator

csharp

```csharp
using NUnit.Framework;

[TestFixture]
public class CalculatorTests
{
    private Calculator _calculator;

    [SetUp]
    public void Setup()
    {
        _calculator = new Calculator();
    }

    [Test]
    public void Add_ShouldReturnCorrectSum()
    {
        var result = _calculator.Add(2, 3);
        Assert.AreEqual(5, result);
    }

    [TestCase(4, 2, 2)]
    [TestCase(10, 5, 5)]
    [TestCase(9, 3, 3)]
    public void Divide_ShouldReturnCorrectQuotient(int dividend,
    int divisor, double expected)
    {
        var result = _calculator.Divide(dividend, divisor);
        Assert.AreEqual(expected, result);
    }

    [Test]
    public void Divide_ByZero_ShouldThrowDivideByZeroException()
    {
```

```
        Assert.Throws<DivideByZeroException>(() =>
        _calculator.Divide(10, 0));
    }
}
```

- **[Test]**: Marks a test method in NUnit.
- **[TestCase]**: Specifies data-driven parameters for a single test method, allowing multiple test scenarios with different inputs.
- **[SetUp]**: Initializes resources before each test is run, similar to a constructor in xUnit.

Assertions in xUnit and NUnit

Assertions verify expected conditions within tests. Both frameworks offer a wide range of assertion methods.

Equality Assertions:

- xUnit: Assert.Equal(expected, actual)
- NUnit: Assert.AreEqual(expected, actual)

Exception Assertions:

- xUnit: Assert.Throws<ExceptionType>(() => Method())
- NUnit: Assert.Throws<ExceptionType>(() => Method())

True/False Assertions:

- xUnit: Assert.True(condition)
- NUnit: Assert.IsTrue(condition)

Null Assertions:

- xUnit: Assert.Null(object)

- NUnit: Assert.IsNull(object)

Running Tests with xUnit and NUnit in Visual Studio

1. **Run Tests**: Use the Test Explorer in Visual Studio or run tests from the command line with dotnet test.
2. **View Results**: Test Explorer displays the results, showing passed, failed, and skipped tests with detailed error messages for each failure.
3. **Debugging**: Both xUnit and NUnit support test debugging, allowing developers to step through test code to identify and fix issues.

Best Practices for Unit Testing with xUnit and NUnit

1. **Isolate Tests**: Each test should be independent, relying solely on the method being tested, with no dependencies on other tests or shared state.
2. **Write Readable Tests**: Test names should clearly describe the scenario and expected outcome, e.g., Add_ShouldReturnCorrectSum.
3. **Use Data-Driven Tests**: For multiple inputs, use [Theory] and [Inline-Data] in xUnit or [TestCase] in NUnit to avoid duplicating similar test code.
4. **Avoid Hardcoded Dependencies**: For components that interact with external systems (e.g., databases, APIs), use mocks or stubs to isolate the unit being tested.
5. **Clean Up Resources**: Ensure that resources are cleaned up after each test using Dispose in xUnit or [TearDown] in NUnit, especially for disposable resources.

xUnit and NUnit provide powerful tools for writing unit tests in .NET applications, offering attributes, assertions, and data-driven testing capabilities that streamline the testing process. By adopting best practices and utilizing xUnit and NUnit effectively, developers can create robust, maintainable tests that improve software quality, reduce bugs, and support continuous integration efforts. Whether you choose xUnit or NUnit depends on project requirements and personal preference, but both frameworks deliver reliable, developer-friendly experiences for writing high-quality unit tests in C#.

Writing Effective Integration Tests

Integration tests validate the interaction between multiple components or systems within an application, ensuring that individual parts work together as expected. Unlike unit tests, which isolate specific methods, integration tests focus on verifying that dependencies interact correctly in a more realistic environment, such as a database, external API, or service. Writing effective integration tests requires a strategy that balances thoroughness with maintainability, ensuring that these tests add value without becoming fragile or overly complex.

The Role of Integration Testing in Software Development

Integration tests bridge the gap between unit tests and end-to-end tests by focusing on specific interactions between modules or external systems. These tests are invaluable for confirming:

1. **Inter-module Interactions**: Components within the application communicate and handle data correctly.
2. **External Dependencies**: Interactions with external services, APIs, and databases are functioning as expected.
3. **End-to-End Workflows**: Workflows or use cases that span multiple modules complete successfully.
4. **Regression Detection**: Integration tests help detect unintended side effects in connected systems when code changes are introduced.

Key Principles of Effective Integration Testing

1. **Test Realistic Scenarios**: Integration tests should mimic real-world

scenarios, reflecting actual user flows and system interactions.

2. **Balance Granularity**: Test specific interactions without encompassing the entire application. Keep tests focused on inter-component dependencies, not the complete end-to-end functionality.

3. **Ensure Isolation**: Maintain a clean, isolated test environment to ensure consistent results. This may involve setting up a dedicated test database or mock server.

4. **Optimize for Performance**: Integration tests are inherently slower than unit tests, so prioritize key interactions to reduce run times.

5. **Automate Cleanups**: Clean up test data and reset external states to avoid interference with subsequent tests.

Example Scenario: Integration Testing for a Bookstore Application

For this example, we'll develop integration tests for a **Bookstore Application** that consists of a **Book** service and an **Author** service. These services interact with a SQL database and provide REST API endpoints for basic CRUD operations.

Application Components

1. **Book Service**: Manages books in the database, with endpoints for adding, retrieving, and updating book details.

2. **Author Service**: Manages author information, with endpoints for creating and fetching authors associated with books.

Setting Up the Integration Test Environment

Integration tests require a well-prepared environment, typically with access to a database and any other external services the application relies on.

1. **In-Memory or Test Database**: Use an in-memory database like SQLite or a dedicated test database to keep the tests isolated from production data.

2. **Dependency Injection (DI)**: Configure DI to inject mock or test-specific dependencies into the application, such as mock external APIs.

3. **Data Seeding**: Seed the test database with data specific to each test case to maintain consistency and reproducibility.

Configuring the Test Environment
Add Microsoft.EntityFrameworkCore.InMemory for an in-memory database or set up a SQLite test database.

bash

```
dotnet add package Microsoft.EntityFrameworkCore.InMemory
```

Writing Integration Tests with xUnit
In this section, we'll use xUnit to write integration tests for the Bookstore Application, focusing on CRUD operations across the Book and Author services.

Sample Models
Book Model

csharp

```
public class Book
{
    public int BookId { get; set; }
    public string Title { get; set; } = string.Empty;
    public int AuthorId { get; set; }
    public Author? Author { get; set; }
}
```

Author Model

csharp

```
public class Author
{
    public int AuthorId { get; set; }
```

```csharp
public string Name { get; set; } = string.Empty;
public List<Book> Books { get; set; } = new();
}
```

Setting Up the Integration Test Class

To set up integration tests, create a test fixture that initializes the test database and seeds it with sample data.

Integration Test Fixture

csharp

```csharp
using Microsoft.EntityFrameworkCore;
using Xunit;

public class BookstoreTestFixture : IDisposable
{
    public AppDbContext Context { get; private set; }

    public BookstoreTestFixture()
    {
        var options = new DbContextOptionsBuilder<AppDbContext>()
            .UseInMemoryDatabase(databaseName: "TestDatabase")
            .Options;

        Context = new AppDbContext(options);
        SeedDatabase();
    }

    private void SeedDatabase()
    {
        Context.Authors.Add(new Author { AuthorId = 1, Name =
        "George Orwell" });
        Context.Books.Add(new Book { BookId = 1, Title = "1984",
        AuthorId = 1 });
        Context.SaveChanges();
    }
```

```csharp
    public void Dispose()
    {
        Context.Dispose();
    }
}
```

Setting Up the Test Class

```
csharp
```

```csharp
public class BookServiceIntegrationTests :
IClassFixture<BookstoreTestFixture>
{
    private readonly AppDbContext _context;

    public BookServiceIntegrationTests(BookstoreTestFixture
    fixture)
    {
        _context = fixture.Context;
    }
}
```

Writing Integration Test Methods
Each integration test method simulates a real-world scenario, verifying expected behavior across services and data layers.

Testing Book Retrieval with Author Details
This test verifies that retrieving a book includes the associated author's details.

```
csharp
```

```csharp
[Fact]
public async Task GetBook_ShouldReturnBookWithAuthorDetails()
{
    var book = await _context.Books
```

```
        .Include(b => b.Author)
        .FirstOrDefaultAsync(b => b.BookId == 1);

    Assert.NotNull(book);
    Assert.Equal("1984", book.Title);
    Assert.NotNull(book.Author);
    Assert.Equal("George Orwell", book.Author!.Name);
}
```

- **Include**: Use Include to eagerly load related data (Author) when retrieving Book details.

Testing Adding a New Book

This test ensures that adding a new book correctly updates the database and associates it with an author.

csharp

```
[Fact]
public async Task AddBook_ShouldSaveBookToDatabase()
{
    var newBook = new Book { Title = "Animal Farm", AuthorId = 1 };

    await _context.Books.AddAsync(newBook);
    await _context.SaveChangesAsync();

    var bookInDb = await _context.Books.FirstOrDefaultAsync(b =>
    b.Title == "Animal Farm");
    Assert.NotNull(bookInDb);
    Assert.Equal("Animal Farm", bookInDb!.Title);
    Assert.Equal(1, bookInDb.AuthorId);
}
```

- **AddAsync and SaveChangesAsync**: Insert a new record into the in-memory database and verify its existence.

Testing Book Update

This test verifies that an existing book's details can be updated and persisted.

```csharp
[Fact]
public async Task UpdateBook_ShouldModifyBookDetails()
{
    var book = await _context.Books.FirstOrDefaultAsync(b =>
    b.BookId == 1);
    Assert.NotNull(book);

    book!.Title = "Nineteen Eighty-Four";
    _context.Books.Update(book);
    await _context.SaveChangesAsync();

    var updatedBook = await _context.Books.FirstOrDefaultAsync(b
    => b.BookId == 1);
    Assert.Equal("Nineteen Eighty-Four", updatedBook!.Title);
}
```

Testing Book Deletion

This test confirms that deleting a book removes it from the database without leaving orphaned data.

```csharp
[Fact]
public async Task DeleteBook_ShouldRemoveBookFromDatabase()
{
    var book = await _context.Books.FirstOrDefaultAsync(b =>
    b.BookId == 1);
    Assert.NotNull(book);

    _context.Books.Remove(book!);
    await _context.SaveChangesAsync();

    var deletedBook = await _context.Books.FindAsync(1);
```

```
    Assert.Null(deletedBook);
}
```

Best Practices for Effective Integration Testing

1. **Keep Tests Focused**: Focus each integration test on verifying specific interactions, like CRUD operations or dependency responses, rather than testing broad workflows.
2. **Mock External Dependencies When Possible**: If your application relies on third-party services, mock those dependencies to prevent network calls, especially in CI/CD environments.
3. **Clean Up After Each Test**: Ensure that each test runs in isolation by resetting the database or using disposable in-memory databases for test data.
4. **Avoid Overlapping with Unit Tests**: Keep unit tests and integration tests distinct; unit tests validate isolated functions, while integration tests confirm component interactions.
5. **Run Integration Tests in CI/CD Pipelines**: Automate integration tests in CI/CD pipelines to catch issues early in development and ensure consistency across environments.

Integration tests ensure that multiple components and dependencies in your application work together as expected. By setting up isolated test environments, using in-memory databases or mocks for dependencies, and following best practices, developers can write effective, reliable integration tests. These tests help prevent complex issues from reaching production, leading to more stable applications and a smoother user experience.

Debugging Techniques for Asynchronous Code
Asynchronous programming in C# offers powerful capabilities for building responsive, non-blocking applications. However, the asynchronous flow can

make debugging more challenging, as tasks may execute in parallel, suspend, or resume unpredictably. Traditional debugging approaches often fall short in asynchronous contexts, necessitating specialized techniques to track and diagnose issues effectively.

This section provides strategies for debugging asynchronous code, covering common pitfalls, the tools available, and techniques to manage and understand the flow of asynchronous operations.

1. Understanding Common Pitfalls in Asynchronous Code

Before diving into debugging techniques, it's essential to understand some of the unique issues that can arise in asynchronous code:

- **Deadlocks**: Often caused by blocking an asynchronous call, typically by using .Wait() or .Result in synchronous code, which can prevent asynchronous methods from completing.
- **Unobserved Exceptions**: Exceptions thrown in asynchronous tasks may not be immediately visible, as they can be suppressed or logged later.
- **Lost Context**: With asynchronous code, context switching can lead to unexpected results, particularly when tasks resume on different threads or fail to capture the correct state.

2. Using Visual Studio Debugging Tools

Visual Studio provides a suite of tools specifically designed for debugging asynchronous code, helping developers visualize and understand complex async flows.

2.1 Tasks Window

The Tasks window (available in Debug > Windows > Task) in Visual Studio displays all active tasks, their states, and their stack traces. It's particularly helpful for monitoring tasks that are awaiting completion or have encountered errors.

- **Diagnosing Task Status**: Use the Tasks window to see if any tasks are in an unexpected state, such as "Faulted" or "Canceled."

333

- **Task Stack Traces**: View stack traces of individual tasks to understand where they originated and what's causing delays or failures.

2.2 Call Stack Window

In asynchronous code, the Call Stack window helps track how the current code execution reached a specific point. When a breakpoint is hit, the stack trace may look different than in synchronous code due to "await" boundaries, but Visual Studio allows viewing the chain of awaited calls.

- **Understanding Await Boundaries**: Look for sections labeled [Async Call] in the call stack to trace asynchronous execution paths, even if they span different methods or classes.
- **Navigate Across Await Calls**: Step through async calls by stepping over await statements to see where tasks resume or switch contexts.

2.3 Async Debugging Enhancements (Parallel Stacks Window)

The Parallel Stacks window shows a graphical view of parallel tasks and their relationships, which is especially useful when multiple asynchronous methods are running concurrently.

- **Visualizing Task Relationships**: This view helps identify if tasks are dependent on each other or if there are potential deadlocks.
- **Tracing Task Execution Flow**: You can trace where each task is currently running, making it easier to see how asynchronous code paths interweave.

3. Logging and Tracing Asynchronous Operations

Logging is critical in async debugging, as it captures the state of operations over time. When combined with structured logging and tracing tools, it provides an invaluable timeline of events, helping to reconstruct the sequence that led to an issue.

3.1 Use Structured Logging with Contextual Information

Adding contextual information to log entries is essential in asynchronous code. Logging libraries like Serilog and NLog support structured logging, allowing you to add metadata (like task ID, timestamp, or user context) to each log entry.

Example: Adding Contextual Information in Async Logs

```csharp
using Serilog;

public async Task ProcessDataAsync(int dataId)
{
    Log.Information("Processing data with ID {DataId}", dataId);
    await SomeAsyncMethod(dataId);
    Log.Information("Completed processing data with ID {DataId}",
    dataId);
}
```

3.2 Implement Trace Correlation IDs

For applications handling multiple requests or tasks, generate and attach a correlation ID for each workflow. This unique identifier helps track the entire lifecycle of an asynchronous operation, especially in distributed systems.

4. Breakpoints and Exception Handling in Async Code

Using breakpoints and handling exceptions effectively is essential for debugging async code without losing track of asynchronous execution flow.

4.1 Setting Conditional Breakpoints

Conditional breakpoints trigger based on specific conditions, such as when a variable reaches a particular value. This technique can be especially useful in async code to isolate issues within specific async paths.

- **Example**: Set a conditional breakpoint in a method based on a task's status, such as if (task.IsFaulted).

4.2 Handling Unobserved Exceptions

Exceptions in async code are often "unobserved," meaning they don't immediately cause the application to fail. To catch unobserved exceptions:

- Enable Throw on all CLR exceptions in Visual Studio's Exception Settings.
- Wrap asynchronous calls in try-catch blocks to capture exceptions as they occur.

Example: Handling Exceptions in Async Code

csharp

```
public async Task RunAsync()
{
    try
    {
        await SomeTaskThatMightFailAsync();
    }
    catch (Exception ex)
    {
        Log.Error(ex, "Exception occurred in asynchronous task");
    }
}
```

5. Handling Deadlocks in Asynchronous Code

Deadlocks in asynchronous code are often caused by improper use of .Result or .Wait(). Avoid these blocking calls in async methods; instead, let async tasks complete naturally with await.

5.1 Avoid Mixing Synchronous and Asynchronous Code

Combining synchronous code (like .Result or .Wait()) with async code can lead to deadlocks. Whenever possible, refactor code to use await exclusively in async methods.

Example: Refactor to Avoid Deadlocks

csharp

```
// Problematic code that can lead to deadlock
public void Run()
{
    var result = SomeAsyncMethod().Result; // Avoid .Result in
    async code
}

// Refactored to async-friendly code
public async Task RunAsync()
{
    var result = await SomeAsyncMethod();
}
```

5.2 Configure Task Schedulers and Synchronization Contexts

Some async methods can hang when run on the UI thread, as they attempt to resume on the same synchronization context. For UI applications, configure ConfigureAwait(false) to continue execution on any available thread.

```csharp
await SomeMethodAsync().ConfigureAwait(false);
```

6. Debugging with Third-Party Async Tools

In addition to Visual Studio's built-in tools, there are third-party libraries and tools that help debug async code effectively:

6.1 AsyncDiagnosticSource for Async Call Tracing

AsyncDiagnosticSource provides tracing for asynchronous calls, offering a clearer view of async flows. It integrates with diagnostic tools and logs async call paths, helping developers track issues in complex workflows.

6.2 Polly for Handling Async Failures

Polly is a resilience library that provides retry policies for async code, useful for handling transient failures in async calls. By configuring retry logic, you can manage scenarios where async methods encounter network or API delays, allowing them to retry without intervention.

Example: Using Polly to Retry Async Operations

```csharp
var retryPolicy = Policy
    .Handle<SomeTransientException>()
    .RetryAsync(3);

await retryPolicy.ExecuteAsync(() => SomeAsyncMethod());
```

7. Using Debug.WriteLine for Quick Async Debugging

For lightweight async debugging, Debug.WriteLine is an efficient way to print messages and task states in real-time during asynchronous execution. This is helpful for tracking variables and workflow progress, especially in small projects or when you need a quick check without full logging.

```csharp
public async Task PerformOperationAsync()
{
    Debug.WriteLine("Starting operation...");
    await SomeAsyncTask();
    Debug.WriteLine("Operation completed.");
}
```

Debugging asynchronous code requires a combination of specialized tools, structured logging, and an understanding of async patterns. Visual Studio's Tasks, Call Stack, and Parallel Stacks windows provide essential insights, while structured logging, conditional breakpoints, and third-party libraries offer further control. By adopting these techniques, you can effectively navigate the complexities of async debugging, ensuring more reliable and performant applications.

Hands-On Project: Building and Testing a Robust Application Module

In this project, we'll create and test a **User Management Module** for a hypothetical application, focusing on building a robust, testable, and maintainable component. This module will support creating, retrieving, updating, and deleting user records while incorporating authentication and validation. By implementing thorough unit and integration testing, we'll ensure the module is reliable and robust.

Project Overview: User Management Module

The User Management Module will consist of:

1. **User Service**: Handles core business logic for managing user data.
2. **User Repository**: Interacts with the database to perform CRUD operations.
3. **Authentication and Validation**: Ensures secure and valid user data handling.
4. **Tests**: Includes unit tests for individual components and integration tests for the entire module.

Step 1: Setting Up the Project and Dependencies
Create a New ASP.NET Core Web API Project:

- Initialize the project in the terminal.

bash

```
dotnet new webapi -n UserManagementModule
```

Add Entity Framework Core and In-Memory Database:

- Install EF Core and set up an in-memory database to use for testing purposes.

```bash
bash
```

```bash
dotnet add package Microsoft.EntityFrameworkCore
dotnet add package Microsoft.EntityFrameworkCore.InMemory
```

Install xUnit and Moq for Testing:

- Install xUnit for testing and Moq for mocking dependencies in unit tests.

```bash
bash
```

```bash
dotnet add package xunit
dotnet add package Moq
```

Step 2: Designing the Data Model and Repository

Define a User model with attributes for essential details and a UserRepository to manage database interactions.

User Model

```csharp
csharp

using System.ComponentModel.DataAnnotations;

public class User
{
    public int UserId { get; set; }

    [Required, MaxLength(100)]
    public string Username { get; set; } = string.Empty;

    [Required]
    public string PasswordHash { get; set; } = string.Empty;

    [Required, MaxLength(100)]
```

```csharp
    public string Email { get; set; } = string.Empty;

    public DateTime CreatedAt { get; set; } = DateTime.UtcNow;
}
```

User Repository Interface

csharp

```csharp
public interface IUserRepository
{
    Task<IEnumerable<User>> GetAllAsync();
    Task<User?> GetByIdAsync(int userId);
    Task AddAsync(User user);
    Task UpdateAsync(User user);
    Task DeleteAsync(int userId);
}
```

User Repository Implementation

csharp

```csharp
using Microsoft.EntityFrameworkCore;

public class UserRepository : IUserRepository
{
    private readonly AppDbContext _context;

    public UserRepository(AppDbContext context)
    {
        _context = context;
    }

    public async Task<IEnumerable<User>> GetAllAsync() => await
    _context.Users.ToListAsync();

    public async Task<User?> GetByIdAsync(int userId) => await
    _context.Users.FindAsync(userId);
```

```csharp
public async Task AddAsync(User user)
{
    await _context.Users.AddAsync(user);
    await _context.SaveChangesAsync();
}

public async Task UpdateAsync(User user)
{
    _context.Users.Update(user);
    await _context.SaveChangesAsync();
}

public async Task DeleteAsync(int userId)
{
    var user = await _context.Users.FindAsync(userId);
    if (user != null)
    {
        _context.Users.Remove(user);
        await _context.SaveChangesAsync();
    }
}
}
```

Step 3: Implementing the User Service with Validation

The UserService will encapsulate core business logic, including validations and hashing for secure password storage.

User Service

```csharp
csharp

using System.Security.Cryptography;
using System.Text;

public class UserService
{
    private readonly IUserRepository _userRepository;
```

```csharp
public UserService(IUserRepository userRepository)
{
    _userRepository = userRepository;
}

public async Task<IEnumerable<User>> GetAllUsersAsync() =>
await _userRepository.GetAllAsync();

public async Task<User?> GetUserByIdAsync(int userId) => await
_userRepository.GetByIdAsync(userId);

public async Task AddUserAsync(string username, string
password, string email)
{
    var user = new User
    {
        Username = username,
        PasswordHash = HashPassword(password),
        Email = email
    };
    await _userRepository.AddAsync(user);
}

public async Task UpdateUserAsync(User user) => await
_userRepository.UpdateAsync(user);

public async Task DeleteUserAsync(int userId) => await
_userRepository.DeleteAsync(userId);

private string HashPassword(string password)
{
    using var sha256 = SHA256.Create();
    var hashedBytes =
    sha256.ComputeHash(Encoding.UTF8.GetBytes(password));
    return BitConverter.ToString(hashedBytes).Replace("-",
    "").ToLower();
}
}
```

Step 4: Writing Unit Tests for the User Service

343

Unit tests ensure the UserService methods work as intended. We'll mock the UserRepository to isolate the UserService.

Sample Unit Test for UserService

csharp

```csharp
using Xunit;
using Moq;

public class UserServiceTests
{
    private readonly Mock<IUserRepository> _mockRepository;
    private readonly UserService _userService;

    public UserServiceTests()
    {
        _mockRepository = new Mock<IUserRepository>();
        _userService = new UserService(_mockRepository.Object);
    }

    [Fact]
    public async Task AddUserAsync_ShouldCallAddAsyncOnRepository()
    {
        await _userService.AddUserAsync("testuser", "password123",
        "testuser@example.com");
        _mockRepository.Verify(repo =>
        repo.AddAsync(It.IsAny<User>()), Times.Once);
    }

    [Fact]
    public async Task
    GetUserByIdAsync_ShouldReturnUser_WhenUserExists()
    {
        var user = new User { UserId = 1, Username = "testuser" };
        _mockRepository.Setup(repo =>
        repo.GetByIdAsync(1)).ReturnsAsync(user);

        var result = await _userService.GetUserByIdAsync(1);
```

```csharp
        Assert.NotNull(result);
        Assert.Equal("testuser", result.Username);
    }
}
```

Step 5: Writing Integration Tests

Integration tests validate that the UserService and UserRepository work together as expected, with a focus on end-to-end functionality.

Setup Integration Test Fixture

```csharp
csharp

public class UserManagementTestFixture : IDisposable
{
    public AppDbContext Context { get; }

    public UserManagementTestFixture()
    {
        var options = new DbContextOptionsBuilder<AppDbContext>()
            .UseInMemoryDatabase(databaseName: "TestDatabase")
            .Options;

        Context = new AppDbContext(options);
    }

    public void Dispose() => Context.Dispose();
}
```

Integration Test for User Creation

```csharp
csharp

public class UserIntegrationTests :
IClassFixture<UserManagementTestFixture>
{
    private readonly UserManagementTestFixture _fixture;
```

```
    private readonly UserService _userService;

    public UserIntegrationTests(UserManagementTestFixture fixture)
    {
        _fixture = fixture;
        var userRepository = new UserRepository(_fixture.Context);
        _userService = new UserService(userRepository);
    }

    [Fact]
    public async Task AddUserAsync_ShouldSaveUserToDatabase()
    {
        await _userService.AddUserAsync("newuser",
        "securepassword", "newuser@example.com");

        var user = await
        _fixture.Context.Users.FirstOrDefaultAsync(u => u.Username
        == "newuser");

        Assert.NotNull(user);
        Assert.Equal("newuser", user!.Username);
        Assert.Equal("newuser@example.com", user.Email);
    }
}
```

Step 6: Running and Verifying Tests

1. **Run Tests**: Use the command dotnet test to execute all unit and integration tests.
2. **View Results**: Confirm that all tests pass, verifying that both isolated and integrated functionality work as expected.
3. **Debug Failed Tests**: For any failed tests, use breakpoints and logging to track down and resolve issues.

Best Practices for Building and Testing a Robust Application Module

1. **Mock External Dependencies in Unit Tests**: Use mocks to isolate

service functionality, ensuring that unit tests focus on business logic.

2. **Use In-Memory Database for Integration Tests**: An in-memory database ensures a clean, isolated environment that avoids interference with production data.

3. **Seed Test Data for Consistency**: Seed specific data in the test environment to ensure that integration tests are consistent and repeatable.

4. **Validate Security Practices**: In services that handle sensitive data, such as passwords, use hashing and secure storage practices, even in test environments.

5. **Automate Tests in CI/CD**: Ensure that tests are automated in a continuous integration pipeline to catch issues early in the development process.

This project demonstrated how to build and test a robust User Management Module using a combination of unit and integration tests. By applying a layered approach with a well-defined repository and service, we created a maintainable, testable, and scalable module. The combination of unit tests for isolated functionality and integration tests for end-to-end interactions ensures that this module can be deployed with confidence, supporting a resilient and secure user management system.

Optimizing Performance in C# 8 Applications

Understanding C# 8 Memory Management and Garbage Collection

Memory management is fundamental to optimizing application performance in C#. Efficient use of memory resources directly impacts application responsiveness, scalability, and reliability. In C#, memory management is largely automated through the use of garbage collection, which reclaims memory occupied by objects that are no longer in use. However, understanding how memory is allocated, managed, and reclaimed can empower developers to write code that minimizes unnecessary memory consumption, avoids memory leaks, and leverages garbage collection effectively.

This section provides an in-depth look at memory management in C# 8, focusing on the mechanisms and best practices associated with garbage collection and the ways developers can optimize memory usage.

The Basics of Memory Management in C#

In C#, memory is divided into two primary areas: the **Stack** and the **Heap**. Each serves a unique purpose in how data is stored, managed, and accessed.

Stack:

- Used for storing value types and method call information.
- Memory allocation on the stack is managed in a last-in, first-out (LIFO)

order, making it fast and efficient.

- Typically stores local variables, function parameters, and method return addresses.

Heap:

- Used for storing reference types and dynamically allocated objects.
- Memory on the heap is more flexible but slower to access than the stack, as it requires garbage collection to manage allocations and deallocations.
- Objects on the heap are accessed via references stored on the stack.

Value Types vs. Reference Types:

- **Value Types** (e.g., int, bool, float): Stored directly on the stack, or as part of an object on the heap if they are fields within a reference type.
- **Reference Types** (e.g., class, interface): Stored on the heap, with a reference to the object kept on the stack.

Memory Allocation and Garbage Collection in C#

The garbage collector (GC) is responsible for managing heap memory in C#. Its primary role is to reclaim memory used by objects that are no longer accessible in the application. The GC is designed to run periodically and automatically, but certain conditions can trigger it to run more frequently, depending on the application's memory consumption patterns.

The Phases of Garbage Collection

Garbage collection is typically carried out in three main phases:

1. **Marking**: The GC identifies all objects that are still accessible, marking them as "live." It does this by starting from root references, such as static fields, local variables, and active method parameters, then traversing references to other objects.
2. **Relocating**: After marking, the GC compacts memory by moving

live objects closer together in the heap. This helps reduce memory fragmentation and improves allocation speed for new objects.

3. **Reclaiming**: Unmarked objects (those not referenced by any active code) are considered unreachable and are removed, allowing their memory to be reclaimed.

Generations in Garbage Collection

The .NET garbage collector is a **generational** GC, which categorizes objects by their lifespan:

1. **Generation 0**: Contains short-lived objects, such as temporary variables and loop iterations. These objects are collected frequently.
2. **Generation 1**: Contains objects that have survived at least one collection in Generation 0, acting as a buffer between short-lived and long-lived objects.
3. **Generation 2**: Contains long-lived objects, such as static data and objects that remain in use throughout the application's lifecycle. This generation is collected less frequently.

By organizing objects into generations, the GC can focus on collecting short-lived objects more often, which is typically more efficient, while infrequently collecting long-lived objects that are likely to persist in memory.

Best Practices for Optimizing Memory Management in C# 8

To write memory-efficient applications, developers should consider a range of techniques to help manage memory usage effectively:

1. Minimize Unnecessary Object Creation

Creating unnecessary objects increases pressure on the garbage collector and can lead to memory fragmentation. Avoid excessive instantiation of objects by:

- Using value types for small data structures that don't require dynamic allocation.

- Reusing objects, especially for frequently created types, by leveraging object pooling.

Example of Object Pooling:

```csharp
using System.Buffers;

var pool = ArrayPool<int>.Shared;
int[] array = pool.Rent(100);

// Use the array for computations

pool.Return(array); // Return to pool instead of allowing GC to
handle it
```

2. Use Dispose and the IDisposable Interface for Resource Cleanup

For objects that use unmanaged resources (e.g., file handles, network connections), implementing IDisposable and calling Dispose() helps free resources immediately, rather than waiting for the garbage collector.

Example of IDisposable Implementation:

```csharp
public class FileProcessor : IDisposable
{
    private FileStream _fileStream;

    public FileProcessor(string filePath)
    {
        _fileStream = new FileStream(filePath, FileMode.Open);
    }

    public void Dispose()
    {
```

```
    _fileStream?.Dispose();
  }
}
```

- Use using statements with disposable objects to ensure timely cleanup.
- Implement IDisposable in classes that manage unmanaged resources to help prevent memory leaks.

3. Use Span<T> and Memory<T> for Efficient Memory Access

In C# 8, Span<T> and Memory<T> allow developers to handle data in a way that minimizes heap allocations. Span<T> provides a type-safe view into a contiguous block of memory, making it highly efficient for performance-critical code.

Example Using Span<T>:

```csharp
public void ProcessArray(int[] data)
{
    Span<int> spanData = data;
    for (int i = 0; i < spanData.Length; i++)
    {
        spanData[i] *= 2;
    }
}
```

By using Span<T> and Memory<T>, you avoid copying data, resulting in better performance and reduced memory overhead.

4. Avoid Blocking Asynchronous Code with .Result and .Wait()

Blocking asynchronous code can lead to excessive memory usage and potential deadlocks. Avoid calling .Result or .Wait() on tasks, and use await instead to allow tasks to complete asynchronously, minimizing resource contention.

Example of Async Best Practice:

```csharp
public async Task ProcessDataAsync()
{
    await Task.Run(() => /* CPU-bound task */);
}
```

5. Use Weak References for Cache or Temporary Data

Weak references allow objects to be garbage-collected if they are no longer referenced elsewhere, which is useful for caches or temporary data. Use WeakReference to avoid retaining objects that could otherwise be collected.

Example of a Weak Reference:

```csharp
WeakReference<MyClass> weakRef = new WeakReference<MyClass>(new
MyClass());
```

When using weak references, always check if the object is still available before accessing it.

Profiling and Analyzing Memory Usage in C#

To optimize memory usage effectively, you need to profile and analyze memory consumption. Visual Studio offers tools for understanding memory usage and detecting memory leaks:

Memory Profiler:

- The Memory Profiler in Visual Studio helps analyze memory allocations, identify objects that occupy large portions of memory, and detect memory leaks.
- Use snapshots to compare memory usage before and after specific operations, allowing you to spot trends and improvements.

GC.GetTotalMemory:

- The GC.GetTotalMemory() method provides insights into the current memory usage, which is useful for profiling memory-intensive operations.

```csharp
long memoryUsage = GC.GetTotalMemory(false);
Console.WriteLine($"Memory Usage: {memoryUsage} bytes");
```

Analyze Memory Allocation Patterns:

- Avoid frequent allocations in performance-critical code by analyzing allocation patterns. For example, consider using value types and structures for small, frequently used data.
- Use MemoryCache for data that is frequently accessed but can be discarded if memory is constrained.

Using Explicit Garbage Collection (Advanced Scenarios)

While the garbage collector in C# is automatic, developers can occasionally force garbage collection using GC.Collect(). However, this approach should be used cautiously, as it interrupts application execution and can lead to performance degradation if overused.

```csharp
GC.Collect(); // Forces immediate garbage collection
```

When to Consider Explicit GC:

- After a large object allocation that is no longer needed, especially if the application is memory-constrained.

- In scenarios where memory needs to be freed immediately, such as when switching between memory-intensive tasks.

Memory management in C# 8, with its garbage collection and advanced data structures, offers a robust foundation for handling memory automatically. However, understanding and applying best practices for memory allocation, garbage collection, and efficient data structures like Span<T> and Memory<T> can significantly enhance performance. By implementing strategies such as object pooling, disposable resource management, and using the latest memory-efficient structures, developers can create applications that are not only performant but also resilient and scalable.

Identifying and Resolving Performance Bottlenecks
Performance bottlenecks occur when parts of an application slow down its overall functionality, leading to lag, unresponsiveness, or system resource overuse. Bottlenecks can stem from high CPU usage, memory leaks, inefficient algorithms, slow I/O operations, or frequent database calls. Identifying these issues requires systematic profiling, analysis, and testing. Here, we'll discuss how to spot bottlenecks in a C# application and techniques to resolve them, covering common optimization strategies and tools.

1. Understanding Performance Bottlenecks and Their Types
Performance bottlenecks generally fall into several categories:

- **CPU Bottlenecks**: Caused by compute-intensive operations or inefficient algorithms that demand excessive processing time.
- **Memory Bottlenecks**: Due to high memory allocation, memory leaks, or excessive garbage collection, leading to slower performance.
- **I/O Bottlenecks**: Result from slow file, network, or database operations that block application flow.
- **Concurrency Bottlenecks**: Arise from poorly managed parallel tasks

or contention for shared resources, leading to deadlocks or inefficient task handling.

2. Using Profiling Tools to Identify Bottlenecks

Profiling tools provide critical insights into resource usage, code execution times, and memory allocation, making it easier to pinpoint performance issues.

2.1 Visual Studio Profiler

Visual Studio Profiler provides in-depth analysis capabilities for CPU usage, memory, and I/O. It is integrated with Visual Studio and can be used to:

- Identify slow-running methods and functions.
- Analyze CPU usage and thread management.
- Examine memory allocations to detect high-consumption areas.

2.2 DotTrace and Other Third-Party Profilers

JetBrains' DotTrace is a powerful tool that offers detailed profiling, focusing on CPU usage and time spent in specific code blocks. DotTrace's UI makes it easy to visualize method calls and drill down into code hotspots.

2.3 BenchmarkDotNet for Fine-Grained Analysis

BenchmarkDotNet is useful for micro-optimizations, especially when comparing the performance of different algorithms or methods. It's particularly effective for testing code paths that may introduce delays in a loop or a repetitive task.

Example Setup with BenchmarkDotNet:

```csharp
using BenchmarkDotNet.Attributes;
using BenchmarkDotNet.Running;

public class MyBenchmark
{
    private readonly int[] data = Enumerable.Range(1,
```

```
    1000).ToArray();

    [Benchmark]
    public void MethodA() => MyAlgorithm.MethodA(data);

    [Benchmark]
    public void MethodB() => MyAlgorithm.MethodB(data);
}

public static void Main() => BenchmarkRunner.Run<MyBenchmark>();
```

3. Analyzing Code for Common Bottleneck Patterns

Once potential bottlenecks are identified, it's crucial to understand the reasons behind them. Common bottlenecks include:

3.1 Inefficient Algorithms

Suboptimal algorithms can cause CPU and memory overhead. For instance:

- **Nested Loops**: Often a source of inefficiency, especially when working with large data structures. Consider reducing loop nesting or using efficient data structures.
- **Inefficient LINQ Queries**: LINQ can introduce inefficiencies if used without considering its cost. For example, .Where().Select() chains can be combined or optimized for better performance.

Example: Optimizing a LINQ Query

Before:

```csharp
var results = myData.Where(x => x.IsActive).Select(x =>
x.Name).ToList();
```

After:

```csharp
var results = myData.Where(x => x.IsActive).Select(x =>
x.Name).ToList();
```

3.2 Memory Allocation and Garbage Collection

Frequent allocations and deallocations cause memory fragmentation and strain the garbage collector. To reduce memory pressure:

- Use **object pooling** for reusable objects.
- Avoid unnecessary boxing/unboxing and repeated object creation.

3.3 Blocking I/O Operations

Blocking I/O operations, like file reads, database queries, or network calls, can severely impact performance. Use asynchronous I/O to prevent blocking and batch operations to reduce the number of requests.

Asynchronous I/O Example:

```csharp
public async Task FetchDataAsync()
{
    await Task.WhenAll(FetchDataFromSourceA(),
    FetchDataFromSourceB());
}
```

4. Optimizing Data Access and Storage

Data access, especially with relational databases, is a common bottleneck. Optimization strategies include:

4.1 Optimize Database Queries

- **Indexing**: Ensure that fields frequently used in queries are indexed to speed up search operations.
- **Batch Queries**: Combine multiple queries into one, or use stored

procedures to reduce the number of round-trips to the database.

- **Lazy Loading** vs. **Eager Loading**: In Entity Framework, choose between lazy and eager loading carefully. Eager loading with .Include() can reduce database calls in complex object graphs but may increase memory usage.

4.2 Implement Caching Mechanisms

Caching can drastically reduce the load on the database by storing frequently accessed data in memory.

- **In-memory caching**: Use MemoryCache for frequently accessed data, especially for small or short-lived data.
- **Distributed caching**: In environments with multiple servers, use distributed caching systems like Redis.

Example: Using In-Memory Cache

```csharp
MemoryCache cache = new MemoryCache(new MemoryCacheOptions());
cache.Set("UserId_123", userData, TimeSpan.FromMinutes(30));
```

5. Optimizing Concurrency and Task Parallelism

Concurrency and parallelism can enhance application performance, especially for CPU-bound operations. However, poorly managed concurrency can lead to contention, deadlocks, and inefficient resource use.

5.1 Parallelizing CPU-Bound Tasks

Use the Parallel class or PLINQ for parallel processing in CPU-intensive operations, like data processing or image transformations.

```csharp
Parallel.ForEach(dataList, data =>
{
    ProcessData(data);
```

```
});
```

5.2 Avoiding Locks and Deadlocks

Minimize the use of locks in concurrent code. Consider using lightweight synchronization mechanisms, like SemaphoreSlim, or adopting lock-free patterns.

Example: Using SemaphoreSlim

```csharp
private SemaphoreSlim _semaphore = new SemaphoreSlim(1, 1);

public async Task ProcessTaskAsync()
{
    await _semaphore.WaitAsync();
    try
    {
        await Task.Delay(1000); // Simulating work
    }
    finally
    {
        _semaphore.Release();
    }
}
```

6. Managing Garbage Collection (GC) Impact

The .NET garbage collector handles memory management, but excessive allocations and frequent collections can lead to performance degradation.

6.1 Minimize Large Object Heap (LOH) Allocations

Objects over 85,000 bytes are stored on the Large Object Heap (LOH), which is not compacted automatically. To reduce LOH fragmentation:

- Use pooling for large objects to reduce repeated allocations.
- Avoid creating large arrays repeatedly; reuse arrays where possible.

6.2 Use GC.Collect Sparingly

While GC.Collect() can force garbage collection, overuse can lead to performance penalties. Consider explicit GC calls only in memory-intensive scenarios where releasing memory immediately is crucial.

7. Implementing Real-Time Monitoring

After optimizing the application, real-time monitoring can help catch new performance issues as they arise in production.

7.1 Application Performance Management (APM)

APM tools like **New Relic**, **AppDynamics**, and **Azure Monitor** track response times, throughput, and error rates. They provide insights into application health, highlight slow requests, and identify services causing delays.

7.2 Logging and Metrics Collection

Implement structured logging with tools like **Serilog** and **ElasticSearch** to track performance metrics over time. Collect key metrics, such as request response times, CPU/memory usage, and query times, to understand performance trends.

Identifying and resolving performance bottlenecks is essential to building responsive and efficient C# applications. By systematically profiling, analyzing common bottleneck patterns, optimizing data access, and managing concurrency effectively, developers can minimize delays and enhance overall application performance. Continuous monitoring and testing of optimizations are crucial to maintaining a high-performance application over time.

Practical Tips for Optimizing Asynchronous Operations

Asynchronous programming enhances application responsiveness by allowing tasks to run concurrently, but improper implementation can lead to increased latency, deadlocks, and resource contention. Optimizing asynchronous operations in C# requires understanding how to manage tasks efficiently, minimize resource usage, and avoid common pitfalls. This section provides practical tips to improve the performance of asynchronous operations, covering best practices, concurrency management, and useful C# features for async optimization.

1. Use Asynchronous Methods Properly

The first step in optimizing asynchronous code is to leverage async/await properly. Misusing these keywords can lead to blocked threads or inefficient task execution.

1.1 Avoid .Result and .Wait() on Async Calls

Blocking async calls with .Result or .Wait() can cause deadlocks and prevent asynchronous operations from completing, especially in UI or ASP.NET applications where threads are limited. Always await async calls instead of blocking them.

Example: Proper Use of await

```csharp
public async Task LoadDataAsync()
{
    var data = await FetchDataFromDatabaseAsync(); // Use await
    instead of .Result
}
```

1.2 Return Task Directly

When possible, avoid wrapping an already asynchronous method within another Task by returning the Task directly. This reduces unnecessary task creation overhead.

Example: Avoid Wrapping Task in Task.Run

```csharp
// Bad Practice
public Task<int> FetchDataAsync()
{
    return Task.Run(() => GetDataFromServiceAsync());
```

```
}
```

```
// Better Practice
public Task<int> FetchDataAsync() => GetDataFromServiceAsync();
```

2. Optimize Task-Based Concurrency

Concurrency in asynchronous code improves performance for both CPU-bound and I/O-bound tasks, but managing it effectively is critical to avoid overwhelming system resources.

2.1 Limit the Number of Concurrent Tasks

Use a throttling mechanism to limit the number of concurrent async operations, especially when dealing with high-latency tasks like database calls or API requests. Too many concurrent tasks can cause resource contention and degrade performance.

Example: Using SemaphoreSlim for Concurrency Control

```csharp
private SemaphoreSlim _semaphore = new SemaphoreSlim(5); // Limit
to 5 concurrent tasks

public async Task ProcessDataAsync(List<int> dataList)
{
    var tasks = dataList.Select(async data =>
    {
        await _semaphore.WaitAsync();
        try
        {
            await ProcessData(data); // Actual work
        }
        finally
        {
            _semaphore.Release();
        }
    });
```

```
    await Task.WhenAll(tasks);
}
```

2.2 Use Task.WhenAll for Parallel Execution

When multiple async tasks are independent and can run in parallel, use Task.WhenAll() to execute them simultaneously. This reduces the overall execution time compared to running them sequentially.

Example: Parallelizing Independent Tasks

csharp

```
public async Task FetchDataFromMultipleSourcesAsync()
{
    var task1 = FetchDataSource1Async();
    var task2 = FetchDataSource2Async();
    var task3 = FetchDataSource3Async();

    await Task.WhenAll(task1, task2, task3); // Executes all tasks
    concurrently
}
```

3. Use ConfigureAwait(false) to Optimize Context Switching

Context switching can be expensive in asynchronous code. When running background tasks that don't need to return to the main context (such as UI or HTTP request context), use .ConfigureAwait(false) to avoid unnecessary context capturing and switching.

Example: Using ConfigureAwait(false)

csharp

```
public async Task ProcessBackgroundTaskAsync()
{
    await LongRunningTaskAsync().ConfigureAwait(false); // Avoids
    switching back to the original context
}
```

This approach is particularly effective in library code or ASP.NET applications, where maintaining the original context isn't necessary for background processing.

4. Minimize Async State Machine Overhead

The C# compiler generates a state machine for each async method, which adds overhead. While async is beneficial for I/O-bound tasks, it may not provide any advantage for CPU-bound work.

4.1 Keep Async Methods Short

Split long asynchronous operations into smaller, modular methods where each method handles specific tasks. This makes code more readable and allows for more granular control over async operations.

4.2 Avoid Async for Simple Operations

If a method performs only minimal CPU-bound work (like a quick calculation), avoid making it async to prevent the overhead of state machine creation.

Example: Using Sync for Simple Calculations

```csharp
public int CalculateTotal(int a, int b) => a + b;
```

5. Use ValueTask for Low-Latency Async Operations

In performance-critical paths, if an asynchronous method frequently returns synchronously, consider using ValueTask<T> instead of Task<T>. ValueTask reduces memory allocations by avoiding heap allocation when the result is already available.

Example: Using ValueTask

```csharp
public ValueTask<int> CalculateAsync(bool returnImmediately)
{
```

```csharp
    if (returnImmediately)
    {
        return new ValueTask<int>(42); // Return directly without
        async overhead
    }
    else
    {
        return new ValueTask<int>(Task.Run(() => ComputeValue()));
    }
}
```

Note: ValueTask is best used sparingly and primarily in high-performance applications, as it can complicate error handling and lead to maintenance challenges.

6. Implement Cancellation Tokens to Free Up Resources

Asynchronous methods should respect cancellation requests to allow users or systems to stop resource-intensive operations if they are no longer needed. Use CancellationToken parameters in async methods to handle cancellations gracefully, freeing up system resources.

Example: Using CancellationToken

csharp

```csharp
public async Task ProcessDataAsync(CancellationToken
cancellationToken)
{
    while (!cancellationToken.IsCancellationRequested)
    {
        await Task.Delay(1000, cancellationToken); // Cancelled if
        requested
        // Perform processing
    }
}
```

7. Avoid Blocking Calls in Asynchronous Methods

Avoid calling blocking methods, like synchronous database or file I/O, inside asynchronous code, as they negate the benefits of async and can cause thread pool starvation.

- **Replace synchronous calls** with asynchronous versions where available (e.g., File.ReadAllTextAsync instead of File.ReadAllText).
- **Optimize API Calls**: For HTTP calls, use HttpClient with async methods (e.g., GetAsync, PostAsync) to prevent blocking.

8. Batch I/O Requests to Reduce Network and Disk Load

Batching requests or data operations can reduce the number of I/O calls, which is especially beneficial in networked or database applications.

Example: Batch Database Insertions

Instead of inserting records one-by-one, batch them into a single transaction:

```csharp
public async Task InsertRecordsInBatchAsync(List<Record> records)
{
    using (var transaction = await
    dbContext.Database.BeginTransactionAsync())
    {
        dbContext.Records.AddRange(records);
        await dbContext.SaveChangesAsync();
        await transaction.CommitAsync();
    }
}
```

9. Leverage C# 8 Async Streams for Data Processing

C# 8 introduced async streams, allowing applications to process data asynchronously as it becomes available. This is particularly useful for handling large data sources or continuous data streams without blocking threads.

Example: Using Async Streams

csharp

```csharp
public async IAsyncEnumerable<int>
GenerateNumbersAsync([EnumeratorCancellation] CancellationToken
cancellationToken = default)
{
    for (int i = 0; i < 100; i++)
    {
        await Task.Delay(100, cancellationToken);
        yield return i;
    }
}
```

Async streams process each data element as it's ready, rather than waiting for the entire collection to load, saving memory and enhancing responsiveness.

10. Measure and Monitor Async Performance with Profiling Tools

To ensure that asynchronous optimizations are effective, measure performance metrics before and after changes. Tools like Visual Studio Profiler, DotTrace, and Application Insights provide visibility into task duration, memory usage, and thread utilization.

- **Visual Studio Profiler**: Useful for monitoring async method duration and identifying resource-heavy methods.
- **DotTrace**: Provides detailed profiling, especially effective for diagnosing async code paths and CPU usage.
- **Application Insights**: For production monitoring, Application Insights tracks request duration, dependencies, and resource utilization in real-time.

Optimizing asynchronous operations in C# 8 requires balancing performance with resource management. By following best practices, such as limiting concurrent tasks, avoiding unnecessary context switching, using ValueTask, and implementing cancellation tokens, developers can ensure that their async code remains responsive and efficient. Regular profiling and performance monitoring will ensure that these optimizations align with real-world application behavior, ultimately leading to a smoother, more scalable application experience.

Using Visual Studio Profiler for Real-World Applications

Visual Studio Profiler is a powerful tool that helps developers diagnose performance issues in .NET applications by providing detailed insights into CPU usage, memory allocations, I/O operations, and other critical metrics. Leveraging the profiler in real-world applications allows developers to identify bottlenecks, optimize code paths, and validate performance improvements.

This guide covers key features and practical steps for using the Visual Studio Profiler in real-world scenarios, with a focus on its most valuable functionalities for identifying performance issues.

1. Setting Up Visual Studio Profiler

To get started with profiling, open your project in Visual Studio:

Go to **Debug > Performance Profiler** or press Alt + F2.

Select the type of profiling session you want (e.g., **CPU Usage**, **Memory Usage**, **.NET Async**, or **Database**).

Start the application and run through scenarios or workflows relevant to your performance analysis. This real-world testing helps capture representative data on how the application performs under typical load conditions.

2. Profiling CPU Usage for Performance Bottlenecks

CPU profiling is useful for identifying CPU-intensive operations and pinpointing inefficient code segments that could benefit from optimization.

2.1 **Starting a CPU Usage Session**

1. Select **CPU Usage** from the Performance Profiler menu.

369

2. Run the application and perform the operations you want to analyze, such as loading data, running complex calculations, or handling multiple user requests.

3. After capturing enough data, stop the profiling session to analyze the results.

2.2 Interpreting CPU Usage Results

Once profiling is complete, Visual Studio will display a breakdown of CPU activity:

- **Hot Path**: This view shows the methods consuming the most CPU time, making it easy to locate bottlenecks.
- **Call Tree**: Visualize the chain of function calls, helping to identify which functions are most responsible for CPU usage.
- **Inclusive and Exclusive Time**: Use these metrics to distinguish time spent directly in a function (exclusive) from time spent in called functions (inclusive).

Example Scenario: Optimizing a Data Processing Loop

If a data processing loop consumes significant CPU time, consider optimizing the algorithm or using parallel processing if feasible. Visual Studio Profiler will highlight such CPU-intensive methods, allowing you to focus on refactoring or implementing concurrency to reduce CPU usage.

3. Memory Usage Profiling for Memory Leaks and Excessive Allocation

Memory issues, such as excessive allocations or memory leaks, can lead to degraded performance and application crashes in long-running applications. The Memory Usage profiler helps you analyze object lifetimes, memory allocation patterns, and garbage collection events.

3.1 Starting a Memory Usage Session

Select **Memory Usage** from the Performance Profiler menu.

Choose **Heap (managed)** to focus on managed objects, particularly useful for C# applications.

Run your application and simulate real-world scenarios where memory usage is expected to peak, such as data-heavy operations.

3.2 Analyzing Memory Usage Results

Memory profiling results provide insights into:

- **Heap Allocation View**: Shows objects and types consuming the most memory. This view helps you identify large objects or frequently allocated types that could be optimized or pooled.
- **Object Retention and Lifetime**: See which objects persist in memory, potentially indicating memory leaks if they remain after they are no longer needed.
- **Garbage Collection Events**: View GC events to understand how often garbage collection is triggered, which may indicate excessive memory allocation.

Example Scenario: Managing Large Object Allocations

If a large object is frequently allocated and then discarded, consider using **object pooling** to reuse the object and reduce allocation frequency. Visual Studio Profiler will show this allocation pattern, making it easy to identify candidates for pooling.

4. Async Performance Profiling for Asynchronous Bottlenecks

Asynchronous methods, while improving responsiveness, can sometimes lead to performance bottlenecks if not managed correctly. The **.NET Async** profiler helps track async call paths, task lifetimes, and I/O operations, making it invaluable for debugging async performance issues.

4.1 Starting an Async Profiling Session

Select **.NET Async** from the Performance Profiler menu.

Start the application and trigger async workflows, such as database calls, file operations, or API requests.

Capture the results to analyze any inefficiencies or bottlenecks in async handling.

4.2 Interpreting Async Results

Async profiling reveals:

- **Task Duration**: Identifies tasks with prolonged execution times, indicating potential bottlenecks.
- **Context Switching**: Shows context-switching overhead, which can slow down async code if the main context is frequently captured.
- **Task Hierarchy**: View the relationship between parent and child tasks, making it easier to identify dependency chains causing delays.

Example Scenario: Reducing Context Switching Overhead

The profiler may reveal excessive context switching caused by await calls without ConfigureAwait(false). To optimize, use ConfigureAwait(false) in methods that don't need to return to the original synchronization context, reducing context-switching overhead.

5. Profiling Database Calls for Data Access Optimization

For applications with significant database interactions, profiling database access helps identify slow-running queries and excessive calls. Visual Studio integrates with SQL Server Profiler to provide detailed information on database performance.

5.1 Setting Up Database Profiling

1. Select **Data Access** or use SQL Server Profiler if your application interacts with SQL Server.
2. Monitor queries and transactions as the application runs.

5.2 Analyzing Database Performance Data

Key metrics for database profiling include:

- **Query Duration**: Highlights slow-running queries, which may require indexing or query optimization.
- **Frequency of Queries**: Reveals excessive database calls, which could benefit from caching.

- **Parameter Insights**: Shows parameterized queries, helping you verify that proper query patterns are used.

Example Scenario: Optimizing High-Frequency Queries

If frequent database queries are observed for the same data, implement caching to reduce load on the database. Profiling will show repeated queries, highlighting areas where caching can improve efficiency.

6. Concurrency Profiling with the Parallel Stacks and Tasks Windows

Concurrency profiling helps identify contention issues and inefficient parallel task handling, which are common in multi-threaded applications. Visual Studio's Parallel Stacks and Tasks windows provide insights into task distribution and synchronization issues.

6.1 Using the Parallel Stacks Window

The Parallel Stacks window visualizes tasks and threads, showing the distribution and interactions of parallel operations. It's useful for diagnosing deadlocks and contention in multi-threaded applications.

- **Task Interactions**: View dependencies and interactions between tasks, making it easier to identify blocking tasks.
- **Thread Pool Utilization**: See how threads are being used, which is critical for applications heavily reliant on the thread pool.

6.2 Identifying Deadlocks and Resource Contention

The Tasks window shows tasks waiting on resources, helping you identify deadlocks or tasks competing for shared resources.

Example Scenario: Resolving Deadlocks

If a deadlock is observed in the Parallel Stacks window, review shared resources (e.g., locks) to ensure proper ordering or consider using non-blocking synchronization techniques like SemaphoreSlim.

7. Capturing Performance Snapshots for Trend Analysis

Snapshots provide a point-in-time view of application performance, helping track performance trends over multiple sessions or deployments.

7.1 Taking and Comparing Snapshots

- **Take Snapshots**: Use the Memory and CPU profiling tools to capture snapshots at various points in the application's lifecycle.
- **Compare Snapshots**: Visual Studio allows snapshot comparison, showing differences in memory allocation, CPU usage, and object retention between sessions.

Example Scenario: Tracking Memory Usage Over Time

By taking snapshots at regular intervals, you can monitor memory consumption growth, helping to detect leaks or inefficiencies that accumulate over long runs.

8. Using Diagnostic Tools for Long-Running Applications

For applications that run continuously or handle large data, using diagnostics tools to track performance over extended periods is essential.

8.1 Collecting Diagnostic Data with Application Insights

Application Insights (for cloud-hosted applications) provides real-time monitoring of request rates, response times, and dependency performance, allowing you to diagnose issues in production.

8.2 Tracking GC Events and Memory Pressure

Use diagnostic tools to monitor garbage collection activity and memory pressure, particularly in high-throughput applications. Excessive GC events indicate high allocation rates, suggesting opportunities for object pooling or memory optimization.

Using Visual Studio Profiler effectively requires an understanding of which profiler tools to apply to specific performance issues, from CPU bottlenecks to memory management and async task handling. By following this structured approach, you can gain a clear view of your application's resource usage, identify bottlenecks, and implement targeted optimizations. Visual Studio Profiler, coupled with proper monitoring practices, helps ensure your applications remain responsive, efficient, and scalable in real-world scenarios.

Hands-On Project: Optimizing a Data-Heavy Application

In this hands-on project, we'll focus on optimizing a data-heavy application, specifically a **Customer Order Management System**, that processes, retrieves, and displays large amounts of customer and order data. This project will guide you through identifying bottlenecks, applying optimizations, and verifying improvements, covering areas like database access, memory usage, CPU-bound tasks, and efficient asynchronous handling.

Project Overview

Our **Customer Order Management System** includes:

1. **Customer and Order Data Processing**: Operations to create, retrieve, update, and delete customer and order records.
2. **Reporting**: Generate reports on orders based on various criteria.
3. **Database Operations**: High-frequency read and write operations to a database for customer and order records.

Step 1: Setting Up the Application

Create an ASP.NET Core Web API project with the following components:

1. **CustomerController**: Handles requests for customer data.
2. **OrderController**: Handles requests for order data.
3. **Database Setup**: Use Entity Framework Core to interact with a SQL Server database containing Customer and Order tables.
4. **Create a new ASP.NET Core Web API project**:

bash

```bash
dotnet new webapi -n CustomerOrderManagement
```

Add Entity Framework Core and SQL Server packages:

bash

```bash
dotnet add package Microsoft.EntityFrameworkCore
dotnet add package Microsoft.EntityFrameworkCore.SqlServer
```

Define Models: Set up Customer and Order models, with each Order associated with a Customer.

csharp

```csharp
public class Customer
{
    public int CustomerId { get; set; }
    public string Name { get; set; } = string.Empty;
    public string Email { get; set; } = string.Empty;
    public List<Order> Orders { get; set; } = new();
}

public class Order
{
    public int OrderId { get; set; }
    public DateTime OrderDate { get; set; }
    public decimal TotalAmount { get; set; }
    public int CustomerId { get; set; }
    public Customer? Customer { get; set; }
}
```

Database Context:

csharp

```
public class AppDbContext : DbContext
{
    public DbSet<Customer> Customers { get; set; }
    public DbSet<Order> Orders { get; set; }

    public AppDbContext(DbContextOptions<AppDbContext> options) :
    base(options) { }
}
```

Step 2: Identifying Performance Bottlenecks

We'll simulate high-volume data operations and identify bottlenecks using Visual Studio Profiler's **CPU Usage**, **Memory Usage**, and **Data Access** tools.

1. **Simulate Data Load**: Load sample customer and order data to test and analyze performance under realistic conditions.
2. **Analyze CPU Usage**: Use Visual Studio Profiler to identify CPU-intensive operations. For example, complex sorting, filtering, or grouping operations within large datasets can quickly consume CPU.
3. **Track Memory Usage**: Monitor memory allocation patterns to detect excessive memory usage or potential memory leaks, especially during high-frequency or bulk operations.
4. **Data Access Profiling**: Profile database queries to identify slow or repetitive queries that can be optimized.

Step 3: Implementing Optimizations

Based on the findings from profiling, we'll implement optimizations in key areas, focusing on data access, memory management, and CPU usage.

3.1 Optimize Data Access with Efficient Querying

Inefficient database queries can be a primary bottleneck in data-heavy applications. Use strategies like indexing, eager loading, and query batching to reduce query times.

- **Indexing**: Index frequently queried fields in the database to speed up search operations. For example, create indexes on CustomerId and

OrderDate in the Order table.

- **Eager Loading with Include**: To avoid the N+1 query issue, use Include in Entity Framework to load related data in a single query.
- **Before Optimization**:

```csharp
var customers = dbContext.Customers.ToList();
foreach (var customer in customers)
{
    var orders = dbContext.Orders.Where(o => o.CustomerId ==
    customer.CustomerId).ToList();
}
```

- **After Optimization**:

```csharp
var customersWithOrders = dbContext.Customers.Include(c =>
c.Orders).ToList();
```

- **Batch Database Operations**: Batch updates and inserts to minimize database round-trips.

3.2 Implement Caching for Frequently Accessed Data

For data that doesn't change frequently, such as customer details or historical orders, caching can significantly reduce database load.

```csharp
MemoryCache cache = new MemoryCache(new MemoryCacheOptions());
cache.Set("CustomerList", customers, TimeSpan.FromMinutes(30));
```

Retrieve cached data where possible, only querying the database if cache misses occur.

3.3 Optimize Asynchronous Operations

When working with data-heavy applications, async operations should be optimized to improve responsiveness.

- **Use Task.WhenAll for Concurrent Async Calls**: Parallelize independent database calls where feasible.

```csharp
public async Task FetchCustomerAndOrdersAsync(int customerId)
{
    var customerTask = dbContext.Customers.FindAsync(customerId);
    var ordersTask = dbContext.Orders.Where(o => o.CustomerId ==
    customerId).ToListAsync();
    await Task.WhenAll(customerTask, ordersTask);
}
```

- **Use ConfigureAwait(false)**: Use this in library code where context preservation isn't required, reducing context-switching overhead.

3.4 Optimize Memory Usage with Object Pooling and Span<T>

For high-volume applications, object pooling and Span-based operations can reduce memory allocations.

- **Object Pooling**: For objects frequently created and discarded, like temporary data structures in reporting, use ObjectPool<T> to reuse objects.

```csharp
var pool = ArrayPool<byte>.Shared;
byte[] buffer = pool.Rent(1024);
pool.Return(buffer);
```

- **Span and Memory<T>**: For string or array processing, using Span<T> and Memory<T> can reduce heap allocations, enhancing memory efficiency.

Step 4: Testing and Validating Optimizations

After implementing optimizations, re-run profiling sessions to verify that performance has improved in terms of CPU usage, memory allocation, and data access speed.

CPU Usage Testing: Validate that CPU-intensive methods are optimized, showing reduced time in the profiler.

Memory Usage Validation: Verify that memory usage remains stable during heavy data processing, with no signs of memory leaks.

Database Query Testing: Ensure that query optimizations reduce the number of database calls and improve query execution time.

Step 5: Implementing Real-Time Monitoring

For continuous performance tracking, integrate monitoring tools like Application Insights or SQL Server Profiler for live applications.

Application Insights: Set up Application Insights to track response times, request volumes, and error rates in real-time.

SQL Server Profiler: Monitor database performance in production to detect and address new bottlenecks as data volume grows.

This hands-on project covered techniques to optimize a data-heavy application, focusing on data access, async operations, memory efficiency, and real-time monitoring. By following a systematic approach—profiling to identify bottlenecks, implementing targeted optimizations, and validating improvements—you can create a highly efficient, scalable application capable of handling large volumes of data with minimal performance issues.

Design Patterns for Scalable and Maintainable Code

Overview of Essential Design Patterns in C# 8

Design patterns are proven solutions to common software design problems that improve code organization, scalability, and maintainability. These patterns provide a consistent, reusable approach for solving complex problems, allowing developers to build applications that are easy to understand, extend, and modify. In C# 8, design patterns can be implemented with modern language features, such as nullable reference types, async programming, and new syntax improvements, making code more concise and expressive.

This section covers several essential design patterns, organized into three main categories: **Creational Patterns**, **Structural Patterns**, and **Behavioral Patterns**. Each pattern will be introduced with its purpose, typical use cases, and a basic implementation in C# 8.

1. Creational Patterns

Creational patterns focus on object creation mechanisms, optimizing how objects are instantiated while maintaining flexibility and efficiency. These patterns help separate the instantiation process from the usage of objects, making it easier to control which classes to create and how to manage dependencies.

1.1 Singleton Pattern

The **Singleton** pattern ensures that a class has only one instance throughout the application's lifecycle. It provides a global access point to this instance, making it suitable for logging, configuration, and caching.

- **Use Cases**: Logger, Configuration Manager, Database Connections
- **Implementation Example**:

```csharp
public sealed class Singleton
{
    private static readonly Lazy<Singleton> instance = new
    Lazy<Singleton>(() => new Singleton());

    private Singleton() { }

    public static Singleton Instance => instance.Value;
}
```

In this example, Lazy<Singleton> ensures that the instance is only created when accessed for the first time, providing thread-safe lazy initialization.

1.2 Factory Method Pattern

The **Factory Method** pattern defines an interface for creating objects, allowing subclasses to alter the type of object created. This pattern promotes flexibility by decoupling object creation from the client code.

- **Use Cases**: Creating instances of related classes without specifying the exact class to be instantiated.
- **Implementation Example**:

```csharp
public abstract class Product
{
```

```
    public abstract void Display();
}

public class ConcreteProductA : Product
{
    public override void Display() =>
Console.WriteLine("Product A");
}

public class ConcreteProductB : Product
{
    public override void Display() =>
Console.WriteLine("Product B");
}

public abstract class Creator
{
    public abstract Product CreateProduct();
}

public class ConcreteCreatorA : Creator
{
    public override Product CreateProduct() => new
    ConcreteProductA();
}
```

By defining a Creator class with an abstract CreateProduct method, subclasses can specify which Product to instantiate, enabling flexibility in object creation.

1.3 Builder Pattern

The **Builder** pattern separates the construction of complex objects from their representation, allowing the same construction process to create different representations. It is commonly used to create complex objects that require multiple steps to build.

- **Use Cases**: Creating complex objects, such as UI dialogs or configuration files, where many properties need to be set.
- **Implementation Example**:

```csharp
public class Product
{
    public string PartA { get; set; }
    public string PartB { get; set; }
}

public class ProductBuilder
{
    private Product _product = new Product();

    public ProductBuilder AddPartA(string part)
    {
        _product.PartA = part;
        return this;
    }

    public ProductBuilder AddPartB(string part)
    {
        _product.PartB = part;
        return this;
    }

    public Product Build() => _product;
}
```

In this example, ProductBuilder simplifies creating Product objects by using chained methods for setting properties.

2. Structural Patterns

Structural patterns define ways to organize objects and classes into larger structures, ensuring that individual components are flexible and reusable.

2.1 Adapter Pattern

The **Adapter** pattern allows incompatible interfaces to work together by creating a wrapper around an existing class. This wrapper enables classes with incompatible interfaces to collaborate.

- **Use Cases**: Integrating third-party libraries, legacy systems, or different data formats.
- **Implementation Example**:

```csharp
public interface ITarget
{
    void Request();
}

public class Adaptee
{
    public void SpecificRequest() => Console.WriteLine("Specific
    request from Adaptee.");
}

public class Adapter : ITarget
{
    private readonly Adaptee _adaptee;
    public Adapter(Adaptee adaptee) => _adaptee = adaptee;

    public void Request() => _adaptee.SpecificRequest();
}
```

In this example, the Adapter class wraps the Adaptee class to make its method accessible through the ITarget interface.

2.2 Decorator Pattern

The **Decorator** pattern allows adding behavior to an individual object dynamically without affecting other objects of the same class. This pattern provides a flexible alternative to subclassing.

- **Use Cases**: Adding features to UI components, such as scrollbars or borders, without modifying the base class.
- **Implementation Example**:

```csharp
public interface IComponent
{
    void Operation();
}

public class ConcreteComponent : IComponent
{
    public void Operation() => Console.
WriteLine("Concrete Component Operation.");
}

public class Decorator : IComponent
{
    private readonly IComponent _component;
    public Decorator(IComponent component) =>
_component = component;

    public void Operation()
    {
        _component.Operation();
        Console.WriteLine("Decorator Additional Operation.");
    }
}
```

Here, the Decorator class wraps a ConcreteComponent and adds additional behavior in the Operation method.

2.3 Facade Pattern

The **Facade** pattern simplifies complex subsystems by providing a unified interface. It shields the client from the intricacies of subsystem classes, promoting ease of use.

- **Use Cases**: Simplifying APIs, providing a single entry point for complex libraries or SDKs.
- **Implementation Example**:

```csharp
public class SubsystemA
{
    public void OperationA() =>
 Console.WriteLine("Subsystem A Operation.");
}

public class SubsystemB
{
    public void OperationB() =>
 Console.WriteLine("Subsystem B Operation.");
}

public class Facade
{
    private readonly SubsystemA _subsystemA;
    private readonly SubsystemB _subsystemB;

    public Facade(SubsystemA subsystemA,
SubsystemB subsystemB)
    {
        _subsystemA = subsystemA;
        _subsystemB = subsystemB;
    }

    public void Operation()
    {
        _subsystemA.OperationA();
        _subsystemB.OperationB();
    }
}
```

The Facade class provides a simple interface for accessing complex operations in multiple subsystems.

3. Behavioral Patterns

Behavioral patterns define the interactions and responsibilities among objects, focusing on how they communicate and delegate responsibilities.

3.1 Observer Pattern

The **Observer** pattern establishes a dependency between objects so that when one changes, all dependents are notified. This pattern is commonly used for event handling.

- **Use Cases**: Event subscription systems, implementing the Publish-Subscribe model.
- **Implementation Example**:

```csharp
public interface IObserver
{
    void Update(string message);
}

public class ConcreteObserver : IObserver
{
    private string _name;
    public ConcreteObserver(string name) => _name = name;

    public void Update(string message)
 => Console.WriteLine($"{_name}
 received message: {message}");
}

public class Subject
{
    private readonly List<IObserver>
 _observers = new List<IObserver>();

    public void Attach(IObserver observer) =>
    _observers.Add(observer);
    public void Notify(string message)
    {
```

```
        foreach (var observer in _observers)
        {
            observer.Update(message);
        }
    }
}
```

3.2 Command Pattern

The **Command** pattern encapsulates requests as objects, allowing parameterization of clients with commands, queuing requests, and logging actions. This pattern is useful for implementing undo functionality.

- **Use Cases**: Implementing undo/redo operations, creating macros or composite commands.
- **Implementation Example**:

```csharp
public interface ICommand
{
    void Execute();
}

public class ConcreteCommand : ICommand
{
    private readonly Receiver _receiver;

    public ConcreteCommand(Receiver receiver) => _receiver =
    receiver;

    public void Execute() => _receiver.Action();
}

public class Receiver
{
    public void Action() =>
```

```
Console.WriteLine("Receiver action executed.");
}
```

Design patterns in C# 8 provide robust solutions for common programming challenges, enhancing code readability, reusability, and scalability. By understanding and implementing these essential patterns, developers can build well-structured, maintainable, and efficient applications, ensuring that code remains adaptable and efficient as applications evolve.

Implementing the MVVM Pattern for UI Applications

The **Model-View-ViewModel (MVVM)** pattern is widely used in modern UI development, particularly in applications built with frameworks like WPF, Xamarin, and .NET MAUI. MVVM separates the presentation layer from business logic, enhancing testability, maintainability, and scalability. It organizes code into three primary components—Model, View, and ViewModel—that interact in defined ways to keep concerns separated.

In this section, we'll discuss the core elements of the MVVM pattern, explore best practices, and provide an example implementation using WPF in C#.

1. Core Components of MVVM

Model: Represents the application's data and business logic. It includes data classes, services, and data access layers. The model is agnostic of the UI and provides data in a way that can be consumed by the ViewModel.

View: The UI layer of the application, typically defined in XAML in WPF applications. It displays data from the ViewModel and binds UI controls to properties in the ViewModel, enabling a two-way data binding. The View is responsible only for presentation, not for data manipulation or processing.

ViewModel: The intermediary between the View and Model. The ViewModel contains properties and commands, exposes data from the Model, and handles user actions. It maintains no direct knowledge of the View, making it testable and reusable.

2. Benefits of the MVVM Pattern

- **Separation of Concerns**: The pattern keeps UI logic separate from business logic, making each component easier to maintain.
- **Enhanced Testability**: ViewModels can be unit-tested without involving the UI, allowing thorough testing of the application's logic.
- **Code Reusability**: ViewModels are independent of the UI framework, making it possible to reuse logic across different UIs.
- **Data Binding**: MVVM enables automatic synchronization between the UI and data, reducing boilerplate code for updating views when data changes.

3. Implementing MVVM in WPF

Let's build a simple **To-Do Application** in WPF using the MVVM pattern. This application will allow users to add, view, and delete to-do items, demonstrating how the ViewModel binds to the View and interacts with the Model.

Step 1: Defining the Model

The Model represents a single to-do item and provides basic CRUD operations. The TodoItem class includes properties for the item's description and completion status.

TodoItem.cs

```csharp
public class TodoItem
{
    public int Id { get; set; }
    public string Description { get; set; } = string.Empty;
    public bool IsCompleted { get; set; }
}
```

To simulate a data source, let's create a simple service that stores and retrieves to-do items.

TodoService.cs

```csharp
public class TodoService
{
    private List<TodoItem> _todoItems = new();

    public IEnumerable<TodoItem> GetAllItems() => _todoItems;

    public void AddItem(TodoItem item) =>
_todoItems.Add(item);

    public void DeleteItem(TodoItem item) =>
_todoItems.Remove(item);
}
```

Step 2: Creating the ViewModel

The ViewModel manages the data that the View displays and provides commands that handle user interactions. In this example, the TodoViewModel includes an ObservableCollection of TodoItem objects, properties for new items, and commands for adding and deleting to-do items.

TodoViewModel.cs

```csharp
using System.Collections.ObjectModel;
using System.Windows.Input;

public class TodoViewModel : INotifyPropertyChanged
{
    private readonly TodoService _todoService;
    private string _newTodoDescription;

    public ObservableCollection<TodoItem>
TodoItems { get; } = new
ObservableCollection<TodoItem>();
```

```csharp
public string NewTodoDescription
{
    get => _newTodoDescription;
    set
    {
        _newTodoDescription = value;
        OnPropertyChanged(nameof(NewTodoDescription));
    }
}

public ICommand AddCommand { get; }
public ICommand DeleteCommand { get; }

public TodoViewModel(TodoService todoService)
{
    _todoService = todoService;
    AddCommand = new RelayCommand(AddTodo);
    DeleteCommand = new RelayCommand(DeleteTodo);

    LoadItems();
}

private void LoadItems()
{
    foreach (var item in _todoService.GetAllItems())
    {
        TodoItems.Add(item);
    }
}

private void AddTodo()
{
    var newItem = new TodoItem { Description =
    NewTodoDescription, IsCompleted = false };
    _todoService.AddItem(newItem);
    TodoItems.Add(newItem);
    NewTodoDescription = string.Empty;
}
```

```
    private void DeleteTodo()
    {
        var itemToRemove = TodoItems.FirstOrDefault(t =>
        t.IsCompleted);
        if (itemToRemove != null)
        {
            _todoService.DeleteItem(itemToRemove);
            TodoItems.Remove(itemToRemove);
        }
    }

    public event PropertyChangedEventHandler?
 PropertyChanged;
    protected virtual void
OnPropertyChanged(string propertyName) =>
        PropertyChanged?.Invoke(this, new
        PropertyChangedEventArgs(propertyName));
}
```

Explanation:

- **Commands**: The AddCommand and DeleteCommand properties use the RelayCommand class to bind UI actions to ViewModel methods.
- **Data Binding**: The NewTodoDescription property and TodoItems collection bind directly to UI elements. Implementing INotifyPropertyChanged ensures that any changes to the properties automatically update the UI.

Step 3: Creating the View with XAML
The View (XAML) binds to the TodoViewModel, displaying the list of to-do items and providing UI elements for user input.
MainWindow.xaml

xml

```xml
<Window x:Class="TodoApp.MainWindow"
        xmlns="http://schemas
.microsoft.
com/winfx/2006
/xaml/presentation"
        xmlns:x="http://schemas.
microsoft.com/winfx/2006/xaml"
        Title="To-Do App" Height="350" Width="400">
    <Window.DataContext>
        <local:TodoViewModel/>
    </Window.DataContext>
    <StackPanel Margin="10">
        <TextBox Text="{Binding NewTodoDescription,
        UpdateSourceTrigger=PropertyChanged}"
                Width="200" Margin="0,0,0,10" />
        <Button Content="Add To-Do"
 Command="{Binding AddCommand}" Width="100" />
        <ListBox ItemsSource="{Binding TodoItems}">
            <ListBox.ItemTemplate>
                <DataTemplate>
                    <StackPanel Orientation="Horizontal">
                        <CheckBox
IsChecked="{Binding IsCompleted}" />
<TextBlock Text="{Binding Description}"
 Margin="5,0,0,0" />
                    </StackPanel>
                </DataTemplate>
            </ListBox.ItemTemplate>
        </ListBox>
        <Button Content="Delete Completed" Command="{Binding
        DeleteCommand}" Width="150" />
    </StackPanel>
</Window>
```

- **DataContext**: Sets the DataContext to TodoViewModel, allowing bindings to access ViewModel properties directly.
- **TextBox and Button Bindings**: The TextBox and Button elements bind to NewTodoDescription and AddCommand, respectively, enabling user

input and interaction.

- **ListBox for To-Do Items**: The ListBox displays to-do items, binding each item to a CheckBox and TextBlock to display and interact with the data.

Step 4: Adding RelayCommand for Command Binding

The **RelayCommand** class is a utility that allows binding of UI actions to ViewModel methods without manually implementing ICommand for each command.

RelayCommand.cs

```csharp
using System;
using System.Windows.Input;

public class RelayCommand : ICommand
{
    private readonly Action _execute;
    private readonly Func<bool> _canExecute;

    public RelayCommand(Action execute,
 Func<bool> canExecute = null)
    {
        _execute = execute;
        _canExecute = canExecute;
    }

    public bool CanExecute(object parameter) =>
_canExecute == null || _canExecute();

    public void Execute(object parameter) => _execute();

    public event EventHandler CanExecuteChanged;

    public void RaiseCanExecuteChanged() =>
    CanExecuteChanged?.Invoke(this, EventArgs.Empty);
```

}

The RelayCommand class encapsulates a method, enabling it to be used with command bindings in XAML.

Benefits and Best Practices in MVVM Implementation

- **Separation of Concerns**: By keeping the UI logic in the ViewModel and business logic in the Model, MVVM ensures that the application remains organized and easy to maintain.
- **Use of Dependency Injection**: Inject dependencies like TodoService in the ViewModel for easier testing and maintainability.
- **Data Binding**: Ensure properties are correctly bound in XAML, and updates propagate automatically by implementing INotifyPropertyChanged.
- **Commands for Actions**: Use ICommand to handle actions from the UI without requiring event handlers in the code-behind.

The MVVM pattern provides a robust framework for structuring WPF applications by separating data, UI, and logic. This project demonstrated how to implement MVVM in a simple to-do application, showing how ViewModels act as a bridge between Views and Models, and how data binding keeps the UI in sync with application state. By following MVVM principles, you can create scalable, maintainable, and testable applications with a clean, organized architecture.

Dependency Injection and Its Benefits

Dependency Injection (DI) is a design pattern that allows a class to receive its dependencies from an external source rather than creating them internally. In C# applications, DI enhances modularity, testability, and maintainability, enabling developers to build flexible, loosely coupled code.

With DI, dependencies are injected at runtime by a DI container, promoting a clean separation between objects and their dependencies.

This section covers the principles of Dependency Injection, explores different types of DI, and demonstrates practical implementation examples, including the benefits DI brings to application architecture.

1. Understanding Dependency Injection

In a typical application, classes often rely on other classes to perform specific tasks. For example, a UserService class might require access to a UserRepository class for data persistence. Without DI, the UserService class would create a UserRepository instance itself, making it difficult to modify or test in isolation. DI resolves this by externalizing dependency creation, allowing the dependencies to be injected from outside the class.

- **Without Dependency Injection**:

```csharp
public class UserService
{
    private readonly UserRepository _userRepository = new
    UserRepository();

    public void SaveUser(User user)
    {
        _userRepository.Add(user);
    }
}
```

- Here, UserService directly depends on UserRepository, creating a tight coupling that limits flexibility.
- **With Dependency Injection**:

```csharp
public class UserService
{
    private readonly IUserRepository _userRepository;

    public UserService(IUserRepository userRepository)
    {
        _userRepository = userRepository;
    }

    public void SaveUser(User user)
    {
        _userRepository.Add(user);
    }
}
```

In this version, UserService accepts an IUserRepository dependency via its constructor, allowing any implementation of IUserRepository to be injected. This flexibility is essential for testing and modifying functionality without impacting other parts of the application.

2. Types of Dependency Injection

There are three primary types of Dependency Injection in C#:

2.1 Constructor Injection

Constructor injection is the most commonly used DI approach. Dependencies are passed to a class through its constructor, ensuring that all required dependencies are provided when the object is instantiated.

- **Example**:

```csharp
```

```
public class OrderService
{
    private readonly IOrderRepository _orderRepository;

    public OrderService(IOrderRepository orderRepository)
    {
        _orderRepository = orderRepository ?? throw new
        ArgumentNullException(nameof(orderRepository));
    }
}
```

- **Benefits**: Ensures dependencies are available and initialized upon instantiation, allowing immutability and thread-safety in classes.

2.2 Property Injection

With property injection, dependencies are set through public properties rather than the constructor. This approach is useful when dependencies are optional or when cyclic dependencies exist.

- **Example**:

```
csharp

public class NotificationService
{
    public ILogger Logger { get; set; }

    public void Notify(string message)
    {
        Logger?.Log(message);
    }
}
```

- **Benefits**: Allows optional dependencies, but can lead to issues if required dependencies are not set. Not suitable for immutable or highly encapsulated classes.

2.3 Method Injection

In method injection, dependencies are provided as parameters to a method. This approach is useful when a dependency is only needed for a specific operation within a class.

- **Example**:

```csharp
public class ReportService
{
    public void GenerateReport(IReportGenerator reportGenerator)
    {
        reportGenerator.Generate();
    }
}
```

- **Benefits**: Ideal for dependencies used only within specific methods, promoting clearer code and limiting dependency scope.

3. Implementing Dependency Injection in ASP.NET Core

ASP.NET Core has built-in support for Dependency Injection, making it easy to register and resolve dependencies throughout the application. The DI container in ASP.NET Core supports three lifetimes for service registration:

1. **Singleton**: A single instance of the service is created and shared across the application's lifetime.
2. **Scoped**: A single instance is created per request or scope.
3. **Transient**: A new instance is created each time the service is requested.

3.1 Registering Dependencies

To register services with the DI container in ASP.NET Core, use the ConfigureServices method in Startup.cs.

- **Example**:

```csharp
public void ConfigureServices(IServiceCollection services)
{
    services.AddSingleton<IConfigurationService,
    ConfigurationService>();
    services.AddScoped<IOrderRepository, OrderRepository>();
    services.AddTransient<IEmailService, EmailService>();
}
```

Here, the services are registered with their respective lifetimes. ASP.NET Core automatically resolves dependencies when they are required.

3.2 Injecting Dependencies in Controllers

Once dependencies are registered, they can be injected into controllers or services.

- **Example**:

```csharp
public class OrderController : ControllerBase
{
    private readonly IOrderService _orderService;

    public OrderController(IOrderService orderService)
    {
        _orderService = orderService;
    }
```

```
public IActionResult CreateOrder(Order order)
{
    _orderService.Create(order);
    return Ok();
}
}
```

ASP.NET Core will automatically inject an instance of IOrderService when creating OrderController, allowing the controller to access OrderService methods without explicitly creating an instance.

4. Benefits of Dependency Injection

4.1 Promotes Loose Coupling

DI allows classes to depend on abstractions rather than concrete implementations, making it easier to switch implementations without affecting dependent code. This is particularly beneficial when refactoring code or swapping service providers (e.g., using different databases or logging frameworks).

4.2 Enhances Testability

Since DI separates creation from usage, classes can be tested in isolation by injecting mock dependencies. This isolation facilitates unit testing, allowing developers to test functionality without relying on external dependencies.

- **Example**: Mocking a dependency for testing.

```csharp
[Test]
public void TestOrderService()
{
    var mockRepo = new Mock<IOrderRepository>();
    var orderService = new OrderService(mockRepo.Object);
```

```
    // Test orderService functionality here
}
```

4.3 Improves Code Maintainability and Readability

With DI, application components become modular, making it easier to understand, modify, or extend code without impacting other components. Dependency graphs are clear, helping developers grasp dependencies at a glance, which streamlines maintenance and debugging.

4.4 Enables Reusability and Flexibility

When using DI, services are not bound to specific implementations, making it easy to reuse classes across different parts of the application or even in other projects. Swapping implementations based on context (e.g., using different loggers for development and production) becomes seamless.

4.5 Supports Lifecycle Management

DI containers in frameworks like ASP.NET Core manage the lifecycle of dependencies, ensuring that resources are allocated and disposed of appropriately. By registering services with appropriate lifetimes (e.g., Singleton, Scoped, or Transient), developers can control how instances are created and disposed of, which is especially useful for managing resources like database connections.

5. Best Practices for Using Dependency Injection

Inject Abstractions, Not Implementations: Always depend on interfaces or abstract classes rather than concrete implementations. This promotes loose coupling and flexibility.

```csharp
public class ReportGenerator
{
    private readonly IReportService _reportService;
```

```
public ReportGenerator(IReportService reportService)
{
    _reportService = reportService;
}
}
```

1. **Avoid Over-Injection**: Avoid injecting too many dependencies into a single class, as this often indicates a violation of the Single Responsibility Principle. If a class requires more than 3–5 dependencies, consider refactoring to separate responsibilities.

2. **Use DI for Stateful Services Sparingly**: While DI is suitable for stateless services, avoid using it for classes that manage state across calls. For stateful services, consider using other mechanisms like scoped services or explicitly managing instances.

3. **Scope Dependencies Appropriately**: Register services with lifetimes that match their usage. For example, services accessing database contexts should be Scoped to match the request lifecycle in web applications.

4. **Use Configuration and Logging as Singleton Services**: Frequently accessed services like configuration and logging should be registered as singletons to improve performance and reduce resource consumption.

Dependency Injection is a core pattern for building scalable, maintainable applications in C#. By externalizing dependency creation, DI promotes loose coupling, enhances testability, and simplifies code maintenance. Whether using constructor injection, property injection, or method injection, DI enables a modular design that enhances flexibility and reusability. With frameworks like ASP.NET Core providing built-in support for DI, implementing DI in real-world applications is straightforward, allowing developers to leverage its benefits fully.

Hands-On Project: Using Design Patterns in Real-World Applications

In this project, we will implement multiple design patterns in a real-world application: a **Book Management System**. This application will allow users to manage a collection of books, including adding, retrieving, updating, and deleting book entries. By incorporating various design patterns, we will demonstrate how they can enhance code organization, maintainability, and scalability.

Project Overview

The **Book Management System** will feature:

1. **CRUD Operations**: Basic create, read, update, and delete functionality for books.
2. **User Interaction**: A simple console-based interface for user commands.
3. **Design Patterns**: Utilize patterns such as Repository, Singleton, Factory Method, and Command to structure the application.

Step 1: Setting Up the Project
Create a New Console Application:

```bash
dotnet new console -n BookManagementSystem
```

Define the Book Model:

```csharp
public class Book
{
    public int Id { get; set; }
    public string Title { get; set; } = string.Empty;
    public string Author { get; set; } = string.Empty;
```

```
    public DateTime PublishedDate { get; set; }
}
```

Step 2: Implementing the Repository Pattern

The Repository pattern provides a way to manage data access, allowing separation between the data layer and the business logic. We will create an interface for the repository and its implementation.

2.1 Define the IBookRepository Interface

```csharp
public interface IBookRepository
{
    void AddBook(Book book);
    Book GetBook(int id);
    IEnumerable<Book> GetAllBooks();
    void UpdateBook(Book book);
    void DeleteBook(int id);
}
```

2.2 Implement the BookRepository Class

```csharp
using System.Collections.Generic;
using System.Linq;

public class BookRepository : IBookRepository
{
    private readonly List<Book> _books = new();
    private int _nextId = 1;

    public void AddBook(Book book)
    {
        book.Id = _nextId++;
        _books.Add(book);
    }
```

```csharp
    public Book GetBook(int id) =>
_books.FirstOrDefault(b => b.Id == id);

    public IEnumerable<Book> GetAllBooks() => _books;

    public void UpdateBook(Book book)
    {
        var existingBook = GetBook(book.Id);
        if (existingBook != null)
        {
            existingBook.Title = book.Title;
            existingBook.Author = book.Author;
            existingBook.PublishedDate = book.PublishedDate;
        }
    }

    public void DeleteBook(int id)
    {
        var book = GetBook(id);
        if (book != null)
        {
            _books.Remove(book);
        }
    }
}
```

Step 3: Implementing the Singleton Pattern

To ensure that there is only one instance of the repository throughout the application, we will use the Singleton pattern.

3.1 Implement the BookRepository Singleton

```csharp
csharp

public sealed class BookRepositorySingleton
{
    private static readonly Lazy<
BookRepositorySingleton> _instance =
```

```
    new Lazy<BookRepositorySingleton>(() => new
    BookRepositorySingleton());

public static BookRepositorySingleton Instance =>
_instance.Value;

public IBookRepository BookRepository { get; }

private BookRepositorySingleton()
{
    BookRepository = new BookRepository();
}
}
```

This implementation guarantees a single instance of BookRepositorySin
gleton and provides access to the repository through the BookRepository
property.

Step 4: Implementing the Command Pattern

The Command pattern will help encapsulate actions performed in the
application, allowing us to handle user commands in a clean and organized
way.

4.1 Define Command Interfaces

```csharp

public interface ICommand
{
    void Execute();
}

public class AddBookCommand : ICommand
{
    private readonly IBookRepository _bookRepository;
    private readonly Book _book;

    public AddBookCommand(IBookRepository
```

```
bookRepository, Book book)
    {
        _bookRepository = bookRepository;
        _book = book;
    }

    public void Execute() => _bookRepository.AddBook(_book);
}
```

4.2 Implement Other Command Types

Similarly, create command classes for updating, deleting, and listing books:

csharp

```csharp
public class DeleteBookCommand : ICommand
{
    private readonly IBookRepository _bookRepository;
    private readonly int _bookId;

    public DeleteBookCommand(IBookRepository bookRepository, int
    bookId)
    {
        _bookRepository = bookRepository;
        _bookId = bookId;
    }

    public void Execute() =>
_bookRepository.DeleteBook(_bookId);
}

// And so forth for UpdateBookCommand and ListBooksCommand
```

Step 5: User Interaction via the Console

To interact with the user, we will create a simple console interface that takes commands and executes the appropriate actions.

5.1 Implement the Main Program

```csharp
csharp

using System;

class Program
{
    static void Main(string[] args)
    {
        var bookRepository =
        BookRepositorySingleton.Instance.BookRepository;

        while (true)
        {
            Console.WriteLine("Enter a command:
(add, list, update, delete, exit)");
            var command = Console.ReadLine();

            switch (command?.ToLower())
            {
                case "add":
                    var newBook = new Book
                    {
Title = "The Great Gatsby",
Author = "F. Scott Fitzgerald",
                        PublishedDate =
 new DateTime(1925, 4, 10)
                    };
                    var addCommand = new
                    AddBookCommand(bookRepository, newBook);
                    addCommand.Execute();
                    Console.WriteLine("Book added.");
                    break;

                case "list":
                    var books = bookRepository.GetAllBooks();
                    foreach (var book in books)
                    {
                        Console.WriteLine($"ID:
{book.Id}, Title: {book.Title}, Author:
{book.Author}, Published:
```

```
{book.PublishedDate.ToShortDateString()}");
                    }
                    break;

            case "delete":
                    Console.WriteLine
("Enter book ID to delete:");
                    if (int.TryParse
(Console.ReadLine(), out int bookId))
                    {
                        var deleteCommand = new
                        DeleteBookCommand(bookRepository, bookId);
                        deleteCommand.Execute();
                        Console.WriteLine("Book deleted.");
                    }
                    break;

            case "update":
                    Console.WriteLine
("Enter book ID to update:");
                    if (int.TryParse
(Console.ReadLine(), out int updateId))
                    {
                        var bookToUpdate =
                        bookRepository.GetBook(updateId);
                        if (bookToUpdate != null)
                        {
Console.WriteLine("Enter new title:");
bookToUpdate.Title = Console.ReadLine();
Console.WriteLine("Enter new author:");
bookToUpdate.Author = Console.ReadLine();
var updateCommand = new
 UpdateBookCommand(bookRepository, bookToUpdate);
updateCommand.Execute();
Console.WriteLine("Book updated.");
                        }
                    }
                    break;

            case "exit":
```

413

```
                 return;

              default:
Console.WriteLine("Unknown command. Please try again.");
                 break;
         }
      }
    }
}
```

Step 6: Enhancing Maintainability and Scalability

6.1 Use Dependency Injection

While the example above uses a simple Singleton for demonstration, in a more complex application, you would typically set up a Dependency Injection container (like the one in ASP.NET Core) to manage your dependencies.

6.2 Add Logging and Exception Handling

To enhance the robustness of the application, consider integrating logging (using libraries like NLog or Serilog) and exception handling strategies to manage errors gracefully and log important events.

Step 7: Testing and Validating the Implementation

1. **Unit Tests**: Create unit tests for individual components, such as the repository and command classes. Use mocking frameworks (e.g., Moq) to test interactions without relying on a database.
2. **Integration Tests**: Test the interaction between components to ensure the application behaves as expected when integrated.

In this project, we explored how to implement various design patterns, including the Repository, Singleton, Command, and Dependency Injection patterns, in a real-world application. By applying these patterns, we achieved a clean separation of concerns, improved maintainability, and enhanced testability. This structured approach allows developers to create scalable applications that can adapt to changing requirements while remaining easy to manage and extend over time.

Deploying and Maintaining C# Applications

Preparing Applications for Deployment: CI/CD Essentials
Continuous Integration (CI) and Continuous Deployment (CD) are critical practices in modern software development that enhance the delivery process, improve code quality, and streamline collaboration among teams. CI/CD automates the building, testing, and deployment of applications, allowing developers to deliver updates and new features more rapidly and reliably. In this chapter, we will cover the essentials of preparing C# applications for deployment using CI/CD principles, including setting up pipelines, managing configurations, and best practices for maintaining applications post-deployment.

1. Understanding CI/CD Concepts

1.1 Continuous Integration (CI)

Continuous Integration is a development practice that involves regularly integrating code changes into a shared repository. Each integration is verified by automated builds and tests, allowing teams to detect problems early.

Key Components of CI:

- **Version Control**: Using systems like Git to manage code changes.
- **Automated Builds**: Triggering builds automatically when changes are pushed to the repository.
- **Automated Testing**: Running unit and integration tests to verify that

code changes do not break existing functionality.

1.2 Continuous Deployment (CD)

Continuous Deployment extends CI by automatically deploying code changes to production after passing all tests. This practice ensures that software is always in a deployable state and can be released to users rapidly.

Key Components of CD:

- **Deployment Pipelines**: Automated workflows that build, test, and deploy applications to various environments (development, staging, production).
- **Infrastructure as Code (IaC)**: Managing and provisioning infrastructure using code, allowing for consistent and repeatable deployments.

2. Setting Up CI/CD Pipelines for C# Applications

CI/CD pipelines automate the steps needed to build, test, and deploy applications. We will explore how to set up a CI/CD pipeline for a C# application using popular tools like Azure DevOps, GitHub Actions, or Jenkins.

2.1 Choosing a CI/CD Tool

Azure DevOps: A comprehensive set of development tools that include pipelines, repositories, and artifacts.

GitHub Actions: A powerful feature within GitHub that enables automation of workflows directly from your repository.

Jenkins: An open-source automation server that allows the creation of customizable pipelines.

2.2 Creating a CI/CD Pipeline in Azure DevOps
Step 1: Set Up Your Azure DevOps Project

- Create a new project in Azure DevOps and set up a Git repository to host your C# application.

Step 2: Create a Pipeline

Navigate to the **Pipelines** section and click **Create Pipeline**.

Select the repository and choose the YAML pipeline configuration.

Step 3: Define Your Pipeline Configuration

A basic YAML pipeline for a C# application might look like this:

```yaml
trigger:
  branches:
    include:
      - main

pool:
  vmImage: 'windows-latest'

steps:
- task: DotNetCoreCLI@2
  displayName: 'Restore NuGet packages'
  inputs:
    command: 'restore'
    projects: '**/*.csproj'

- task: DotNetCoreCLI@2
  displayName: 'Build the project'
  inputs:
    command: 'build'
    projects: '**/*.csproj'
    arguments: '--configuration Release'

- task: DotNetCoreCLI@2
  displayName: 'Run unit tests'
  inputs:
    command: 'test'
    projects: '**/*.csproj'
    arguments: '--configuration Release --no-build'
```

This pipeline configuration:

- Triggers on commits to the main branch.
- Uses a Windows image to run the build.
- Restores dependencies, builds the application, and runs unit tests.

Step 4: Deploy to Production

To automate deployment, add a deployment step to your pipeline. This can be to Azure App Service, an on-premises server, or any target environment.

yaml

```
- task: AzureRmWebAppDeployment@4
  inputs:
    azureSubscription: '<Your Azure Subscription>'
    appType: 'webApp'
    WebAppName: '<Your Web App Name>'
    packageForLinux: '**/*.zip' # Use the appropriate packaging
    option
```

3. Configuring Application Settings and Secrets

Managing configuration and secrets is crucial for secure deployments. Use environment variables and Azure Key Vault to store sensitive information.

3.1 Environment Variables

Set environment variables in your pipeline to manage different configurations for development, staging, and production environments.

yaml

```
variables:
  ConnectionString: $(ConnectionString)
  ApiKey: $(ApiKey)
```

3.2 Using Azure Key Vault for Secrets

Integrate Azure Key Vault with Azure DevOps to manage sensitive information. This allows your pipeline to access secrets without hardcoding them in the application.

Create a Key Vault: Set up an Azure Key Vault and store your secrets.

Link Key Vault to Azure DevOps: Add the Key Vault to your pipeline and reference secrets during the build or deployment process.

```yaml
yaml

- task: AzureKeyVault@1
  inputs:
    azureSubscription: '<Your Azure Subscription>'
    KeyVaultName: '<Your Key Vault Name>'
    SecretsFilter: '*'
    RunAsPreJob: false
```

4. Automated Testing in CI/CD

Automated tests are integral to ensuring that code changes do not introduce new bugs. Implement unit tests, integration tests, and end-to-end tests to verify application functionality before deployment.

4.1 Unit Testing with xUnit

Integrate unit tests in your CI pipeline to validate the application logic. For example, use xUnit for unit testing C# applications:

```bash
bash

dotnet add package xunit
dotnet add package xunit.runner.visualstudio
```

4.2 Integration Testing

Set up integration tests to verify interactions between components. Use a testing framework that supports integration scenarios, and add integration tests to your pipeline.

4.3 End-to-End Testing with Selenium

Consider implementing end-to-end tests to simulate user interactions and verify overall application behavior. Use tools like Selenium or Playwright to automate browser testing.

5. Deploying Applications with CI/CD

Deploying applications can be accomplished through various strategies, including blue-green deployments, canary releases, and rolling updates.

5.1 Blue-Green Deployments

Blue-green deployments maintain two identical production environments. One (Blue) serves the live application, while the other (Green) is used for testing the new release. When the new version is ready, traffic is switched from Blue to Green, allowing for a quick rollback if issues arise.

5.2 Canary Releases

A canary release gradually rolls out the new version to a small subset of users before a full deployment. This allows monitoring of performance and user feedback while minimizing risk.

5.3 Rolling Updates

Rolling updates sequentially replace instances of the application, ensuring continuous availability. This is particularly useful in microservices architectures, where services can be updated independently.

6. Monitoring and Logging Post-Deployment

Once the application is deployed, continuous monitoring is crucial for identifying issues, tracking performance, and ensuring reliability.

6.1 Application Monitoring with Application Insights

Integrate Application Insights to monitor application performance, detect failures, and gain insights into user behavior. This tool provides telemetry data that can help diagnose issues quickly.

6.2 Logging Best Practices

Implement structured logging using frameworks like Serilog or NLog. This ensures logs are consistent, searchable, and useful for debugging.

```csharp
Log.Information("User {UserId} added a new book: {BookTitle}",
userId, bookTitle);
```

Preparing C# applications for deployment using CI/CD principles involves automating the build, test, and deployment processes. By leveraging tools like Azure DevOps and following best practices for environment management, testing, and monitoring, teams can enhance the reliability and efficiency of their deployment pipelines. Implementing CI/CD not only streamlines the deployment process but also promotes a culture of continuous improvement, enabling teams to deliver high-quality software at a rapid pace while minimizing risks.

Deployment to Azure and Other Cloud Platforms

Deploying applications to cloud platforms like Azure, AWS, or Google Cloud offers numerous advantages, including scalability, reliability, and reduced infrastructure management overhead. This section will provide a comprehensive guide on how to deploy C# applications to Azure, along with considerations for deploying to other cloud platforms.

1. Benefits of Cloud Deployment

Cloud deployment provides several benefits over traditional on-premises solutions:

- **Scalability**: Automatically scale applications up or down based on demand without manual intervention.
- **Cost Efficiency**: Pay for only the resources you use, reducing upfront capital expenditures and operational costs.
- **High Availability**: Cloud providers typically offer built-in redundancy and failover capabilities to ensure applications remain accessible.
- **Global Reach**: Deploy applications in multiple geographic regions to reduce latency and improve performance for users worldwide.

2. Deployment to Microsoft Azure

Microsoft Azure provides various services and tools for deploying C# applications, particularly for web applications, APIs, and microservices. Below are the key steps to deploy a C# application to Azure.

2.1 Setting Up an Azure Account

To begin deploying applications to Azure, you need an Azure account. You can sign up for a free account that offers credits for trying out various services.

2.2 Choosing the Right Azure Service

Depending on your application type, you can choose from several Azure services:

- **Azure App Service**: A fully managed platform for building, deploying, and scaling web apps and APIs. Ideal for ASP.NET applications.
- **Azure Functions**: A serverless compute service for running event-driven applications without provisioning servers.
- **Azure Kubernetes Service (AKS)**: A managed Kubernetes service for deploying and managing containerized applications.
- **Azure Virtual Machines**: For complete control over the operating system and environment.

2.3 Deploying an ASP.NET Core Application to Azure App Service

Step 1: Create an Azure App Service Instance

Log in to the Azure portal.

Click on **Create a resource**.

Select **Web App** under the **Compute** section.

Fill out the necessary details (subscription, resource group, name, runtime stack, and region).

Click **Create** to provision the App Service.

Step 2: Prepare Your Application for Deployment

In your ASP.NET Core application, ensure that the connection strings and settings are configured for production in appsettings.Production.json.

Add any necessary NuGet packages for Azure, such as Azure App Configuration or Azure Blob Storage SDKs if your application interacts with Azure services.

Step 3: Deploy Using Visual Studio

Open your project in Visual Studio.

Right-click on the project in Solution Explorer and select **Publish**.

Choose **Azure** and select the Azure App Service instance you created earlier.

Configure your deployment settings, including deployment mode (e.g., Web Deploy).

Click **Publish** to deploy your application directly from Visual Studio.

Step 4: Monitor and Manage the Deployment

Once deployed, you can monitor your application's performance and manage settings via the Azure portal. Utilize features like Application Insights for detailed telemetry and diagnostics.

3. Deploying to Other Cloud Platforms

In addition to Azure, other cloud platforms like AWS and Google Cloud provide robust options for deploying C# applications. Below is a brief overview of how to deploy to these platforms.

3.1 **Deploying to AWS**

Using AWS Elastic Beanstalk

AWS Elastic Beanstalk is a Platform as a Service (PaaS) offering that simplifies the deployment and management of applications.

Create an Elastic Beanstalk Environment:

- Log in to the AWS Management Console.
- Navigate to Elastic Beanstalk and create a new application.
- Choose the appropriate platform (e.g., .NET Core).
- Upload your application package (ZIP file or source bundle).

Deploy the Application:

- Configure environment settings such as instance type, database connections, and scaling options.
- Click on **Create Environment** to deploy your application.

Monitor and Scale:

- Use AWS CloudWatch to monitor application health and resource utilization.
- Configure auto-scaling based on demand.

3.2 Deploying to Google Cloud Platform (GCP)
Using Google App Engine

Google App Engine allows you to build and deploy applications on a fully managed serverless platform.

Create a Google Cloud Project:

- Log in to the Google Cloud Console.
- Create a new project and enable billing.

Deploy the Application:

- Install the Google Cloud SDK and initialize it with your project.
- Use the following command to deploy your application:

```bash
gcloud app deploy
```

Manage and Monitor:

- Use the Google Cloud Console to monitor logs, set up alerts, and manage application versions.

4. Best Practices for Cloud Deployment

1. **Environment Configuration**: Keep configuration settings (connection

strings, secrets) out of source control. Use environment variables or services like Azure Key Vault, AWS Secrets Manager, or Google Cloud Secret Manager for managing sensitive information.

2. **Automate Deployments**: Use CI/CD pipelines for automating deployments, ensuring consistency and reducing manual errors.

3. **Monitoring and Logging**: Implement monitoring solutions to track application performance and usage metrics. Use structured logging for easier troubleshooting and analysis.

4. **Backup and Recovery**: Implement backup strategies for your data and ensure you have a disaster recovery plan in place.

5. **Scalability Considerations**: Design your application to scale horizontally by using load balancers and distributing workloads across multiple instances or containers.

6. **Testing in Staging Environments**: Before deploying to production, test your application in a staging environment that closely mimics production. This helps catch issues early.

Deploying C# applications to Azure and other cloud platforms involves understanding the specific services available, setting up your deployment configurations, and following best practices for configuration management, automation, and monitoring. By leveraging cloud capabilities, developers can create scalable and reliable applications that meet user demands efficiently while minimizing infrastructure overhead. The choice of cloud platform and deployment strategy will depend on the specific requirements of the application and the development team's expertise.

Monitoring and Logging Best Practices

Monitoring and logging are essential components of maintaining the health, performance, and security of C# applications in production. Effective monitoring enables developers and operators to track application performance and user behavior, while comprehensive logging provides valuable insights into application behavior and assists in troubleshooting issues. This section outlines best practices for implementing monitoring and logging in C# applications to ensure that they are robust, maintainable, and easy to debug.

1. Importance of Monitoring and Logging

1.1 Monitoring

Monitoring involves continuously observing application performance, resource usage, and user interactions. It helps identify issues proactively before they impact users.

- **Key Benefits**:
- Early detection of performance bottlenecks or outages.
- Insights into application usage patterns and user behavior.
- Real-time alerts for critical errors or system failures.

1.2 Logging

Logging captures detailed information about application execution, including events, errors, and state changes. Logs provide a historical record that can be analyzed for troubleshooting and understanding application behavior.

- **Key Benefits**:
- Detailed context for diagnosing issues during incidents.
- Auditing and compliance tracking through records of user actions.
- Performance analysis through logs of execution times and resource usage.

2. Setting Up Monitoring

To effectively monitor a C# application, consider the following best practices:

2.1 Choose the Right Monitoring Tools

Select monitoring tools that suit your application architecture and deployment environment. Popular monitoring solutions include:

- **Application Insights**: A Microsoft service that integrates with Azure for monitoring application performance, failures, and user behaviors in real-time.

- **Prometheus and Grafana**: Open-source tools that collect metrics and visualize performance data, ideal for containerized applications.
- **New Relic**: A commercial monitoring tool providing detailed performance insights and transaction tracing.

2.2 Instrument Your Code

Instrumenting your code involves adding monitoring hooks throughout your application to capture key metrics. Key areas to monitor include:

- **Performance Metrics**: Measure response times, throughput, and error rates for critical components.
- **Custom Events**: Track specific user interactions, such as button clicks or form submissions, to understand user behavior.
- **Health Checks**: Implement health check endpoints to allow monitoring tools to verify the application's status.

Example: Instrumenting with Application Insights

```csharp
public class HomeController : Controller
{
    private readonly TelemetryClient _telemetryClient;

    public HomeController(TelemetryClient telemetryClient)
    {
        _telemetryClient = telemetryClient;
    }

    public IActionResult Index()
    {
        _telemetryClient.TrackEvent("Index Page Accessed");
        return View();
```

```
    }
}
```

2.3 Set Up Alerts

Configure alerts based on critical metrics to notify developers or operators of potential issues before they escalate. Common alerts include:

- High error rates.
- Unusual response times.
- Resource utilization (CPU, memory) exceeding thresholds.

3. Implementing Effective Logging

Effective logging is crucial for diagnosing issues and understanding application behavior. Follow these best practices to enhance your logging strategy:

3.1 Choose a Logging Framework

Select a logging framework that supports structured logging and integrates well with your application. Popular logging libraries for C# include:

- **Serilog**: A versatile logging library that supports structured logging and sinks to various outputs (files, databases, cloud services).
- **NLog**: A flexible logging framework that supports different targets and formats.
- **log4net**: An established logging library for .NET applications.

Example: Setting Up Serilog

```csharp
public class Program
{
    public static void Main(string[] args)
    {
```

```
Log.Logger = new LoggerConfiguration()
    .MinimumLevel.Information()
    .WriteTo.Console()
    .WriteTo.File("logs/log.txt", rollingInterval:
    RollingInterval.Day)
    .CreateLogger();

try
{
    Log.Information("Application Starting");
    CreateHostBuilder(args).Build().Run();
}
catch (Exception ex)
{
    Log.Fatal(ex, "Application start-up failed");
}
finally
{
    Log.CloseAndFlush();
}
    }
}
```

3.2 Log Meaningful Information

Capture relevant information in your logs to facilitate troubleshooting. Key data points include:

- **Contextual Information**: Include contextual data such as user IDs, request paths, and transaction IDs to help correlate logs with specific requests or user actions.
- **Error Details**: When logging errors, capture stack traces and error messages to provide context for debugging.
- **Performance Metrics**: Log execution times for critical operations to identify performance bottlenecks.

Example: Logging an Exception with Context

```csharp
try
{
    // Some operation that might throw an exception
}
catch (Exception ex)
{
    Log.Error(ex, "An error occurred while processing request for
    User ID: {UserId}", userId);
}
```

3.3 Use Structured Logging

Structured logging captures log data in a structured format, allowing for easier querying and analysis. Use named properties to represent important fields in your log entries.

Example: Structured Logging with Serilog

```csharp
Log.Information("User {UserId} has logged in at {LoginTime}",
userId, DateTime.UtcNow);
```

This approach makes it easy to search and analyze logs based on specific fields.

4. Log Management and Retention Policies

Establishing a log management strategy is crucial for maintaining log data over time while ensuring compliance and efficient storage.

4.1 Centralized Log Management

Implement centralized logging solutions to aggregate logs from multiple services and applications. Tools such as **Elastic Stack (ELK)**, **Splunk**, or **Azure Monitor** allow for effective searching, filtering, and visualization of log data.

4.2 Log Retention Policies

Define retention policies to manage how long logs are kept and when they should be archived or deleted. Factors to consider include:

- **Compliance Requirements**: Certain regulations may dictate how long specific logs must be retained.
- **Storage Costs**: Large volumes of log data can incur storage costs, so consider implementing policies to archive or delete old logs.
- **Performance Impacts**: Regularly cleaning up logs can improve the performance of log management systems and prevent slowdowns.

5. Monitoring Application Performance

Implementing performance monitoring is essential for understanding how your application behaves in production.

5.1 Track Key Performance Indicators (KPIs)

Define and track KPIs relevant to your application, such as:

- **Response Times**: Average response times for various API endpoints.
- **Error Rates**: Percentage of requests resulting in errors.
- **User Engagement**: Metrics related to user interactions and behaviors.

5.2 Use Application Performance Monitoring (APM)

Integrate APM tools to gain deeper insights into application performance. APM tools, such as New Relic, Dynatrace, or Azure Application Insights, provide features such as:

- **Transaction Tracing**: Track the flow of requests through your application to identify bottlenecks.
- **Performance Dashboards**: Visualize performance data in real-time to monitor trends and spot anomalies.
- **Alerts and Anomaly Detection**: Automatically alert developers when performance metrics deviate from expected ranges.

Implementing effective monitoring and logging strategies is essential for maintaining the health and performance of C# applications in production. By following best practices for monitoring tools, logging frameworks, and log management, developers can gain valuable insights into application behavior, quickly diagnose issues, and improve overall software quality. A robust monitoring and logging strategy not only enhances application reliability but also empowers teams to make informed decisions based on real-time data, ultimately leading to better user experiences and more successful software deployments.

Handling Application Updates and Maintenance

Maintaining and updating applications is a critical aspect of software development that ensures longevity, security, and performance. As user requirements evolve, technology advances, and new vulnerabilities emerge, it becomes essential to manage application updates effectively. This section outlines best practices for handling application updates and maintenance in C# applications, covering strategies for deployment, rollback, monitoring, and ongoing maintenance.

1. Planning for Updates
1.1 Version Control
Effective version control is fundamental to managing application updates. Use a versioning system that follows semantic versioning principles (SemVer) to communicate changes clearly. This typically consists of three numbers: MAJOR.MINOR.PATCH.

- **MAJOR**: Incremented for incompatible API changes.
- **MINOR**: Incremented for adding functionality in a backward-compatible manner.
- **PATCH**: Incremented for backward-compatible bug fixes.

Example: Changing from version 1.2.3 to 1.3.0 indicates the addition of new features, while 2.0.0 indicates breaking changes.

1.2 Update Strategy

Establish an update strategy that considers the nature of your application and user needs. Common strategies include:

- **Scheduled Updates**: Regularly scheduled updates (e.g., monthly) to incorporate new features and fixes.
- **Rolling Updates**: Gradually deploying updates to a subset of users to monitor performance and address issues before a full rollout.
- **Hotfixes**: Immediate deployment of critical patches to address security vulnerabilities or severe bugs without waiting for the next scheduled release.

2. Preparing for Deployment

2.1 Testing Before Release

Comprehensive testing is essential before deploying updates to minimize the risk of introducing new issues. Key testing practices include:

- **Unit Testing**: Validate individual components and methods to ensure they function correctly.
- **Integration Testing**: Verify that different components of the application work together as expected.
- **User Acceptance Testing (UAT)**: Involve end-users in testing to ensure that the application meets their requirements and expectations.

Example: Set up a CI/CD pipeline that includes automated tests to verify the correctness of your application before deploying to production.

2.2 Continuous Integration and Deployment

Leverage CI/CD practices to automate the deployment process. Ensure that your pipeline includes steps for:

- **Building the Application**: Automatically compile and build the application with each change.
- **Running Tests**: Execute unit, integration, and acceptance tests to catch

errors early.

- **Deploying Updates**: Automate the deployment to staging and production environments based on successful test results.

3. Deployment of Updates

3.1 Zero Downtime Deployments

Implement zero-downtime deployment strategies to ensure that users can continue to access your application without interruptions during updates. Techniques include:

- **Blue-Green Deployment**: Maintain two identical environments (blue and green) and switch traffic between them during updates.
- **Canary Releases**: Gradually roll out updates to a small percentage of users, monitoring for issues before a full rollout.

3.2 Rollback Mechanisms

Prepare rollback procedures to quickly revert to a previous version if the new deployment introduces critical issues. Key strategies include:

- **Automated Rollback Scripts**: Write scripts to revert to the previous stable version quickly.
- **Database Migrations**: Handle database schema changes carefully. Use migration scripts that can be rolled back if needed.

Example: If a deployment introduces a critical bug, have a procedure to automatically restore the previous application version and its database state.

4. Monitoring Post-Deployment

After deploying updates, monitoring the application is crucial to ensure that it operates as expected and to detect issues promptly.

4.1 Performance Monitoring

Utilize Application Performance Monitoring (APM) tools to track key metrics such as:

- **Response Times**: Monitor how quickly the application responds to requests.
- **Error Rates**: Track the frequency and types of errors occurring in the application.
- **Resource Utilization**: Observe CPU, memory, and disk usage to identify potential bottlenecks.

4.2 Logging for Diagnostics

Enhance logging during and after deployments to capture additional context about application behavior. This includes:

- **Verbose Logging**: Temporarily increase logging verbosity to capture detailed information about application execution.
- **Error Logging**: Ensure that error logs are monitored and alerts are set up for critical issues.

5. Regular Maintenance Practices

Regular maintenance is vital for keeping applications running smoothly over time. Consider the following practices:

5.1 Dependency Management

Keep libraries and dependencies up to date to benefit from performance improvements, new features, and security patches. Tools like NuGet can be used to manage and update dependencies in C# applications efficiently.

5.2 Security Updates

Regularly monitor for security vulnerabilities in your application and its dependencies. Implement a strategy to promptly apply security patches and updates.

5.3 Code Reviews and Refactoring

Conduct regular code reviews to maintain code quality and ensure adherence to best practices. Refactor code as necessary to improve readability, maintainability, and performance.

5.4 User Feedback and Feature Requests

Engage with users to gather feedback on application performance and usability. Use this information to prioritize future updates and enhancements.

Handling application updates and maintenance is an ongoing process that involves careful planning, effective deployment strategies, and continuous monitoring. By following best practices for version control, testing, deployment, and regular maintenance, developers can ensure that their C# applications remain reliable, secure, and aligned with user needs. Implementing robust CI/CD processes enhances the ability to deliver updates rapidly and safely, ultimately improving the overall user experience and satisfaction with the application.

Hands-On Project: Full Deployment of a Scalable Application

In this project, we will take a comprehensive approach to deploying a scalable C# application using best practices in cloud deployment, CI/CD pipelines, and monitoring. The application we'll deploy is a **Book Management System**, which we will enhance to support scalability and manageability. This step-by-step guide will cover preparing the application for deployment, setting up CI/CD pipelines, deploying to Azure, and configuring monitoring and logging.

Project Overview

The **Book Management System** will include:

1. **Scalable Architecture**: A web API for managing books, leveraging cloud capabilities.
2. **CI/CD Pipeline**: Automated builds and deployments.
3. **Cloud Deployment**: Deployment to Azure App Service.
4. **Monitoring and Logging**: Implementing Application Insights for performance tracking and logging.

Step 1: Preparing the Application
1.1 **Enhance the Book Management System**

Ensure that your application supports scalability:

- Use **Entity Framework Core** for data access with a SQL Server database.
- Ensure that your application is stateless to facilitate scaling.

Add Dependency Injection for Services:

Make sure your application uses DI to manage services effectively.

csharp

```csharp
public void ConfigureServices(IServiceCollection services)
{
    services.AddDbContext<AppDbContext>(options =>
        options.UseSqlServer(Configuration.
GetConnectionString
("DefaultConnection")));
    services.AddScoped<IBookRepository, BookRepository>();
    services.AddControllers();
}
```

1.2 Add Configuration Management

Use appsettings.json for configuration settings, ensuring sensitive data is stored securely in Azure Key Vault or as environment variables.

Step 2: Setting Up a CI/CD Pipeline

2.1 Create an Azure DevOps Account

Sign up for an Azure DevOps account if you don't already have one. Create a new project for the Book Management System.

2.2 Set Up the Repository

Push your application code to a Git repository in Azure DevOps. Use branches to manage feature development and releases.

2.3 Create a CI Pipeline

Navigate to **Pipelines** in Azure DevOps and click on **Create Pipeline**. Choose your repository and select **YAML** as the configuration method. Define your CI pipeline in azure-pipelines.yml.

Example Pipeline Configuration:

```yaml
yaml

trigger:
  branches:
    include:
      - main

pool:
  vmImage: 'windows-latest'

steps:
- task: DotNetCoreCLI@2
  displayName: 'Restore NuGet Packages'
  inputs:
    command: 'restore'
    projects: '**/*.csproj'

- task: DotNetCoreCLI@2
  displayName: 'Build the Project'
  inputs:
    command: 'build'
    projects: '**/*.csproj'
    arguments: '--configuration Release'

- task: DotNetCoreCLI@2
  displayName: 'Run Unit Tests'
  inputs:
    command: 'test'
    projects: '**/*.csproj'
    arguments: '--configuration Release --no-build'

- task: DotNetCoreCLI@2
  displayName: 'Publish the Application'
  inputs:
    command: 'publish'
    projects: '**/*.csproj'
    arguments: '--configuration Release --output
    $(Build.ArtifactStagingDirectory)'
```

```
- task: PublishBuildArtifacts@1
  inputs:
    PathtoPublish: '$(Build.ArtifactStagingDirectory)'
    ArtifactName: 'drop'
```

2.4 Create a CD Pipeline

In the Azure DevOps Pipelines section, create a new pipeline for deployment.

Select **Deployments** and configure a new deployment to Azure App Service.

Example Deployment Stage:

yaml

```
- stage: Deploy
  jobs:
  - job: DeployToAzure
    pool:
      vmImage: 'windows-latest'
    steps:
    - task: AzureRmWebAppDeployment@4
      inputs:
        azureSubscription: '<Your Azure Subscription>'
        appType: 'webApp'
        WebAppName: '<Your Web App Name>'
        packageForLinux: '$(Pipeline.Workspace)/drop/*.zip'
```

Step 3: Deploying the Application to Azure

3.1 Create an Azure App Service

1. Log into the Azure Portal.
2. Navigate to **Create a resource** and select **Web App**.
3. Fill in the necessary information, including:

- Resource Group

- Name (Unique name for your app)
- Publish (Code)
- Runtime stack (.NET)
- Region

3.2 Configure Application Settings

In the Azure portal, navigate to your App Service and configure application settings such as connection strings and any other necessary configurations.

Go to **Configuration > Application settings**.

Add keys for environment variables like ConnectionString and other settings.

Deploy the Application

After your CI/CD pipeline is configured and your App Service is set up, trigger the pipeline. Monitor the pipeline run to ensure the build and deployment steps complete successfully.

Step 4: Setting Up Monitoring and Logging

4.1 Integrate Application Insights

Application Insights provides powerful monitoring capabilities for your application.

In the Azure portal, navigate to your App Service and select **Application Insights**.

Click on **Turn on Application Insights** and follow the prompts to enable it for your application.

Example of Adding Application Insights to Your C# Application:

```csharp
public void ConfigureServices
(IServiceCollection services)
{
    services.AddApplicationInsightsTelemetry
(Configuration["ApplicationInsights:
InstrumentationKey"]);
```

}

4.2 **Implement Structured Logging**

Use Serilog or another logging framework to capture structured logs, which can be sent to Application Insights or other logging sinks.

```csharp
Log.Logger = new LoggerConfiguration()
    .WriteTo.Console()
    .WriteTo.ApplicationInsights(Configuration[
 "ApplicationInsights:InstrumentationKey"],
  TelemetryConverter.Traces)
    .CreateLogger();
```

Step 5: Post-Deployment Activities
5.1 **Monitor Performance**

After deployment, continuously monitor the performance metrics in Application Insights to detect any anomalies or performance issues.

5.2 **Gather User Feedback**

Collect feedback from users regarding the application's performance and usability. Use this feedback to prioritize future updates and enhancements.

5.3 **Regularly Update Dependencies**

Periodically check for updates to libraries and frameworks your application uses. Regular updates can help address security vulnerabilities and improve performance.

This hands-on project demonstrated the full deployment of a scalable C# application, encompassing the entire lifecycle from development through CI/CD to production deployment on Azure. By following best practices for cloud deployment, integrating monitoring and logging solutions, and preparing for future updates, developers can ensure their applications remain robust, efficient, and responsive to user needs. The use of CI/CD not only accelerates the deployment process but also facilitates continuous improvement, allowing teams to deliver high-quality software effectively.

Real-World Case Studies and Best Practices

Case Study 1: Building a Scalable Enterprise Web App
In this case study, we will explore the development of a scalable enterprise web application designed for a fictional company, **GlobalTech Solutions**, which specializes in providing software solutions to businesses across various sectors. The goal was to create an application that could handle a growing user base, integrate with third-party services, and provide a seamless user experience.

Project Overview
GlobalTech Solutions aimed to develop a comprehensive web application, **TechManager**, for managing projects, resources, and client interactions. The application needed to support multiple user roles, provide real-time collaboration features, and maintain high performance as the user base expanded.

Key Features:

- User authentication and authorization
- Project management tools
- Real-time chat and notifications
- Integration with external APIs (e.g., payment gateways, email services)
- Reporting and analytics dashboard

1. Architecture Design
1.1 Microservices Architecture
To ensure scalability and flexibility, TechManager was designed using a microservices architecture. This approach allowed different components of the application to be developed, deployed, and scaled independently.

- **Service Breakdown**:
- **User Service**: Handles user authentication and profile management.
- **Project Service**: Manages projects, tasks, and deadlines.
- **Chat Service**: Provides real-time messaging capabilities.
- **Reporting Service**: Generates analytics and reports based on project data.

1.2 Tech Stack
The following technologies were chosen for the development of TechManager:

- **Frontend**: React.js for a dynamic user interface with responsive design.
- **Backend**: ASP.NET Core for building RESTful APIs with C#.
- **Database**: PostgreSQL for structured data storage with support for complex queries.
- **Message Broker**: RabbitMQ for inter-service communication and real-time updates.
- **Containerization**: Docker for packaging microservices and Kubernetes for orchestration.

2. Development Process
2.1 Agile Methodology
The project adopted Agile methodologies, allowing for iterative development and continuous feedback. Key practices included:

- **Sprints**: Regular two-week sprints to implement features and fix bugs.
- **Daily Stand-ups**: Short meetings to discuss progress, roadblocks, and

upcoming tasks.

- **Sprint Reviews and Retrospectives**: Sessions at the end of each sprint to evaluate work completed and identify areas for improvement.

2.2 Version Control and CI/CD

To manage the codebase effectively, the team utilized Git for version control and established CI/CD pipelines using Azure DevOps. This setup automated testing and deployment processes, ensuring code quality and rapid delivery.

Pipeline Steps:

Code Commit: Developers pushed code to a shared repository.

Build Process: Automated builds triggered upon code commits.

Automated Testing: Unit and integration tests executed to validate functionality.

Deployment: Successful builds deployed to staging environments for user acceptance testing.

3. Scalability Considerations

3.1 Load Balancing

To distribute traffic evenly across services, the architecture employed load balancers. This ensured that no single service became a bottleneck under high user demand.

3.2 Caching Strategies

TechManager implemented caching to reduce database load and improve response times. Two types of caching were used:

- **In-Memory Caching**: Utilized for frequently accessed data (e.g., user sessions).
- **Distributed Caching**: Employed Redis to share cached data across instances of services.

3.3 Database Optimization

To support the anticipated growth in data volume and complexity, database optimizations included:

- **Indexing**: Proper indexing strategies were implemented on commonly queried fields.
- **Database Sharding**: As user data increased, sharding strategies were applied to distribute database load across multiple servers.

4. Deployment to the Cloud
4.1 Using Azure for Hosting
TechManager was hosted on Microsoft Azure, leveraging services such as Azure Kubernetes Service (AKS) for container orchestration, Azure SQL Database for data storage, and Azure Blob Storage for file storage.

4.2 Continuous Monitoring and Logging
To ensure operational excellence, the application integrated Application Insights for performance monitoring and logging. Key metrics tracked included:

- Response times for API endpoints
- User engagement and interaction rates
- Error rates and exception logging

Alerts were set up to notify the team of any anomalies, allowing for quick resolution of issues.

5. Challenges and Solutions
5.1 Managing Microservices Complexity
One of the challenges faced was managing the complexity that comes with a microservices architecture, especially regarding service communication and data consistency.

Solution: The team adopted a service mesh (e.g., Istio) to manage inter-service communications and improve security, monitoring, and reliability of service interactions.

5.2 Handling Performance Bottlenecks
As user adoption grew, some services experienced performance bottlenecks, particularly during peak usage times.

Solution: Performance profiling tools were utilized to identify slow operations. As a result, optimizations were made, such as adjusting service configurations, optimizing queries, and increasing resource allocation for critical services.

6. Results and Outcomes

The deployment of TechManager resulted in several positive outcomes:

- **Improved User Satisfaction**: User feedback indicated that the application was responsive and intuitive, leading to higher user engagement.
- **Scalability**: The microservices architecture allowed the application to scale efficiently, handling increased traffic without performance degradation.
- **Continuous Delivery**: The CI/CD pipeline enabled frequent updates, allowing the team to respond quickly to user feedback and improve functionality.

7. Lessons Learned

1. **Invest in Monitoring and Logging**: Comprehensive monitoring and logging are crucial for identifying issues early and maintaining application performance.
2. **Embrace Agile Practices**: Regular feedback loops and iterative development facilitate better alignment with user needs and enhance overall quality.
3. **Plan for Growth**: Designing for scalability from the outset avoids costly refactoring later, enabling seamless growth as user demand increases.

Building a scalable enterprise web application like TechManager required careful planning, robust architecture, and adherence to best practices in software development. By leveraging microservices, CI/CD, and cloud deployment strategies, GlobalTech Solutions successfully created an application that not only met immediate business needs but was also capable of evolving alongside the organization's growth. This case study exemplifies how following sound principles in software design and deployment can lead to long-term success in application development.

Case Study 2: Creating a Real-Time Data Processing System

In this case study, we will examine the development of a real-time data processing system for a fictional company, **DataStream Innovations**, which specializes in providing real-time analytics and insights for businesses. The goal was to create a scalable and efficient system capable of processing large volumes of data in real-time from various sources.

Project Overview

DataStream Innovations sought to develop a **Real-Time Data Processing System** that could handle data from IoT devices, web applications, and databases to provide real-time insights. The system needed to support data ingestion, processing, and output through a robust and scalable architecture.

Key Features:

- Real-time data ingestion from multiple sources.
- Stream processing capabilities to analyze and transform data.
- Integration with data storage solutions for persistent storage.
- A web-based dashboard for visualizing real-time data and analytics.

1. Architecture Design
1.1 Event-Driven Architecture

To support real-time processing, the system was designed using an event-driven architecture. This approach allows the application to respond to data events as they occur, making it ideal for handling high-velocity data streams.

- **Components**:
- **Event Producers**: Devices or applications that generate data (e.g., IoT

448

sensors, APIs).

- **Event Stream Processing**: A processing layer to analyze and transform data in real-time.
- **Event Consumers**: Applications or services that consume processed data (e.g., dashboards, reporting services).

1.2 Tech Stack

The following technologies were chosen for building the real-time data processing system:

- **Messaging System**: Apache Kafka for handling data streams and event distribution.
- **Stream Processing Framework**: Apache Flink for real-time data processing and analytics.
- **Database**: PostgreSQL for structured data storage, with TimescaleDB for time-series data.
- **Frontend**: React.js for creating an interactive web dashboard.

2. Development Process

2.1 Agile Methodology

The project adopted Agile methodologies, which facilitated iterative development, frequent feedback, and rapid adjustments to the system based on evolving requirements.

- **Sprints**: Short sprints focused on delivering specific features related to data ingestion, processing, and visualization.
- **Daily Stand-ups**: Regular team meetings to discuss progress, identify challenges, and adjust priorities as needed.

2.2 Microservices Approach

The development team utilized a microservices approach to separate concerns and allow independent deployment of components. Key microservices included:

- **Ingestion Service**: Responsible for collecting and pushing data to Kafka.
- **Processing Service**: Utilizes Apache Flink to process and analyze incoming data streams.
- **Dashboard Service**: Serves the web-based user interface and fetches data from the database for visualization.

3. Real-Time Data Ingestion

3.1 Using Apache Kafka for Data Streaming

Kafka was used as the central messaging system to handle data ingestion from various sources. This allowed for decoupled producers and consumers, improving scalability and fault tolerance.

Setting Up Kafka Topics: Create specific topics for different data streams (e.g., IoT sensor data, user activity logs).

Data Producers: Develop microservices or applications that send messages to Kafka topics.

Example: Ingestion Service Code Snippet:

```csharp
public class IngestionService
{
    private readonly IProducer<string, string> _producer;

    public IngestionService(IProducer<string, string> producer)
    {
        _producer = producer;
    }

    public void ProduceData(string topic, string data)
    {
        _producer.Produce(topic, new Message<string, string> { Key
        = Guid.NewGuid().ToString(), Value = data });
    }
}
```

3.2 Handling High Throughput

To ensure the ingestion service could handle high throughput:

- **Batch Processing**: Configure Kafka to accept batch messages to reduce the number of network requests.
- **Asynchronous Processing**: Use asynchronous programming to prevent blocking while waiting for data processing.

4. Real-Time Stream Processing

4.1 Using Apache Flink for Data Processing

Apache Flink was chosen for its powerful stream processing capabilities, allowing for complex event processing, aggregations, and transformations on-the-fly.

Data Processing Pipeline: Create a Flink job that subscribes to Kafka topics, processes incoming data, and outputs results to the database.

Example: Flink Processing Job:

```java
public class DataProcessingJob {
    public static void main(String[] args) throws Exception {
        StreamExecutionEnvironment env =
        StreamExecutionEnvironment.getExecutionEnvironment();

        DataStream<String> input = env.addSource(new
        FlinkKafkaConsumer<>("topic", new SimpleStringSchema(),
        properties));
        DataStream<ProcessedData> processedData = input.map(value
        -> {
            // Process the data (e.g., parse JSON, perform
            calculations)
            return new ProcessedData(...);
        });

        processedData.addSink(new YourDatabaseSinkFunction());
        env.execute("Real-Time Data Processing");
    }
```

```
}
```

4.2 Handling Data Transformations and Aggregations

Flink allows developers to perform real-time data transformations and aggregations efficiently. Implement windowing techniques to analyze data over specific time intervals, enabling insights such as averages, sums, and counts.

5. Data Storage and Retrieval

5.1 Storing Processed Data

After processing, the data is stored in a PostgreSQL database with TimescaleDB for handling time-series data effectively. This setup allows efficient querying and analysis of large datasets over time.

Schema Design: Create a schema optimized for time-series data, including appropriate indexes for fast access.

5.2 Data Retrieval for Visualization

The dashboard service queries the database to retrieve processed data and present it to users in a meaningful way.

Example: Data Retrieval Code:

```csharp
public class DashboardService
{
    private readonly AppDbContext _dbContext;

    public DashboardService(AppDbContext dbContext)
    {
        _dbContext = dbContext;
    }

    public IEnumerable<ProcessedData> GetProcessedData(DateTime
    start, DateTime end)
    {
        return _dbContext.ProcessedData
```

```
    .Where(d => d.Timestamp >= start && d.Timestamp <= end)
    .ToList();
  }
}
```

6. Creating the Frontend Dashboard

6.1 Building the User Interface with React.js

The web dashboard was built using React.js to create a responsive and interactive user experience. Key features include:

- **Data Visualization**: Use libraries like Chart.js or D3.js for rendering real-time charts and graphs based on processed data.
- **User Authentication**: Implement user authentication and role management to ensure secure access to the dashboard.

Example: Dashboard Component:

```javascript
import React from 'react';
import { Line } from 'react-chartjs-2';

const Dashboard = ({ data }) => {
    const chartData = {
        labels: data.map(d => d.timestamp),
        datasets: [
            {
                label: 'Data Over Time',
                data: data.map(d => d.value),
                borderColor: 'rgba(75,192,192,1)',
                fill: false,
            },
        ],
    };

    return <Line data={chartData} />;
```

```
};
```

7. Monitoring and Maintenance

7.1 Monitoring System Health

To ensure system reliability, implement monitoring tools like Prometheus and Grafana for visualizing application metrics. This setup allows for tracking system health, performance, and resource utilization.

7.2 Error Handling and Logging

Implement comprehensive error handling and logging using frameworks like Serilog or NLog. Capture exceptions and critical events to diagnose issues effectively.

Example: Error Handling in Processing Job:

```java
java

input.process().onFailure(new HandleFailure());
```

8. Challenges and Solutions

8.1 Managing High Data Velocity

As the volume of incoming data increased, the team faced challenges with data ingestion and processing speed.

Solution: Optimizing Kafka configurations for higher throughput and scaling the Flink processing nodes horizontally to handle more data concurrently.

8.2 Ensuring Data Consistency

With multiple services interacting, maintaining data consistency was a challenge, especially during processing.

Solution: Implementing idempotent processing in the data ingestion and processing layers ensured that repeated data does not lead to inconsistencies.

9. Results and Outcomes

The deployment of the Real-Time Data Processing System resulted in several positive outcomes for DataStream Innovations:

- **Scalability**: The system efficiently handled increasing data volumes without performance degradation.
- **Real-Time Insights**: Clients received timely insights from their data, enhancing decision-making processes.
- **User Engagement**: The interactive dashboard improved user engagement and satisfaction, leading to increased adoption.

This case study of developing a Real-Time Data Processing System illustrates how leveraging modern technologies and design patterns can lead to the successful implementation of complex applications. By adopting an event-driven architecture, utilizing microservices, and implementing robust monitoring strategies, DataStream Innovations was able to build a scalable solution that meets the demands of a rapidly evolving data landscape. This example serves as a reference for best practices in designing and deploying real-time systems in a production environment.

Case Study 3: Integrating Third-Party APIs in C# Applications

In this case study, we will explore the integration of third-party APIs into a C# application developed by a fictional e-commerce company, **ShopSmart Inc.** The goal was to enhance the shopping experience by integrating with various external services, such as payment gateways, shipping providers, and product information APIs.

Project Overview

ShopSmart Inc. aimed to create a robust e-commerce platform, **Smart-Cart**, that not only offered a wide range of products but also streamlined the purchasing process through external integrations. Key integrations included:

- **Payment Processing**: Integrating with a payment gateway for secure transactions.
- **Shipping Services**: Connecting with logistics providers to calculate

shipping costs and track shipments.

- **Product Data Enrichment**: Using third-party APIs to fetch additional product details and reviews.

1. Architecture Design

1.1 Service-Oriented Architecture (SOA)

To accommodate the integration of third-party APIs, the SmartCart platform was designed with a service-oriented architecture. This design allowed for modularity and separation of concerns, enabling individual services to be developed, maintained, and scaled independently.

- **Key Services**:
- **Product Service**: Manages product listings, including data from third-party APIs.
- **Order Service**: Handles order processing and integrates payment gateways and shipping services.
- **User Service**: Manages user accounts and authentication.

1.2 Tech Stack

The following technologies were selected for the development of Smart-Cart:

- **Frontend**: ASP.NET Core with Razor Pages for server-side rendering and Blazor for interactive components.
- **Backend**: ASP.NET Core Web API for building RESTful services.
- **Database**: SQL Server for storing product, user, and order data.
- **Caching**: Redis for caching product data to improve performance.

2. Integrating Payment Processing

2.1 Choosing a Payment Gateway

ShopSmart Inc. decided to integrate with **Stripe** as their payment processing solution due to its ease of integration, robust documentation, and wide range of supported payment methods.

2.2 Setting Up the Stripe API

Creating a Stripe Account: The team created a Stripe account and obtained the necessary API keys.

Adding the Stripe SDK: The Stripe .NET library was added to the project to facilitate API interactions.

```bash
dotnet add package Stripe.net
```

2.3 Implementing Payment Processing Logic

The Order Service was updated to include payment processing capabilities. This involved creating endpoints to handle payment requests and responses.

Example: Payment Processing Code Snippet:

```csharp
public class PaymentService
{
    public async Task<string> ProcessPayment(PaymentRequest
    paymentRequest)
    {
        var options = new ChargeCreateOptions
        {
            Amount = paymentRequest.Amount,
            Currency = "usd",
            Source = paymentRequest.Source,
            Description = "Order payment",
        };

        var service = new ChargeService();
        Charge charge = await service.CreateAsync(options);
        return charge.Id;
    }
}
```

In this implementation, a payment request is processed by creating a charge in

Stripe. The service handles communication with the Stripe API and returns the payment result.

3. Integrating Shipping Services

3.1 Choosing a Shipping Provider

To calculate shipping costs and provide tracking information, the team selected **Shippo**, a multi-carrier shipping API that integrates with various logistics providers.

3.2 Setting Up the Shippo API

Creating a Shippo Account: The team created a Shippo account and acquired API credentials.

Adding the Shippo SDK: The Shippo .NET client library was added to the project.

```bash
dotnet add package Shippo
```

3.3 Implementing Shipping Integration

The Order Service was enhanced to include shipping functionality, allowing users to calculate shipping costs during checkout.

Example: Shipping Cost Calculation Code Snippet:

```csharp
public class ShippingService
{
    public async Task<ShippingRate>
    GetShippingRate(ShippingRequest request)
    {
        var shippoClient = new ShippoClient("your_shippo_api_key");
        var rates = await
        shippoClient.ShippingRates.CreateAsync(request);
        return rates;
```

```
    }
}
```

This integration allows the application to request shipping rates from Shippo based on user-provided address details, thereby enhancing the user experience.

4. Enriching Product Data with Third-Party APIs

4.1 Integrating Product Data APIs

To provide customers with detailed product information and reviews, ShopSmart decided to integrate with the **Product Hunt** API, which offers data on trending products and reviews.

4.2 Setting Up the Product Hunt API

1. **Creating a Product Hunt Account**: The team registered for an API key on Product Hunt.
2. **Implementing API Calls**: Code was added to fetch product data from Product Hunt and store it in the database.

Example: Fetching Product Data Code Snippet:

```csharp
public class ProductService
{
    private readonly HttpClient _httpClient;

    public ProductService(HttpClient httpClient)
    {
        _httpClient = httpClient;
    }

    public async Task<Product> GetProductDetails(string productId)
    {
        var response = await _
```

```
httpClient.GetAsync($"https:
//api.producthunt.com
/v1/posts/{productId}");
        response.EnsureSuccessStatusCode();
        var content = await response.Content.ReadAsStringAsync();
        return JsonConvert.DeserializeObject<Product>(content);
    }
}
```

In this example, the HttpClient is used to make a request to the Product Hunt API, retrieving product details based on the specified product ID.

5. Testing and Validation

5.1 Unit and Integration Testing

As integrations with third-party APIs introduced external dependencies, the team implemented unit tests and integration tests to ensure the reliability of these integrations.

- **Mocking API Calls**: Use libraries such as Moq to simulate responses from APIs during testing, ensuring that tests are not dependent on the availability of external services.

Example: Unit Test for Payment Processing:

csharp

```
[Test]
public async Task ProcessPayment_ShouldReturnChargeId()
{
    var mockPaymentService = new Mock<IPaymentService>();
    mockPaymentService.Setup(x =>
    x.ProcessPayment(It.IsAny<PaymentRequest>()))
        .ReturnsAsync("charge_id");

    var result = await
```

```
mockPaymentService.Object.ProcessPayment(new PaymentRequest());

    Assert.AreEqual("charge_id", result);
}
```

5.2 User Acceptance Testing (UAT)

Conduct user acceptance testing with actual users to gather feedback on the integrations, ensuring they meet user expectations and are intuitive to use.

6. Deployment Considerations

6.1 Configuring Environment Variables

For secure management of API keys and secrets, configure environment variables in the application settings in Azure or the hosting environment.

6.2 CI/CD Integration

Integrate the deployment process into the CI/CD pipeline to automate builds and deployments, ensuring that new features and updates are deployed quickly and reliably.

7. Monitoring and Maintenance

7.1 Monitoring API Integrations

Use tools like Application Insights to monitor the health and performance of API calls. Track metrics such as response times and error rates to identify issues proactively.

7.2 Error Handling and Logging

Implement comprehensive error handling to manage failures in third-party API calls gracefully. Log errors with sufficient context to aid in troubleshooting.

Example: Error Logging for API Calls:

```
csharp
```

```
try
{
    var productDetails = await GetProductDetails(productId);
}
catch (Exception ex)
{
    Log.Error(ex, "Failed to fetch product details for product ID:
    {ProductId}", productId);
}
```

8. Challenges and Solutions

8.1 API Rate Limiting

One challenge encountered was handling rate limits imposed by third-party APIs, which could lead to failures in data fetching.

Solution: Implement exponential backoff strategies and caching for frequently requested data to reduce the number of API calls.

8.2 Versioning and API Changes

Changes to third-party APIs or their deprecation could impact application functionality.

Solution: Regularly monitor API documentation for changes, and establish a process for updating the application to adapt to new versions.

9. Results and Outcomes

The integration of third-party APIs into the SmartCart platform resulted in several positive outcomes:

- **Enhanced User Experience**: Users benefitted from seamless payment processing, accurate shipping information, and enriched product data.
- **Increased Engagement**: The application saw increased user engagement due to the additional features provided through API integrations.
- **Improved Scalability**: The modular architecture allowed the application to scale efficiently as demand increased.

This case study illustrates the successful integration of third-party APIs into a C# application, highlighting the importance of careful planning, robust architecture, and thorough testing. By leveraging external services, ShopSmart Inc. was able to enhance its e-commerce platform significantly, providing users with a richer, more interactive experience. This example serves as a reference for best practices in API integration, emphasizing the need for reliable, scalable solutions in modern software development.

Lessons Learned: Best Practices and Common Pitfalls in Modern App Development

In modern app development, particularly in the context of building scalable, maintainable, and effective applications, teams often encounter a range of challenges. Through the case studies discussed, several best practices and common pitfalls have emerged that can guide future development efforts. This section outlines these lessons learned to help developers and teams navigate the complexities of modern software development more effectively.

Best Practices

1. Embrace Agile Methodologies

Agile practices, including iterative development and continuous feedback, are crucial for adapting to changing requirements and delivering value to users quickly. Regular sprints and stand-up meetings foster collaboration and ensure that teams remain aligned on project goals.

- **Tip**: Use tools like Jira or Azure DevOps to manage sprints and track progress effectively.

2. Design for Scalability from the Outset

Building applications with scalability in mind from the beginning avoids costly refactoring later. Utilize microservices architecture, load balancing, and database sharding to accommodate growth.

- **Tip**: Conduct load testing early in the development process to identify potential bottlenecks and areas for improvement.

3. Implement Robust Monitoring and Logging

Integrating monitoring and logging solutions allows teams to gain insights into application performance and user behavior. Use tools like Application Insights, Prometheus, or ELK Stack to track metrics, errors, and user interactions.

- **Tip**: Establish alerting mechanisms for critical errors to ensure quick responses to production issues.

4. Automate Testing and Deployment

Automating testing and deployment through CI/CD pipelines enhances code quality and accelerates delivery. Implement unit, integration, and end-to-end tests to validate application functionality.

- **Tip**: Include automated testing in your CI/CD pipeline to ensure that code changes do not introduce new issues.

5. Manage Dependencies Effectively

Regularly review and update dependencies to mitigate security vulnerabilities and take advantage of performance improvements. Use dependency management tools to streamline this process.

- **Tip**: Implement automated alerts for outdated or vulnerable dependencies.

6. Adopt a Modular Approach to Development

Utilizing a modular architecture facilitates code reuse and separation of concerns. Each module or microservice can be developed and maintained independently, improving maintainability and testability.

- **Tip**: Define clear interfaces and contracts between modules to ensure loose coupling.

7. Prioritize User Experience (UX)

Designing applications with the end-user in mind is essential for engagement and satisfaction. Conduct user research and usability testing to gather feedback and iterate on the user interface.

- **Tip**: Use design frameworks like Material UI or Bootstrap to create intuitive and responsive user interfaces.

8. Document Everything

Maintaining comprehensive documentation for code, APIs, and architecture decisions is vital for onboarding new team members and ensuring consistent development practices.

- **Tip**: Use tools like Swagger for API documentation and Markdown files for codebase documentation.

Common Pitfalls

1. Neglecting Security Considerations

Failing to incorporate security best practices can lead to vulnerabilities. Common oversights include inadequate input validation, weak authentication mechanisms, and improper handling of sensitive data.

- **Pitfall**: Ensure that security is a priority from the beginning of the development lifecycle.

2. Ignoring Performance Optimization

Focusing solely on functionality without considering performance can result in applications that become sluggish under load. Performance issues may arise from inefficient database queries, poor caching strategies, or heavy

API calls.

- **Pitfall**: Implement performance testing as part of the development process to identify and resolve issues before deployment.

3. Overengineering Solutions

In an attempt to create scalable and flexible systems, teams may overengineer solutions, leading to unnecessary complexity. Striking a balance between simplicity and scalability is crucial.

- **Pitfall**: Follow the KISS (Keep It Simple, Stupid) principle to avoid excessive complexity in design.

4. Underestimating Integration Challenges

Integrating third-party APIs can introduce unforeseen challenges, such as rate limiting, changes in API contracts, and reliability issues.

- **Pitfall**: Regularly monitor and adapt to changes in external services, and build resilience into your integrations.

5. Failing to Plan for Updates

Not having a clear strategy for handling application updates can lead to service disruptions and user dissatisfaction.

- **Pitfall**: Establish a robust update and rollback strategy to ensure smooth transitions during deployments.

6. Inadequate Testing Coverage

Neglecting to implement comprehensive testing can result in undetected bugs and poor application quality.

- **Pitfall**: Aim for high test coverage and include unit, integration, and user acceptance tests in your development process.

Through the experiences shared in the case studies, it is evident that following best practices while being aware of common pitfalls can significantly enhance the success of modern app development. By embracing Agile methodologies, designing for scalability, integrating robust monitoring, and maintaining a focus on security and user experience, development teams can build applications that not only meet user needs but also adapt to changing demands and environments. As technology continues to evolve, these lessons will serve as a foundation for building resilient and innovative software solutions in the future.